They Did Not Make It Back

Perry County's Civil War Dead

Terry Bender

an imprint of Sunbury Press, Inc.
Mechanicsburg, PA USA

LOCAL HISTORY PRESS

an imprint of Sunbury Press, Inc.
Mechanicsburg, PA USA

Copyright © 2026 by Terry Bender.
Cover Copyright © 2026 by Sunbury Press, Inc.

Sunbury Press supports copyright. Copyright fuels creativity, encourages diverse voices, promotes free speech, and creates a vibrant culture. Thank you for buying an authorized edition of this book and for complying with copyright laws. Except for the quotation of short passages for the purpose of criticism and review, no part of this publication may be reproduced, scanned, or distributed in any form without permission. You are supporting writers and allowing Sunbury Press to continue to publish books for every reader. For information contact Sunbury Press, Inc., Subsidiary Rights Dept., PO Box 548, Boiling Springs, PA 17007 USA or legal@sunburypress.com.

For information about special discounts for bulk purchases, please contact Sunbury Press Orders Dept. at (855) 338-8359 or orders@sunburypress.com.

To request one of our authors for speaking engagements or book signings, please contact Sunbury Press Publicity Dept. at publicity@sunburypress.com.

FIRST LOCAL HISTORY PRESS EDITION: January 2026

Set in Adobe Garamond Pro | Interior design by Crystal Devine | Cover by Lawrence Knorr | Edited by Sarah Peachey.

Publisher's Cataloging-in-Publication Data
Names: Bender, Terry, author.
Title: They did not make it back : Perry County's Civil War dead / Terry Bender.
Description: First trade paperback edition. | Mechanicsburg, PA : Local History Press, 2026.
Summary: While leaders of governments call for war, the common man fights it. Though the chest thumping warmongers gathered in the state capitol, not in the county seat of New Bloomfield, Perry Countians were some of the first to answer President Lincoln's call for volunteers. This book reveals nearly three hundred men, over 1% of the county's total population, who did not make it back.
Identifiers: ISBN : 979-8-88819-366-2 (paperback).
Subjects: HISTORY / Military / Civil War | HISTORY / United States / Civil War Period (1850–1877) | HISTORY / United States / State & Local / Middle Atlantic (DC, DE, MD, NJ, NY, PA)

Designed in the USA
0 1 1 2 3 5 8 13 21 34 55

For the Love of Books!

Contents

Acknowledgments v
Preface vii

I.	The Story of David Neely.	1
II.	First to Volunteer, First to Die	3
III.	The Militia.	8
IV.	The Pennsylvania Reserves	10
V.	The 12th Reserves—41st Pennyslvania Regiment.	24
VI.	Perry County's Bucktails.	28
VII.	The Early Artillery	42
VIII.	More Perry County Artillerymen	46
IX.	The Men	48
X.	The 46th Pennsylvania Regiment	54
XI.	The Deadliest Assignment	58
XII.	The 49th Pennsylvania Regiment	88
XIII.	The 51st Pennsylvania Regiment	93
XIV.	The 53rd Pennsylvania Regiment	95
XV.	The 60th Pennsylvania Regiment (3rd Cavalry)	98
XVI.	The 65th Pennsylvania Regiment (5th Calvary)	100
XVII.	Another from the 77th Pennsylvania Regiment	102
XVIII.	United States Cavalry.	103
XVIX.	Jone's Independent Cavalry	104
XX.	The 7th Pennsylvania Cavalry.	106
XXI.	The 83rd Pennsylvania Regiment	110
XXII.	The 9th Pennsylvania Cavalry.	112
XXIII.	The 93rd Drafted Infantry	129
XXIV.	The 99th Pennsylvania Infantry	130
XXV.	The 101st Pennsylvania Infantry.	131

XXVI.	The 102nd Pennsylvania Regiment	139
XXVII.	The 107th Pennsylvania Regiment	140
XXVIII.	The 112th Pennsylvania Regiment	141
XXIX.	The 12th Pennsylvania Calvary	143
XXX.	The 13th Pennsylvania Calvary	145
XXXI.	The 132nd Pennsylvania Regiment	148
XXXII.	The 133rd Pennsylvania Regiment	149
XXXIII.	The Second Bucktails: 149th Pennsylvania Regiment	166
XXXIV.	The 151st Pennsylvania Regiment	179
XXXV.	158th Pennsylvania Infantry	181
XXXVI.	The 16th and 17th Pennsylvania Cavalry Regiments	183
XXXVII.	The 173rd Pennsylvania Drafted Militia	192
XXXVIII.	The 177th Drafted Militia	194
XXXIX.	The 21st Pennsylvania Cavalry	197
XL.	The 184th Pennsylvania Regiment	198
XLI.	The 186th Pennsylvania Regiment	201
XLII.	The 187th Pennsylvania Regiment	203
XLIII.	No Cannons But We Have Plenty of Muskets	208
XLIV.	New Regiments for Old Reserves	212
XLV.	The 192nd Pennsylvania Regiment	217
XLVI.	The 200th Pennsylvania Regiment	218
XLVII.	The 201st Pennsylvania Regiment	220
XLVIII.	The 202nd Pennsylvania Regiment	223
XLIX.	The 208th Pennsylvania Regiment	226
L.	The 209th Pennsylvania Regiment	237
LI.	An Illinois Soldier with Perry Roots	239
LII.	A Minnesota Lad Returns to Pennsylvania	240
LIII.	Another Grand Old Man	242
LIV.	Conclusion	244
LV.	Personnel List for Soldiers Appearing	247

About the Author 268

Acknowledgments

MOST often, stories have their endings in a cemetery; however, this story, as well as a previous one, *Perry County at Gettysburg*, has its genesis there. A couple of years ago, for reasons I am still uncertain about, I visited Perry County cemeteries and photographed Civil War veterans' gravestones and then placed biographical information on the backs of the photos. This war has always captured my attention, so much so that my kids will tell you virtually all family vacations were to sites rife with history. I have dragged them to Gettysburg numerous times, to Fredericksburg, to Chancellorsville; not to mention my constant stories about where this or that event occurred.

One sunny morning while visiting Buffalo Cemetery at Saville, a particular tombstone grabbed my attention. This inscription on the stone "in memory of Frank Hamilton Hench" reads, "Killed on Round Top Battle of Gettysburg July 3, 1863." Wow! I have no idea why I never connected Perry Countians with that epic battle, but I was mesmerized by the words chiseled into that stone a century and a half earlier. History stared back at me and sent me on a mission to learn more about Frank Hench, as well as any others with comparable stories. That quest has resulted in discovering over one hundred men from the county who were with Private Hench at Gettysburg, including an eyewitness to his death. It also propelled me to discover more than 280 men who suffered a fate like Frank's and did not return to Perry County alive.

Along the way, I have been aided by many. Our county's director of Veterans Affairs, Jim Scott, provided a comprehensive listing of county cemeteries containing Civil War veterans that I have used repeatedly. Jane

Stambaugh shared items about her great-great-grandfather, including the touching letter his widow received announcing her husband's death: a letter still cherished by family members. Adrian Roberts shared information about his ancestors, the Hench brothers, which included the eyewitness account alluded to earlier. Joni Abeling shared information about her great-great-grandfather Henry Foose. Included was a letter written by Captain McKeehan that provided the particulars of Henry's death to his father, Daniel. This letter was sent on May 9, 1865, thirty-eight days after the death. This is representative of the time delays encountered during that era, time delays that caused loved ones back home to wait, wonder, and worry. My sister-in-law Judy Zimmerman edited the manuscript and provided valuable suggestions for phrasing. And of course, the lady who indulged me in all those family vacations, my beautiful wife of fifty years, Donna. Not only has she been there to support me, but also has acted as my sounding board and editor, constantly answering my questions: Does this sound right? Does this make sense? Does this fit the message? I would be nowhere without her, for many reasons.

    I would be remiss if I did not thank Sarah Peachey and Crystal Devine of the Sunbury Press staff. Sarah took my very rough manuscript and edited it into something readable, and Crystal arranged the edited version into book form. These two ladies deserve special mention for aiding a fledgling author.

Preface

ANY Civil War buff from Perry County can list battlegrounds like Antietam, Chancellorsville, Fredericksburg, Gettysburg, and Petersburg. Our ancestors fought and died at these places, so the names are quite familiar. But how about battles like Pocotaligo, Pleasant Hill, or Cedar Creek? Though not as familiar, our ancestors contested those battlefields, and many died in these remote spots and there remain to this day.

This book deals with 288 Perry County soldiers who did not survive the Civil War. Though the 1860 census was never fully compiled due to the war, Perry's population was reported to be just under twenty-three thousand. Therefore, more than one percent of that number fell during the war. That percentage in all probability is higher due to suspect government records, the migration of families to western areas that caused our men to soldier in other states, and my own inadequacies as a researcher.

While the subject may be depressing, it is also meant to be a tribute to these men. These brave souls range in age from fifteen to fifty-three and run the gamut from fresh-faced, youthful exuberance, to middle-aged grit and determination; from the excitement of seeking an adventure, to the harsh reality that family values and lives were on the line—and that many men would perish in the struggle.

This book presents sketches of who these men were. These are not meant to be biographies. These men were too complex to have their lives detailed in a few paragraphs. Hopefully, the sketches will arouse the curiosities of the readers to learn more about Perry County soldiers and their families. I have included, where possible, the locations of burials. A visit to cemeteries where these brave men sleep reveals much.

Some left large families behind to risk their lives so that the nation could be healed and united. Some were too young to appreciate the dangers and horrors that awaited them. As is the case for many today, teenagers had that feeling of invincibility. They desired something more than the monotony of farm chores or of learning a trade. They marched off to war with friends, neighbors, cousins, uncles, and, in some cases, fathers. This, they were certain, would be a lark.

Early on, most northerners felt assured of a quick victory and looked forward to that joyous return home, replete with parades and admiring, flag-waving young girls. Instead, what many received was a return trip in a pine box or hobbling on crutches. Many returned missing limbs, missing comrades, missing brothers, and missing hope. Many never returned and still rest on what was, after secession, foreign soil. Many more remain to this day unidentified but not unremembered.

You will note in the succeeding pages that certain battles were costly. You will also note that diseases took a staggering toll on these men. Perry County's men answered the call in substantial numbers immediately after the opening salvos at Fort Sumter. They were among the first troops to report for duty in Washington. Perry Countians today can be enormously proud of our rich rural heritage and of our ancestors who gave the "last full measure" in a cause that many did not fully understand yet were eager to support.

You will meet a few men who did return to Perry County, albeit only briefly, before dying of wounds or disease. I have included these men because all too often war is viewed as something almost mythical. We sometimes give battlefield deaths an elevated status, something of which family members can be proud. If death came swiftly to these men, possibly there is a sense that they died heroically while facing the enemy. If men lingered with horrible wounds and suffered an agonizing death, the result may seem less glorious, but the outcome is the same. I also wish to provide a sense of the terrible effects that wounds and disease visited upon these men. Lives were cut short. Quality of life was hugely impacted. Men spent their last weeks and months in the throes of disease, their bodies wasting away. Dozens of these men died within a few years after the war. Months spent sleeping on the ground during summer rains and winter snows, eating little but hardtack, and in need of shoes and adequate clothing certainly contributed to early deaths. There is nothing noble about that other than the cause for which they struggled.

We tend to think the war ended on April 9, 1865, with Lee's surrender. It did not. The killing continued for weeks in parts of our nation not named Virginia and continued for months and years. Take the case of Private John A. Gilmore of Liverpool Township. John served with Company A of the 9th PA Cavalry, a unit recruited in Perry County and one we will cite many times later. John was wounded on March 18, 1865, at Black River, North Carolina, as the final days of the conflict played out. Severely wounded in the right shoulder and lung, John was furloughed home. We can only imagine his pain, his struggle to breathe as he endured the next 683 days (nearly two years) until he died on January 30, 1867. In a deposition given in support of his wife's attempt to garner a government pension, John's doctor stated that his death was caused by "wounds received near Black River, N.C." John Gilmore does not appear in the pages of this book that deals with men who died during the Civil War, but he certainly was killed by the war. He rests in Liverpool Cemetery, marked by a government-issued headstone.

Another man, Corporal Samuel A. M. Reed, of Company D of the 47th PA Regiment, made it home to New Bloomfield after serving his time. Samuel was discharged on September 18, 1864, "by reason of expiration of term of service" according to information contained in his widow's application for a pension. Also included in that application were affidavits from doctors, both in the service and later in New Bloomfield, stating Sam's chronic diarrhea was "contracted in the service," and, at the time of discharge, he "was so reduced as to be scarcely able to walk." Corporal Reed led a miserable existence until January 19, 1866, when he passed away and was interred in New Bloomfield Cemetery. Sam Reed left behind wife Elizabeth, who struggled to raise youngsters Eddie and Minnie. The children were later educated in the Andersonburg Orphan's School. Was Sam Reed killed in the war? I contend that he was.

You will meet men who died on their way home from the war. You will meet men who served very briefly as well as men who served from beginning to end. You will also meet men who tragically died in the waning days of the conflict when the outcome already had been decided but still needed to play out until the curtain finally, thankfully, came down on a four-year-long American heartache.

By way of explanation, "enrollment dates" or "enlistment dates" are when the man reported to a recruitment station. "Muster-in dates" are when the soldier officially joined the Federal service and was thus put on the payroll. "Muster-out dates" are when the soldier left the service and payrolls effectively stopped.

Index cards will also be mentioned. These were cards developed by Samuel Bates to chronicle Pennsylvania's soldiers. Some cards are complete with descriptions of the man, enlistment and enrollment dates, and any promotions the man received. These descriptions, when available, show hair and eye color, height, and type of complexion. Interestingly, the Library of Congress has provided a snapshot of the typical Civil War soldier that shows him to be twenty-six years old, standing five feet, eight inches tall, and weighing 143 pounds. You will note, though, that the only thing typical about these men was their devotion to a cause, to each other, and to their families. These cards may also provide the occupation of the man and the location where he enlisted. Sometimes a place of residence is given. Sometimes other than the name, not much information is shown. One constant with governmental records of that period is that there is no consistency.

You will see the terms "Reserves" or "Pennsylvania Reserves." This refers to the fifteen regiments that were held at the ready at Camp Curtin in Harrisburg. In April and May 1861, when the call went out from Washington for volunteers to quell the Southern uprising, the response was overwhelming. Soon more men flooded into Harrisburg and other troop camps than were expected or could be processed immediately. There also, unfortunately, was animosity between fellow Pennsylvanians Governor Andrew Curtin and Secretary of War Simon Cameron which impeded cooperation. After all, the need was only for ninety-day volunteers at that point. That was all the time needed to put these upstart secessionists back in their places.

Governor Andrew Curtin retained these extra men and equipped and trained them rather than turning them away—a prudent decision, as it turned out. They were indeed soon needed, and some, like the Bucktails, became much celebrated in the North and much feared in the South.

Regiments received their numbers in the order of their entrance into the Federal service. So, the first regiment (normally about one thousand men) mustered in was the 1st PA Regiment, the next became the 2nd PA Regiment and so on. The 1st Reserves entered as the 30th PA Regiment, and other reserve regiments were numbered sequentially through the 13th, which became the 42nd PA Regiment, known by many names, including the Kane Rifles, the 1st PA Rifles, or, most often, the Bucktails. The 14th Reserves became the 44th PA Regiment, but it was the first one to be mustered in as a cavalry unit. The 15th was mustered in as an artillery unit, though these men did carry muskets at various times.

Therefore, when you see a regiment with a low number, recognize that these men were some of the first regiments to join the Union Army. However, attrition over the course of the war would require new recruits to replenish older regiments, so not every soldier in a unit with a low number would necessarily have been in the service from the outset. For example, the 104th Regiment had men added to as late as March 1865. In fact, the second Company F of that regiment was comprised of Perry County recruits. Excluding some independent artillery and cavalry units, and some colored regiments, Pennsylvania numbered 215 regiments in all. The 208th, which contained four companies recruited in Perry County, mustered in early in September 1864.

As we discover the men who comprised these regiments, I hope to provide a sense of the devastation that went far beyond the battlefields, and far beyond 1865. The families left behind often were not only hugely emotionally impacted by the loss of loved ones, but were left in dire financial conditions that haunted them for years and decades. Wives and children relied solely upon the man of the family. At the outset of hostilities, women did not work outside the home. Government did not provide financial aid. When the husbands and fathers were out of the picture, the outlook was bleak. Pensions became available later in the war, but garnering one was a painstaking process requiring months and even years. Just the simplest thing, like a signature on the application, became a matter requiring more than one witness to the "mark" most women made, because the majority could neither read nor write. And after all the work required to get a pension, the few dollars per month were often not enough to sustain a family. Many families were forced to live with relatives. Numerous instances exist of families being split apart, with a few children staying with the mother, while a few older ones were housed elsewhere.

We will address these men in the regiments in which they served. A brief overview of the regiment and its battles will also be included, but the primary focus is on the man rather than the unit of service. Here are 288 men who did not come back to their Perry roots, their families, or their lives.

Grand Army of the Republic markers like this are often used to indicate a Civil War soldier's gravesite.

I.

The Story of David Neely

THIS book will provide information on soldiers in order by the regiment number in which they served, from the 2nd PA Regiment through the 210th Regiment of Pennsylvania volunteers. But I will break from that by beginning with a soldier from Company A of the 77th: Private David Neely. Jane Stambaugh, Neely's great-great-granddaughter, has graciously provided me with information, including a letter sent to his widow that announced his death. This letter has been preserved through the generations and is a poignant example of the countless numbers of letters that widows, children, and parents received during the four years of heartache this nation endured. Though it is the only such document cited in this text, thousands of similar letters were sent. And bear in mind that many other families received no notice at all of their loved one's fate. Some men died without benefit of witnesses who were alive to tell their tales. Some families waited until long after the war's end and had only to guess what may have happened. Here is David Neely's story.

There is conflicting information as to the year of David's birth, but based upon his stated age at enlistment, it appears to be 1829. He was born to David and Elizabeth (Clinton) Neely and lived most of his life in the Sheaffer's Valley area of Tyrone Township. The 1850 census shows him living with John Dunbar and John's sister Elizabeth. John was a shoemaker. David was a laborer. Ten years later, the census shows David married Elizabeth and had children Sarah Jane, aged ten; John David, aged eight; and William Henry, aged five. John Dunbar now resided with the Neely family. David was engaged in farming.

You will note a recurring theme throughout this book: lives interconnected by the Civil War. Sarah Jane would later marry William Sheaffer, a veteran of the 47th PA Regiment. One of their children, Lillie Elizabeth, would wed Clark William Gensler in 1903. We will meet C. William Gensler's father later in this volume.

David first enlisted in Loysville as a musician with Company H of the 133rd. This nine-month regiment had a large contingent of Perry Countians. David mustered on August 13, 1862, and was discharged with the regiment on May 25, 1863. As a veteran volunteer, he enlisted in Carlisle on February 26, 1864, and mustered into Company A of the 77th PA Regiment that same day. The 77th was primarily engaged in Tennessee, Kentucky, and Georgia, fighting in some of the bloodiest battles in that sector. They were stationed in Chattanooga from January to April 1864, awaiting new recruits and the return of veterans who had reenlisted and were on furlough. They anticipated the return to fighting that would arrive with the spring weather.

That spring saw the beginning of Sherman's March to the Sea with the 77th, and David took part. Near Atlanta, at Kingston, a sharp skirmish occurred in which David received a mortal stomach wound. David died on May 18, but excerpts from the following letter indicate a date of May 20. David was laid to rest in Marietta National Cemetery, where interment records also indicate a May 20 death date. Here is some of what Chaplain M. H. B. Burlett wrote to David's widow:

> Madam it becomes my painful duty to announce to you the death of your husband David Neely private in company A 77 regt. Pa. Vol. On yesterday while skirmishing with the enemy near this place and driving him howling before us, your companion was shot through the bowels and died this morning in Erwina hospital.

Chaplain Burlett had David's possessions sent home and, in part, offered Elizabeth these final words of hope: "in God through his son Jesus you have a house in Heaven, where friends will never more be parted by Cruel War."

II.

First to Volunteer, First to Die

BARELY one week after the firing on Fort Sumter, the 2nd PA Regiment was formed in Harrisburg on April 21, 1861, recruiting Company D from New Bloomfield. The Orwan family was well represented in the 2nd.

SAMUEL BROWN ORWAN

Brothers George Washington, Martin Van Buren, and Samuel Brown Orwan enlisted, as did Cousin Lewis. All mustered on April 21, making them some of the earliest volunteers. Sadly, Samuel would not fulfill his three-month term with the others, making him one of the earliest volunteers to die. After being sent home, Samuel passed away on July 4, 1861, and was interred at New Bloomfield Cemetery.

The Orwan brothers were the sons of John and Eleanor (Brown) Orwan, farmers in Centre Township. Samuel was born in 1830 per his gravestone, but the 1860 census lists him being born in 1832. In 1860, he was a millwright living in Centre Township with his wife, Elizabeth Myers Orwan, and four-year-old daughter, Emily. The couple had another daughter, Sarah Ida, on August 29, just eight weeks after Samuel's passing. Much later, a teenaged Sarah wed John A. Stambaugh, seventeen years her senior, who was a veteran of Company D of the 1st Battalion. The remaining three Orwans all served again after their muster out in late July, with Lewis and George serving in the 17th PA Cavalry, and Martin serving with the infantry in Company K of the 149th.

THADDEUS RIDER

Another pair of brothers, Thaddeus and Oliver Hazard Perry Rider, of Newport, enlisted in the 2nd Regiment as well. The Rider family, though maybe not as well-known as some others, has a special place in the history of Perry County. The brothers' grandfather Paul, along with his four brothers, moved to Perry from York County. They bought a large tract of land between Big Buffalo and Little Buffalo Creeks. On this land, they erected a mill. The men also laid out the town of Newport, which at the beginning was named Ridersville.

Thaddeus and Oliver were born to Paul David and Dorothy Frank Rider. Oliver was born in 1837, and Thaddeus on May 15, 1840. Both were born on the family farm in Penn Township. Their siblings were Paul, David, Jacob, and Margaret. By 1860, the family resided in Newport Borough. The elder Paul was listed as a butcher, as were sons David, Thaddeus, and Jacob.

Five Rider men served in the war. The elder Paul and David served in Company I of the 6th PA Militia. Jacob later enlisted in the 208th. Father, Oliver, Jacob, and David survived the war; Thaddeus did not. Thaddeus contracted a deadly fever and passed away on July 7, 1861. All sources agree on the date but not the circumstances. One source cites a death at home after being furloughed. Another source says the death was caused by brain fever while in the hospital in Hagerstown. Still another, the U.S. Registers of Deaths of Volunteers, shows he died at the Camden Street General Hospital in Baltimore of "intermittent fever." Thaddeus was laid to rest in the old Newport Cemetery off Fifth Street in town.

LOUIS H. VARNS

The story of Pennsylvania's 3rd Regiment is remarkably like that of the 2nd. It was composed of companies of volunteers that had existed prior to the outbreak of hostilities. Most of the men in the ranks of this unit were from the Altoona, Bedford, Duncansville, and Hollidaysburg areas. The index card for Private Louis H. Varns shows his residence as Duncansville, and that is indeed where he enlisted.

However, Louis is buried in Hill Church Cemetery in Watts Township, where his parents, Abraham and Mary, also are interred. The 1850 census data shows his residence as New Buffalo with his parents. Abraham is listed as an innkeeper. Mary was Abraham's second wife.

We are not sure how or why Louis was in Duncansville in 1861, but we are certain he was among the first to volunteer, doing so on April 20, 1861, and becoming a member of Company A. The 3rd Regiment was a ninety-day unit, so muster-out occurred on July 20. Muster files do not show whether Louis had come down with disease, but he only survived his stint in the army by thirty-three days.

ALLEN S. JACOBS

The 11th PA Regiment was also originally a ninety-day unit mustered on April 23, 1861. It was then re-mustered as a three-year regiment in September 1861. This unit saw action in every major battle in the Eastern Theater of conflict, including Antietam, Fredericksburg, and Gettysburg. The 11th PA's monument is a worthwhile trip. It showcases the most famous member of the regiment, their dog, Sallie. She was the regimental mascot and joined her soldiers at every skirmish and battle, barking furiously at the enemy and keeping watch over her men. Sallie's story of vigilance and dedication to her men is worthy of the reader's time, though not apropos here.

A member of Company A was Lt. Allen S. Jacobs of New Bloomfield. Allen enrolled on October 15, 1861, as a private. He was promoted to commissary sergeant, then commissioned as a second lieutenant on February 1, 1863, and then to first lieutenant on June 3, 1863. He served as the regimental adjutant at Gettysburg until his sick leave furlough.

Allen was born on October 6, 1828, to George and Margaret Jacobs, farmers in Juniata Township. A brother, Samuel, later joined Company E of the 173rd PA and attained the rank of sergeant. The 1860 census shows Allen lived in New Bloomfield as a student.

His term in the army took a toll on his health, and he was sent home for a rest after the Battle of Gettysburg. Some in the borough remarked that he looked better than ever. But he took a turn for the worse and died on October 18, 1863. The *Perry County Democrat* printed the following in his obituary on October 29, 1863: "The deceased returned from the army a few weeks ago and died among his friends and kindred. We knew him long and well and his death cast a gloom over our borough." Allen was married to the former Mary Lauck and was the father of a daughter, Margaret. Burial was in New Bloomfield Cemetery.

ARNOLD LOBAUGH

The John Lobaugh family resided in Adams County, close to the county line between Adams and Cumberland. John had wed Mary John in Adams, where the couple began raising a family before relocating to Juniata Township near Newport in 1832. John again moved his family to Peoria County, Illinois, fifteen years later. However, at least two children stayed in Perry: George and Arnold. George, a Mexican War veteran, kept store near Donnally Mills. Arnold was a clerk in Newport, according to the 1850 census, before being appointed to a postmaster position there in 1852.

Arnold, born in Adams County on November 24, 1818, married Mary Hartzell in Newport. The couple endured tragedy after tragedy with their children. Ephraim, born in 1842, died a year later. An infant died at childbirth in 1845. Emma was born in 1846 and lived only one year. Mary was one year old when she died in 1848. Margaret was born and died in 1856. John R. was three when he died in 1864. Angelia, born in 1844, was only twenty when she passed the same year as brother John R. All are buried in Old Newport Cemetery off Fifth Street.

Possibly seeking escape from those memories, the 1860 census shows Arnold, Mary, Angelia, Travilla, Susan, and Matilda living in Greensburg, where Arnold was a merchant. Arnold enlisted there on April 20, 1861, as a sergeant in the 11th PA Regiment. He, along with most of the men in the regiment, signed on in September as the 11th began a three-year commitment. They mustered on September 20, 1861. One of the first big tests came a year later at Antietam. During the single bloodiest day of the war, Arnold was horrifically wounded on September 17.

He was promoted three days later to first lieutenant, but his wounds were too severe for a recovery. Lieutenant Arnold Lobaugh died of a gunshot wound on September 26 at the regimental hospital near Sharpsburg, Maryland. Some information suggests he is buried in Antietam National Cemetery, but there is also a tombstone in the same Newport cemetery as so many of his children and his wife, Mary.

JACOB D. HETRICK

The 15th PA Regiment was also mustered into service in Harrisburg. Recruited in the capital, these men joined the Union Army on May 1, 1861, and were another ninety-day regiment. Jacob D. Hetrick, of Greenwood Township, was a member of Company E. The son of Adam and Maria Burd Hetrick, Jacob was born on April 6, 1838. He was one of ten children, six of whom were boys. Three served in the Union Army. Amos, who will be covered later, was in Company B of the 36th, and Adam was in Company G of the 151st.

The 15th did a lot of marching and moving around in its three-month term. They moved to the Hagerstown area and back again before finishing their stint in Carlisle. Jacob died on August 3, 1861, in Carlisle, just four days before the regiment mustered out.

The census of 1850 lists Jacob as living with a farm family by the name of Grubb. He and sister Rebecca resided there and worked for them. There is speculation as to where he is buried. Some information suggests that the burial was in St Matthew's Cemetery near Millerstown. Other sources show the burial to have been beside brother Amos in White Church Cemetery in Liverpool Township. In any case, it marks a tragically short army career and life.

III.

The Militia

AN often-overlooked segment of the military is the militia. These units were comprised of local men who were farmers, bankers, businesspeople, laborers—men who would be ready and willing to leave their daily lives in an emergency for the benefit of their community. Throughout the war years, the militia was called upon repeatedly when real or perceived threats were imminent. Such an occasion was in June 1863, when word of Robert E. Lee's second move northward created fear and panic in south-central Pennsylvania.

Men answered Governor Curtin's call by the hundreds, ready to meet the Rebel Army and send them packing. Some men in these militia units had served previously and volunteered readily. For some, it was their only time of service. For others, it led to later service. For still others, it marked the tragic end to a military life.

Company B of the 36th Militia was recruited from Perry County. Men assembled in Harrisburg and were immediately dispatched to Gettysburg, where that pivotal battle was fast-reaching its dramatic conclusion. Though the militia escaped battle, two men in the ranks of Company B did not return to Perry alive.

WILLIAM SHADE

Beneville and Mary Shade were Centre Township farmers who resided with Beneville's father, according to the 1850 census. Beneville (often seen as Beneval) was a carpenter then, as well as ten years later. In the 1860 census, three Shade families were listed as living side by side on farms. Beneville and his family resided between Henry's farm and brother John's farm.

Beneville and Mary had children William, George, Mary, Ellen, and Sarah. William Henry Shade, born in September 1844, was a farm laborer. Despite his youth, William volunteered and served with Company I of the 133rd from August 13, 1862, through May 21, 1863. Home for just over a month, he answered the call and joined the 36th Militia as a corporal, just as the great battle in Adams County was raging.

William, along with the others, was assigned mop-up duties upon reaching the field of battle. As we have seen, Rebel Minié balls were not the only deadly force at work. Corporal William Henry Shade contracted disease and passed away in Gettysburg on August 2, 1863. He was interred at New Bloomfield Union Cemetery, where he rests among other family members.

JOHN SLAUGHTERBECK

Thousands of German immigrants reached America's shores in the early to mid-1800s, with many relocating to central Pennsylvania from the Baden-Württemberg region. Arriving in 1832, Jacob Slaughterbeck Sr. and Jacob Jr. brought their growing families. Their surname is spelled variously as Slaughterback, Slaughterbaugh, or Slaughterbach.

By 1850 they had settled on a farm in Greenwood Township. The younger Jacob was married to Anna Mary, also from the Baden-Württemberg region. Their children in 1850 were Jacob, sixteen; Margaret, fourteen; Susanna, thirteen; John, eleven; Mary, nine; Elizabeth, six; and David, four. Jacob III would enlist in the 101st Regiment toward the end of the war. John joined Company B of the 36th Militia during the Gettysburg crisis.

John, born on March 27, 1839, was twenty-four when he enlisted. He, like William Shade, escaped musket fire only to be felled by disease. The 36th Militia was discharged on August 11, 1863, from their duties at Gettysburg. John died on the seventh, just four days before mustering out. He was brought home and laid to rest in Millerstown Memorial Cemetery.

IV.

The Pennsylvania Reserves

THE Pennsylvania reserves constituted a division and mostly fought together. But from time to time, some units transferred to other arenas during the war. The list of their commanders reads like a who's who of Pennsylvania generals, including George Meade, John F. Reynolds, George McCandless, and Samuel Crawford. The reserves fought in the eastern theater of the war and distinguished themselves in major battles such as South Mountain, Antietam, Fredericksburg, Gettysburg, and the Wilderness. The 30th, along with the 41st and 42nd, fought close to home at Gettysburg and helped turn the tide on July 2 near the Wheatfield, Devil's Den, and the Round Tops.

SAMUEL SCHEIBLEY BAKER

As noted previously, many Perry County families sent multiple sons to war. The Baker family of Tyrone and later Tuscarora Townships outdid most. Five Baker sons fought for the Union. Though not always spelled the same way, all had their mother's birth name, Scheibley, as their middle name. Peter and John fought in the 208th late in the war. James joined the 201st. Abraham was a member of the 173rd. And Samuel Scheibley Baker enrolled with Company H of the 1st PA Reserves on June 8, 1861. That unit mustered into Federal service as the 30th PA Regiment.

Samuel was born to Samuel and Elizabeth Scheibley Baker in Tyrone Township on March 2, 1831, but by the 1860 census, the Baker family was farming in Tuscarora Township near Donnally Mills. That same census shows the younger Samuel living in Carlisle and working as a bricklayer. Samuel fought with the 30th through many large battles, including Gettysburg, but on May 18, 1864, he suffered a mortal wound at Spotsylvania. According to the hospital records at a Staunton Area Hospital, Samuel died from a gunshot wound to the spine just nine days later. His body was "taken home," and he was buried in St. John's Church Cemetery in Markelsville. No record of Samuel being married has been found.

WILLIAM H. BERKSTRESSER/BAXTER

Another member of the 30th was William H. Berkstresser/Baxter, who served in Company I. Millions of Europeans immigrated to America in the nineteenth century, and many "Americanized" their names. These folks wanted to blend in, and they volunteered by the thousands to fight for both sides. Discrimination in the 1800s was not confined only to blacks. Italians, Germans, Irish, and many others were scorned and treated as second-class citizens. Taking a name like Berkstresser and utilizing Baxter instead was just one way of trying not to stand out in society. This family sent quite a few members to the Union Army, and, at various times, seemed to go by both names as well as Bergstresser. William's uncle Samuel Baxter also served with the 30th. William appears on the Pennsylvania Monument at Gettysburg as Baxter, though his tombstone reads Berkstresser. William's father, Solomon, is buried in Sandy Hollow, and his tombstone reads "Solomon Berkstresser Baxter." Mother Margaret's tombstone in New Bloomfield reads "Baxter."

William Harrison Berkstresser was born to Solomon and Margaret McGowan Berkstresser/Baxter on April 26, 1840. He had five sisters: Margaret, Anna Belle, Sarah, Mabel, and Mary Jane. He also had brothers: Calvin, John Wesley, Theodore, and David, a member of the 130th PA. The 1860 census shows William living with his parents in Spring Township and employed as a laborer.

After Gettysburg, William and the rest of the Army of the Potomac dogged Lee's army, fought repeated skirmishes, and pitched battles on Virginia soil. During the Wilderness battles, he suffered a wound to his right knee. This hospitalized William and, though it is not noted as to the exact cause, he died of his wounds in Washington, D.C., at Mount Pleasant Hospital on May 25, 1864. William's tombstone is in Middle Ridge Cemetery, but records indicate he was buried in Washington; therefore, it is unclear whether his body is back home in Perry County.

WILLIAM H. QUIGLEY

Like Berkstresser, William H. Quigley was born and raised in Perry County but was living and working in Carlisle at the outbreak of war. Born to Hugh Whiteford and Sophia Frey Quigley in 1837, William was the oldest of the couple's six children. His mother died in 1853, when she was in her early thirties.

The 1850 census shows William resided with Sophia and Hugh, who was employed as a laborer in Centre Township. Ten years later, William was married with a little daughter, Mary J., and working as a plasterer. He had wed Martha J. Winckers in Carlisle on November 27, 1859.

William was quick to answer Lincoln's call for volunteers, enrolling on June 8, 1861, and mustering on July 26 as a member of the 1st Reserves (30th Regiment). At enlistment, William was 5'9", with dark hair, gray eyes, and a light complexion.

Early in the war, information was not well secured, so we know little of what transpired with Private William H. Quigley. Muster files for the 30th contain this notation: "died date unknown of wounds received at Mechanicsville 6/26/62." The battle at Mechanicsville was the first of the Seven Days Battles during the Peninsula Campaign. It was fought close to Richmond and is also known as the Battle of Beaver Dam Creek. No burial information has been located for William. Martha filed for a widow's pension on November 17, 1864, just ten days before what would have been their fifth wedding anniversary.

JOHN F. ADAMS

The 7th Reserves, or 36th PA Regiment, mustered into service on May 4, 1861. The regiment's Company B was recruited in Perry County with many county men in the ranks coming from the eastern part of the county. Most men of Company B were originally recruited in Liverpool and known as the Biddle Rifles. Seventy-six officers and privates comprised the Liverpool contingent. They volunteered quickly after the fall of Fort Sumter, and then, as the old army adage says, they hurried up and waited. Frustrated with the wait, Captain George K. Scholl, the driving force behind this regiment, telegraphed Governor Curtin that he and his men were reporting for duty. Curtin's reply was direct and succinct:

"Don't attempt to move your men until ordered. No directions to report." Scholl knew he risked losing some of his men if the wait continued, so he garnered a boat and moved them all down the canal and into Harrisburg. There, of course, more waiting ensued, but he forced Curtin's hand.

Many Perry Countians filled the rosters of the 36th Regiment early in the war. John F. Adams was a latecomer, enlisting on January 13, 1864, at the age of twenty-one in Carlisle. His army records also show his middle initial as "T." Much of the information surrounding John's family is uncertain. He was most likely born to David and Sarah McAlester Adams in 1843. David was a weaver in Carroll Township. John's siblings were David A. Patterson, Alexander, Matthew, and Sarah. While his lineage is uncertain, he was a Perry Countian by birth. At enlistment, he gave an address of Cumberland County and stated that he was born in Perry. At the time of his enlistment, counties had a quota to fill, and his muster file shows he was from the 15th Congressional District, which was Perry at the time.

His veterans card file shows that John was a blacksmith standing 5'6" tall, with a florid complexion, gray eyes, and dark hair. His time with the 36th was brief, as he was one of hundreds captured at the Wilderness on May 5, 1864. He was sent to Andersonville Prison. In late winter of 1864, John was sent to Camp Parole in Annapolis, Maryland. This facility was where paroled soldiers were kept after being freed by the Confederates. It was a bit of an honor system, whereby after being exchanged for a Rebel of similar rank, soldiers were housed at Camp Parole, unable to reenter the war but still a soldier and property of the army. Many soldiers were stricken by diseases there, including John. He died of "typhoid fever" on March 10, 1865, and was interred at the national cemetery in Annapolis.

MATTHEW ADAMS

Matthew Adams, an elder statesman born on August 22, 1822, was the son of Joseph and Eliza Adams, who resided in Carroll Township but later moved to Wheatfield Township, where Matthew was employed as a laborer according to the 1850 census. By 1860, Matthew lived in Oliver Township, where he was a wagon maker. He was married to the former Sarah Campbell and had children Mary, Joseph, Jefferson, Alexander, and Luther. Joseph, born in May 1846, later enlisted with the 36th

Emergency Militia in 1863 and then served with Company I of the 7th PA Cavalry from February 1864 through August 23, 1865. Unfortunately, father and son never got to share war stories, as Matthew died in the regimental hospital in Alexandria, Virginia, of "Laryngitis acute" on March 5, 1864.

GEORGE W. BROWN

Another early volunteer for service was George W. Brown, nineteen years old, who enrolled at Liverpool on July 18, 1861, and became a private in Company B of the 7th Reserves nine days later. The 7th mustered in as the 36th PA Regiment on July 27 in Harrisburg. *Haines History of Perry County* shows him to be among the soldiers killed from the county. George Brown was a popular name in the 1800s in general, and in the army especially. A George S. Brown was killed the same day, so information may be intermingled. George's father was also named George. The elder George and Mary were farmers in Watts Township, who, in addition to young George, had children Mary, Anna, Henry, Jesse, and David.

Little is known about George or his demise. The muster file includes this notation after his name: "died of wounds received at the Battle of Gaines Mill, June 27th, 1862." George died just eleven months after mustering in. Burial information has not been located for this Perry County hero.

FRANKLIN B. ELLIS

Is it more tragic when a husband and father goes off to war and doesn't return? Or could it be worse if a promising youth of sixteen enlists only to be shot down before he can make his mark on the world? Obviously, there is no good answer, only sadness and emptiness.

Obadiah Ellis was a millwright in Ferguson Township, Centre County, according to census data. He had wed Sarah Holter and fathered five children with her by that year. The census of 1860 reveals that the family had relocated to Duncannon, where a great need for a man of his skills existed.

Franklin B. Ellis was a fifteen-year-old student. On May 8 of the following year, young Franklin enlisted. Muster files show him to have provided an age of eighteen upon enrolling. He stood 5'7" tall, with brown hair, brown eyes, and a fair complexion. Frank reenlisted as a veteran volunteer in Washington three years later.

The muster files indicate he was "missing in action at Battle of Wilderness 5/5/1864." In reality he had been wounded and succumbed to his wounds on June 16. His brother Thomas enlisted that fall with the 208th Regiment. Obadiah applied for a pension, as did Sarah after her husband had passed away. However, there is no record of the pension being awarded.

STEPHEN F. GLAZE

The Liverpool and Montgomery's Ferry sections of Perry County attracted many people to relocate there. Jobs were plentiful with the Susquehanna River and Pennsylvania Canal within easy walking distance. Boat building and shipping were the main industries, but support businesses were plentiful also. Hotels, general stores, tailor shops, shoemakers, and blacksmith shops were needed. Stephen F. Glaze was a nineteen-year-old blacksmith in Montgomery's Ferry per his enlistment profile. No Glaze family is found in that area's 1860 census, therefore one may assume Stephen moved there to take advantage of the opportunities. Amos Glaze appears in that census in Northumberland County in the Winfield area. He is a farmer with a nineteen-year-old son named Stephen, but it would be a leap to point the finger in that direction.

Stephen enrolled with the Biddle Rifles in May 1861 and was mustered in with the others on July 27, 1861. He was described as being just under 5'7" tall, with dark hair, a light complexion, and blue eyes. He reenlisted on November 10, 1863. Private Stephen Glaze went missing at the Wilderness on May 5, 1864. He had been captured and was incarcerated at Andersonville Prison. Conditions at Andersonville were horrendous all the time, but the Georgia sun would have been especially brutal in summer. In all, more than thirteen thousand Union soldiers died in that prison, with 1,849 hailing from Pennsylvania. The muster file for Company B of the 7th Reserves shows that Stephen was one of those 1,849. However, no cause of death is listed and no burial location has been found. Private Stephen F. Glaze did not get a chance to live out his life on his terms, nor did he receive the dignity due him for his sacrifice.

AMOS HETRICK

Amos was a member of Company B of the 36th. Born on May 21, 1832, Amos was six years older than his brother Jacob (page 7). Amos mustered in at the rank of sergeant just before turning twenty-nine and was later elevated to first sergeant. His index card shows him to be a tall man at 5'10", with a light complexion and blue eyes. His listed occupation was tailor.

The 1850 census shows Amos residing in Liverpool Borough with the Peter Holsman family. Peter was also a tailor. Amos never married. His mother applied for his pension. Amos was killed at the battle of Gaines Mills in Virginia on June 27, 1862. One source says he is buried in White Church Cemetery in Liverpool, while another says St. Matthew's Church in Millerstown.

JAMES MCGLAUGHLIN

Liverpool was a bustling, thriving town during the heyday of the Pennsylvania Canal in the mid-nineteenth century. It became one of the canal's major ports with hotels, taverns, and boat manufacturing and had many townspeople employed in the related industries along the Susquehanna River. Two of the many boatmen in the area were brothers Carson and James McGlaughlin. Sometimes spelled McLaughlin, the brothers were the sons of Sarah: James, born in 1833, and Carson, born in 1836.

Their father was not in the picture at the time of the 1850 census. By 1860, both boys were boatmen helping to support their mother, another brother Henry W., and sister Harriett.

Both enrolled in Company B of the 36th Regiment: James on May 4, 1861, and Carson on January 28, 1862. Similar in appearance, James was half an inch shorter at 5'6". Both had brown hair and a light complexion. Their time serving together would be tragically brief. Carson mustered on March 4, 1862. James died less than eight months later, on October 27, in Annapolis, Maryland, of chronic diarrhea while in the hospital at a parole camp. James is buried in Annapolis National Cemetery.

Carson was discharged on a surgeon's certificate just six days later. Then he reenlisted in Company B on January 28, 1864, and served later in Company K of the 83rd PA. Carson passed away two days after the thirty-fifth anniversary of his brother's death and is buried in Liverpool Cemetery.

JAMES H. MCCROSKEY

Many farmers in Perry County saw one, two, three, or more of their farmhands (sons) go off to war just when crops were ready either to be planted or harvested. This created both heartache and hardship. Some managed to keep the boys down on the farm for a few years, but sooner or later most of them went. James H. McCroskey of Carroll Township probably waited until the fall and winter work was complete before he journeyed over the mountain to Carlisle to offer his services. He did just that on the last day of February in 1864. That day, James became a member of Company A of the 36th Regiment. At enlistment James was 5'7" tall, with dark hair and blue eyes. His time with them was tragically short, as he was one of the hundreds captured at the Battle of the Wilderness.

He was incarcerated at a prisoner of war camp in Florence, South Carolina, where diseases of all kinds were rampant. James died there on November 13, 1864, and is buried in Florence National Cemetery, but no headstone graces his grave, for he was not identified when the bodies were reinterred.

SILAS PORTZLINE

Silas Portzline (sometimes spelled Portzlein or Portsline) was born to Francis and Margaret on August 9, 1838, one of a dozen children. Francis was a mason, but many of the boys chose to be boatmen. The 1860 census shows four Portzline brothers—Silas, William, Abraham, and John—living in Liverpool borough, employed as boatmen. Also living there, in what appears to be a boardinghouse run by H. W. Shuman, were Samuel Cratzer and Lewis Bitting, who were boatmen as well. With the Pennsylvania canal close by, that was a needed skill in the mid-1800s. Bitting, along with William and Silas, enlisted in Company B of the 36th.

Silas was listed at 5'5", with light hair, gray eyes, and a light complexion at enlistment. The year 1862 was an especially costly one for the 36th. That year, in addition to battles at South Mountain, Antietam, and

Fredericksburg, the battle at Gaines Mills hit them hard. Brother William was among the wounded that day. Silas escaped the leaden missiles but could not avoid disease. He was furloughed to go home but died shortly after his return on November 16, 1863. Silas was buried in Portzline Family Cemetery near Mount Pleasant Mills.

THE RICE BROTHERS

We must now meet our second pair of brothers to make this unenviable list. Jeremiah and Catharine (Koser) Rice of Tyrone Township near Landisburg were the parents of ten, including Elias and Josiah. Jeremiah was a miller and farmer.

We will treat these two together since they grew up together, served together, and perished together. Josiah, born in 1841, was two years older than Elias. Information on Elias is more prevalent than on Josiah because Josiah was likely a contract employee rather than a private in the army. When Josiah registered for the draft in June 1863, a notation was entered stating that he "was a contract teamster in the army." His information listed him as being a saddler who was twenty-two and unmarried. Elias's index card shows him as a 5'11"-tall farmer, with dark hair, gray eyes, and a light complexion upon his enlistment on May 4, 1861.

Apart from a brief period in the spring and summer of 1863, the 36th camped, trained, and fought alongside the other reserve regiments. An interesting letter Elias sent home from Camp Green contains a reference to a visit from "a man from Ickesburg, Nicholas Hench who is here to visit his sons." The Hench brothers were in the 41st Regiment. In the letter, Elias says he "had just received pay of twenty dollars and was sending seventeen home with Mr. Hench so it could be mailed to his parents."

Elias was listed as missing in action on May 5, 1864, at the Battle of the Wilderness. He was captured and taken to Andersonville Prison. Josiah was also incarcerated at Andersonville after he was captured on November 25, 1863, at the Orange and Alexandria Railroad. Both men became sick; Elias entered the hospital first. Josiah arrived at the hospital on September 2, 1864, and Elias died the following day of dysentery. Twenty-five days later Josiah joined his brother among the ranks of the fallen.

A memorial stone, or cenotaph, stands in Landisburg Cemetery. It reads that Josiah died a POW in Savannah, Georgia. The place of death may be in question, but not the cause. This entry in the *Religious Intelligence Newspaper*, dated March 23, 1867, may shed some light. It reads, "Two young sons of Jeremiah Rice, of Landisburg, Pa. died of starvation in Andersonville Prison." It adds that a generous "donation to the German Reformed Church by Elias who had become resigned to his fate, was made as one of his last acts on earth."

DAVID SHATTO

The Seven Days Campaign in June 1862 was devastating to the 36th, particularly to Company B. During this fighting, Private David Shatto of Newport was captured. He was the son of farmers Anthony and Mary (Smith) Shatto, and born on February 25, 1838, in Oliver Township.

The 1860 census shows David living with older brother Michael and employed as a plasterer. David married Catherine Cluck, who gave birth to Mary Alice one month before David enlisted in the army. At enlistment, he was described as 5'6" tall, with light hair, gray eyes, and a light complexion. He mustered into Company B on July 27, 1861, in Washington, D.C., where he would return less than a year later. After his parole from a Confederate prison camp, David was hospitalized at Armory Square Hospital in our nation's capital. He died on October 3, 1862, of typhoid fever and was laid to rest in Soldiers' and Airmen's Home Cemetery.

JOHN QUINCEY SNYDER

With a name like John Quincey Snyder, it seems our next man was destined to make his mark in history. His father was George Snyder, who lived near Montgomery's Ferry. George was a saddler who probably taught the trade to John as that was the occupation John gave when he enlisted on May 4, 1861, in Liverpool. John's mother must have died around 1845, because there is a five-year-old brother, Simon, in the house, as well as an older brother, Henry, but no mother shown on the 1850 census.

John was born in 1842 and was active in the Biddle Rifles, a militia unit in Liverpool that became the core of Company B of the 36th PA

Regiment. He enlisted at the rank of sergeant but was quickly promoted to first lieutenant on November 11. His brother, Henry Clay Snyder, was also a lieutenant in the company. A year later, John was elevated to a captaincy. He was described as being 5'7" tall, with light hair, gray eyes, and a light complexion. John was desperately wounded in his left thigh at Fredericksburg, and it required amputation.

He was discharged on a surgeon's certificate on August 20, 1863, but a year later was recommissioned as captain and assigned to the Veterans Reserve Corps. The period from August 1864 until August 1865 is mysterious. It is unclear if he was discharged from the Reserve Corps. At some point, he married Emma V. No children are shown and their time together was brief. John died on August 25, 1865, and is buried in Liverpool Union Cemetery. The 1870 census shows Emma living as a housekeeper with her father-in-law, George, but sadly that didn't last long either as Emma passed away on September 20, 1870, and rejoined her husband.

JOHN WESLEY VAN FOSSEN

Precious little is known about our next man, John Wesley Van Fossen. The census information for both 1850 and 1860 lists him as residing with parents, Abner and Eliza (Holland) Van Fossen in Duncannon. Abner was a merchant. Two of John's sisters were teachers. John's index card shows him as a student when he enlisted in Company H on May 28, 1861, in Cumberland County. He was 5'4½" tall, with brown hair, hazel eyes, and a dark complexion.

Private Van Fossen was killed along with many others on December 13, 1862, in Fredericksburg. John was buried in Evergreen Cemetery in Duncannon, located atop a hill, not unlike the one John and his fellow soldiers tried in vain to assault that freezing day in Virginia.

WILLIAM H. VAN NEWKIRK

William H. Van Newkirk was born to John and Elizabeth (Shinn) Van Newkirk in Oliver Township in 1828. John's family had emigrated from Holland and was in the water transportation business in Newport. William would also become a boatman and live in Oliver Township. He married the former Elizabeth Huggins, and together they had six children; however, a little girl did not survive infancy. They raised five boys, the youngest born early in 1862.

William was a big man, just half an inch short of six feet tall. His index card shows that he had a light complexion, light hair, and blue eyes. He enlisted in Company B of the 36th on May 4, 1861, and was promoted to corporal, but there is no record of exactly when. He was another of the many casualties at Gaines Mills. Wounded twice during the battle, William refused to go to the rear for aid. But he was hit a third time by a shell that mangled his body. Two men tried to carry him to the rear, but the combination of his size and the severity of the wounds prevented that. William was among those killed in action on June 27, 1862. The location of his grave remains in doubt.

JOHN WAGNER

Our next man is an interesting case. It appears he enlisted twice with the same company and regiment and was issued a pension between terms. At least six John Wagners resided in Liverpool and Liverpool Township in 1860. All were between twenty and twenty-five years of age, but our subject is most likely the twenty-four-year-old John Wagner of Liverpool Borough. He was twenty-five when he enrolled with Company B of the 36th on May 4, 1861, and was mustered into the Federal service on July 27. He was a woodchopper who stood 5'4" tall, with dark hair, gray eyes, and a light complexion.

John's veterans card file shows him discharged on a surgeon's certificate on March 3, 1863. He was discharged from the convalescent camp at Alexandria, Virginia, due to "functional disease of the heart and general debility." In July 1863, John registered for the draft in Liverpool Borough. The notation on the draft form recognized his twenty-two months of service in the 36th Regiment: another piece of evidence that this is our man. Two weeks after his discharge, he applied for and apparently was awarded a pension for his disability. One would think that is the end of the story, but it wasn't. John enlisted in Philadelphia on January 28, 1864, and re-joined his old company. His veterans card file shows the two musters, and even though army recordkeeping was slapdash, it seems this is the same man, even though there are two John Wagners listed in the muster file for Company B.

John was among the many unfortunates captured in the Wilderness. He was originally deemed "missing in action." Later, he was shown to have been a prisoner in Florence, South Carolina, where he died from disease on October 4, 1864, and is probably buried among the many unknowns in Florence National Cemetery.

HENRY W. WETHERALD

We know so little about Henry W. Wetherald. In fact, we cannot be sure his middle initial is "W." The 1850 census shows Henry W. The muster file for Company H of the 36th PA Regiment appears to show a "W," but his tombstone has his name as Henry N. Wetherald. That 1850 census shows a family of Wetherald siblings living in Duncannon without parents. Albert, twenty-two, and Rosanna, twenty-five, were a married couple. With them were Edwin, twenty-four; Edgar, twenty; Thomas, eighteen; Henry W., sixteen; and Mary, eleven. Edwin was a puddler, while Albert, Thomas, Henry, and Edgar were nailers. All the men were probably working at the Duncannon Iron Works.

When Henry enlisted on July 18, 1861, he stated he was twenty-four. He stood about 5'7" tall, and had a fair complexion, brown hair, and blue eyes. He was married and had a daughter named Minnie with his wife, Martha (Mattie) Siders Wetherald. Henry was one of hundreds captured during the Battle of the Wilderness. The muster file shows him to be missing as of May 5, 1864. The Wilderness has been described by soldiers as hell on earth. That hell was replaced by the hell that was Andersonville Prison in Georgia. Thousands died there. Henry passed away from what the Register of Deaths of Volunteers cited as "Scorbutus," popularly known as scurvy. Henry died on November 22, 1864, and lies in Andersonville National Cemetery under a tombstone that lists him as Henry N. Wetherald. Mattie wed an ex-Bucktail, James Branyan, in 1866, but would die the following year.

PETER WILLIAMSON

Soldiers joined the army from all levels of society. Though farming, blacksmithing, and other strenuous labors were more often associated with soldiering in the mid-nineteenth century, all jobs were essential. One may not typically think about tailors when contemplating military life, but with hundreds of thousands in uniform, clothing was an essential. A person handy with needle and thread was an asset around the camps, where uniforms became torn and tattered from frequent wear.

A tailor from Liverpool, Peter Williamson joined Company B of the 36th Regiment on May 4, 1861, in his hometown. Brothers Cyrus, Jackson, and Ramsey joined the army later as well. Ramsey enrolled with the 83rd, Cyrus and Jackson with the 36th. Jackson also then transferred to the 190th to complete his term. All were born to John Wesley and Maria (Shell) Williamson. John, Peter, and another brother, Bruce, were all listed as tailors in the 1850 census. John and Maria operated an apparel shop. In 1860 the census shows that Peter, born January 22, 1831, had a wife, Margaret, and children Josephine, John, and Peter.

Peter suffered a mortal wound, but there is conflicting information as to whether it was at South Mountain or at Antietam. The muster rolls state he was shot at South Mountain and died in the hospital at Middletown, Maryland, on September 25, 1862. He is buried with other family members in Liverpool Cemetery.

V.

The 12th Reserves—
41st Pennsylvania Regiment

ICKESBURG and surrounding Saville Township are tucked away in the northern part of western Perry County. That area supplied quite a few recruits to Lincoln's Army, particularly early in the war. Some men journeyed to Harrisburg to enlist, some to Carlisle, some to Juniata County, and some to Chambersburg.

FRANK HAMILTON HENCH

Frank and older brother Nicholas Ickes Hench headed west to Chambersburg to offer their services to the Federal government, enlisting in Company K of the 12th PA Reserves. No muster files exist from this enlistment, but these and other young volunteers were quickly transported to Harrisburg and enrolled on June 15, 1861. They mustered into the Federal ranks on August 10, 1861, and became part of the 41st PA Regiment.

Frank Hamilton Hench had just turned twenty-two on April 8 when President Lincoln issued his call for volunteers to quell the rebellion. No doubt young Frank was eager for the chance to serve as well as to escape the monotony of rural life in 1861. The 1860 census shows Frank residing with the William Jacobs family in Saville Township. That same census reveals that Mr. Jacobs was a blacksmith, and it is probable that Frank was apprenticing there, as the Jacobs property was near to that of Frank's father, the elder Nicholas Hench. As was a normal custom in those days, Frank's middle name was his mother's maiden name. Frank would have the honor of carrying his mother's name in this manner. Catharine passed away in 1856, so it was especially poignant.

Most of these men were transferred to Company A on July 20, 1862, and served in that company from then on. Frank and Nicholas served with their fellow reserves through the battles at Dranesville, Gaines Mills, South Mountain, Antietam, and Fredericksburg, earning acclaim for their fighting abilities and heroism. July 2, 1863, saw the 41st close to home in the pivotal battle at Gettysburg. They were heavily engaged in the Valley of Death, the Slaughter Pens, Devil's Den, and the Round Tops. There the regiment suffered heavy losses, but on Friday, they were stationed atop Big Round Top, where their only action was that of trading sniper fire with Confederate sharpshooters hidden in trees. The battle report from the third day lists a few wounded soldiers and one man killed: Frank Hamilton Hench.

In a letter to his daughter some fifty years after the battle, Nicholas, Frank's older brother, vividly recalled the events of that fateful day.

> My brother, Frank H. Hench remarked he would go down and see where they were. He went down fifty steps from our line right in front of the right wing of our regiment, leaned over the rock, looking to the left, with his gun leaning against him, held by his right hand. He was shot through the head, ball entering at right temple, coming out behind left ear. I went down as soon as I saw it and called and we carried his body up in blanket and took it to the rear of Big Round Top and buried him in a triangular little field, wrapping body in blankets.

Nicholas further recalled that he telegraphed home with the news and that "father made two trips before he found grave." The father referred to here is the same Nicholas Hench whom Elias Rice had entrusted with his pay two years earlier. Frank Hench was brought home to Saville and buried there in Buffalo Cemetery.

WILLIAM ALLEN FRY

In 1861, William Allen Fry and brother Joseph accompanied the Hench brothers to Chambersburg to enlist. William was born on October 12, 1828, to George Fry of Saville Township. The brothers enlisted in Company K of the 12th Reserves and served together in Company A of the

41st Regiment with the Hench brothers. In all, four Fry brothers served in the Union Army. Samuel Lilly Fry enlisted in the 195th, and George Kelly Fry served in the 96th.

The Pennsylvania Archives file lists William as a saddler upon enlistment. He was tall at 5'10" and had a fair complexion. William was married to the former Mary Price at her home in Lewistown on January 20, 1851. When William left for the war, they had sons Francis, Job, and George, and daughters Hannah and Elisa Jane. It is unclear why William enlisted with a large family at home, but in some cases, army pay was an incentive. Indications are that the Fry family held strong religious beliefs, and it could be that William, like thousands of others, felt enlistment was the right thing to do.

He was promoted to corporal shortly after being mustered in, which was not unusual given his age. He served with honor and, though he survived the ordeals of all the battles in the first three years of the war, he contracted disease and died at Harwood Hospital in Washington, D.C., on November 2, 1863, just four months after Frank Hench had passed. The hospital records list the cause as "typho malarial fever." William is another of the many Civil War veterans interred at Buffalo Cemetery. His wife, Mary, later relocated to Kansas, where she obtained a widow's pension.

It is remarkable that at least fourteen Saville Township residents enlisted with the 12th Reserves (41st Regiment), providing evidence of the dedication and patriotism in that tight-knit community. Sadly, their terms of service were marred by tragedy.

DAVID H. GRAHAM

Among the many members who perished in the war was David H. Graham. David was born to Thompson and Elizabeth (Hall) Graham in 1842 and was listed as a nineteen-year-old farmer at enlistment. He was described as having dark hair, gray eyes, and a dark complexion. Unlike the others, he was transferred from Company K to Company E and mustered on June 15, 1861, in Harrisburg.

In the 1850 and 1860 censuses, David's mother was listed as being by herself. Thompson presumably died extremely young. David had a brother, William, who was two years younger, and a sister, Mary, who was four years younger. William served with Company D of the 1st Battalion in 1864. David was killed in action at Antietam on September 17, 1862, and was buried there.

JOHN CALVIN LIGGETT

Another of the young Saville Township men who journeyed to Chambersburg to enlist was John Calvin Liggett. The son of Samuel, a "foundryman," according to the 1860 census, and Ann Milligan Liggett. He had an older brother, Martin, who later served in Company F of the 104th PA Regiment. John had sisters Susanna, Emma, Laura, Carrie, and Ann, as well as a younger brother, George, and a sister, Mary, who died in 1850 at the age of three.

While most of the others were transferred to other companies in the 41st Regiment by July 1862, John would not make it that long and was still in Company K. Born on October 24, 1842, he mustered in on August 10, 1861, as an eighteen-year-old. By his description, he seemed a hardy individual. He stood six feet tall, with fair hair, fair eyes, and a light complexion. He listed his occupation as "moulder," which would imply that he may have been working alongside his father in what was surely a strenuous profession.

Regardless of physical presence, diseases of many types ravaged the soldier encampments, preying upon the weak and strong alike. In what should have been the prime of his life, Private John C. Liggett was felled by "Phthisis Pulmonalis," better known as tuberculosis, on January 6, 1862, while in Camp Pierpont Regimental Hospital in Virginia. The nineteen-year-old was returned to his home and buried in Center Presbyterian Cemetery near what was known at that time as Bixler.

VI.

Perry County's Bucktails

COMPANY B of the 42nd Regiment or 13th Reserves was recruited in Duncannon. Though known by many names—the Morgan Rifles, Company B of the 13th Reserves, Company B of the Kane Rifles—they were most notably Company B of the PA Bucktails. An examination of the headstones showing where these brave souls sleep indicates that most liked the title 1st PA Rifles. Langhorne Wister worked at the Duncannon Iron Works, a family-owned and operated business. When the call went out for volunteers, he was quick to recruit and did so in large numbers from the ranks of the Iron Works. The Duncannon Iron Works was a huge contributor to Perry County's economy. At one point in its history, it employed over seven hundred workers and made, among other things, 140,000 kegs of nails per year.

WILLIAM ALLISON

William Allison was listed in the 1860 census as a master nailer. In that position, William was one of Wister's chief lieutenants of production. Therefore, it was only natural that he should become a lieutenant when Langhorne recruited Company B for the PA Bucktails. That census shows Allison living in a boardinghouse in Duncannon run by Abraham Varnes. William was forty years old and gave his place of birth as Massachusetts. How long he had been in Duncannon is unclear, but long enough to become a respected man in the community: so much so that his name became associated with the VFW Post there, which, ironically, is in the building that once housed the Iron Works offices.

William joined the Bucktails in Harrisburg on June 4, 1861, as a second lieutenant. He was just under 5'10", with dark hair, a light complexion, and blue eyes. He was promoted to first lieutenant due to his ability to lead and was in that capacity at Antietam on September 16, 1862, when he was killed in action. William was brought home to Duncannon and buried at Evergreen Cemetery. Today, he rests near some beautiful, majestic cedar trees that overlook the town.

CHARLES AUSTIN

According to the 1860 census, Private Charles Austin resided in Petersburg (now Duncannon) with wife, Maria, and son, Harry. He was listed as a brewer; however, his enrollment information notes him as a laborer who stood 5'9½" tall, with dark hair, brown eyes, and a light complexion. Little information is available on the Austin family.

Born on May 27, 1831, Charles enlisted on his birthday thirty years later and was mustered into Federal service on June 4, 1861, along with most of Company B. He served with his regiment through all their battles but was wounded on May 7, 1864, near Spotsylvania, Virginia. Charles was hospitalized in a Washington, D.C., hospital, but his condition worsened, and he died on July 28, 1864, seven weeks after his comrades had mustered out of the 42nd.

The burial register for Arlington National Cemetery lists his cause of death as "exhaustion." It also shows his place of birth as England. His body was "taken home," and Charles rests in Evergreen Cemetery in Duncannon. The tombstone is in contradiction with the government's records, as it has a date of death of July 28, 1863; however, the 1864 date is accurate.

THOMAS J. BELTON

Thomas J. Belton was one of those employees of the Iron Works. Born in 1838 in Ireland, he was the type of sturdy individual who was tailor-made to be a Bucktail. Thomas and brother John emigrated in 1849 and quickly settled in Duncannon, where other recent immigrants were living and plying their iron-making skills. At enlistment, he was 5'10", with light hair and gray eyes. Thomas quickly rose through the ranks to become a first sergeant.

The Bucktails gained a reputation for hard fighting and expert marksmanship. Soon after their entry into the war, at the suggestion of Langhorne Wister, they were assigned to a permanent position as skirmishers, armed with breech-loading rifles that southerners quipped, "could be loaded on Sunday and fired all week." They were the shock troops of their era, and through the battles at Dranesville, South Mountain, and Fredericksburg, became famous and feared.

At Gettysburg, Thomas was out front leading his men, as sergeants are supposed to, on Friday, July 3, in the Devil's Den area. Unfortunately, he was shot in the abdomen and died from his wounds. He was laid to rest in the Pennsylvania section of the National Cemetery at Gettysburg, a fitting tribute to a man representing his native country while fighting to preserve his adopted country. A notation in the compiled muster files for Company B states that his body was reinterred at Duncannon, but this author has yet to find documentation to that effect.

Gravestone for Sergeant Thomas J. Belton of the 1st PA Rifles. His tomb is in the Pennsylvania section of the Gettysburg National Cemetery where he fell on July 3, 1863.

GEORGE W. EBRIGHT

George W. Ebright was born to John Hunter and Sophia Clay Ebright on January 29, 1838, in Penn Township. George was one of nine children, one of whom, Samuel Clay Ebright, also fought in the Civil War with the 49th PA Regiment. George's name sometimes is misspelled as Elright, and his index card spells it Eybright. The 1850 census shows George living with Sophia's parents in Wheatfield Township, but by the 1860 census, George had married the former Sarah Ann Hays. The couple wed on May 5, 1858, and had young John Wesley. They would welcome another son, William Otterbein, about six months after George enlisted with Company B of the 42nd on May 27, 1861.

Unfortunately, George's military career was brief. The muster-out files for Company B show that he died on February 28, 1862, of "consumption." This cruel war orphaned vast numbers of young children. John Wesley and William Otterbein were two. In the 1860s, few women worked outside the home, so they relied solely on their husbands for sustenance. Pensions were slow to become something widows could depend upon, so many were left with no means of providing for youngsters. John and William were sent to the Tressler Orphans' Home in Loysville on January 14, 1869. There they received education and care until they were released when they turned sixteen. Private George Ebright was buried in Duncannon Union Cemetery.

PATRICK FORAN

Information is incomplete for Patrick Foran of Duncannon. He was a puddler at the Iron Works who was married to Eliza. Patrick was born in County Tipperary, Ireland, and emigrated to America on July 9, 1850. It was typical at the time for ironworkers to come to the United States because conditions in Europe were less than ideal, and America's fledgling iron industry needed the skills these men possessed, particularly the art of puddling. This skill was typically passed down through generations in the same family. It paid well but carried with it short life expectancies. It involved mixing and stirring the molten iron until achieving the right consistency. These puddlers had to be strong, knowledgeable, and focused for extended periods of time—just the type of men who made ideal Bucktails.

Upon his enlistment, Foran was described as 5'10½" tall, with dark hair, a light complexion, and blue eyes. His stated age was twenty-eight. Like the others, Patrick mustered on June 4, 1861, but his military career was short. The Bucktails were stationed at Manassas Junction on April 13, 1862. Some men broke into rail cars and made off with what they thought was whiskey, but, instead, it was a concoction used for medicinal purposes. The muster-out file contains this note after Patrick's name: "April 13, 1862, Poisoned from drinking alcohol and laudanum at Manassas Va."

Though Patrick was originally buried at Manassas, his body now rests in Arlington National Cemetery. Eliza, who died in 1872 at the age of thirty-eight, was laid to rest in Duncannon Union Cemetery, a final resting place for many of her husband's comrades.

FRANCIS ASBURY FOSTER

Most of the children born to William A. and Sarah Martin Foster spent their early years in northwestern Virginia, an area that became part of the state of West Virginia in 1863. However, by 1860, the family resided in Duncannon, where the census lists William as a "watchman," and sons Martin, Erastus, and Francis were employed as nailers at the Iron Works. A sister, Jane, also lived in the household. In an ironic twist of fate, the three brothers were back in Virginia a year later, but not to renew old acquaintances.

In 1861, Martin, born twenty-five years earlier, enlisted with Company A of the 9th PA Cavalry; Erastus, twenty-three, enlisted with the Bucktails; and Francis, born in 1840, joined Company D of the 46th PA Regiment. All three ended their military careers with regiments different than the ones in which they began service. Martin was discharged on a surgeon's certificate on August 13, 1862, then later enlisted with the 201st Regiment. Erastus was discharged from the 42nd Regiment on a surgeon's certificate sixteen days before Martin's release. He also later enlisted with the 201st. Francis enlisted in the 46th at Harrisburg. The muster files indicate an enlistment date of August 19, but by the first day of September, he had transferred. He joined brother Erastus in Company B of the Bucktails. Francis was described as 5'8" tall, with a sallow complexion, light hair, and blue eyes.

Private Francis Asbury Foster was probably named in honor of Francis Asbury, who broke away from the Methodists and founded the Methodist Episcopal Church. The Foster family attended Duncannon Methodist Episcopal Church. Francis often went by his middle name, leading to the confusion surrounding his military service. On December 20, 1861, Francis suffered two serious leg wounds at Dranesville. He spent the next four months in hospitals before being discharged, by a surgeon's certificate, on May 1, 1862. All three were now out of the service; only two would have the opportunity to reenlist.

Francis returned to Duncannon, still suffering from his wounds at Dranesville. That battle is considered minor by comparison to what occurred later; however, it was fierce and deadly. The men of Company B played a key role in the affair and suffered for it. Saville Township's Absalom Sweger, along with Hiram Wolf and John Pennell of Duncannon, were wounded in the same fire that hit Francis and killed two others from Company B.

Private Francis Asbury Foster succumbed to his wounds before the year was out. He was buried in Young's Methodist Church Cemetery just outside Duncannon. There he rests under a government-issued headstone that simply reads, "F A Foster Co B 1ST Pa Rifles."

SAMUEL GALBRAITH

In many cases, we are not blessed with a lot of information about soldiers who served early and died early in the war. We must consider that our military was quite small on the eve of hostilities and that many of our military personnel chose to cast their lots with the Confederates. Therefore, it seems our government was ill-prepared for the great influx of men into the ranks. Another example is Samuel Galbraith of the Duncannon area. The 1850 census shows Samuel living in Wheatfield Township as a laborer with his wife, the former Elizabeth Abbey Titler, and infant daughters Phebe and Sarah.

The 1860 census shows Samuel living with son Charles in Miller Township. It appears that Phebe had died, and, since no further mention of Sarah exists, one must assume she had also died. Elizabeth and another daughter, Mary, were not shown in Perry County. Later, Elizabeth filed for a widow's pension from Dauphin County, where she remained from then on. In her later years, she resided with Mary in Harrisburg.

The 42nd, as was the case for all the reserves, saw little action for about six months after mustering in. Their first major test came at Dranesville, Virginia, in December 1861. There they acquitted themselves well and claimed a victory, albeit a minor one. During this battle, some of the Bucktails were tasked with storming a house that was being used by Rebel troops as a stronghold. They accomplished that task and then defended it against counterattacks. At the very beginning of this battle, two officers and twenty-six men received wounds. Two men were killed outright, both from Company B. One was Samuel Galbraith.

Samuel had received a promotion to corporal by then. He was killed on December 20, 1861, and buried in Duncannon Presbyterian Cemetery. It is apparent that Elizabeth's life was fraught with tragedy; another heartbreak occurred at war's end when her brother, Samuel, was killed in an explosion on the Ohio River as he was returning from service with the 76th Ohio Regiment.

SAMUEL TITLER

Samuel Titler was born in 1832 to Toboyne Township farmers John and Magdalena Hartman Titler. The Titler family was from Chester County, where they and dozens of other farmers were defrauded of their lands and forced to start over, which many did in Perry and Juniata Counties. This is a fascinating story that doesn't fit this volume's subject but is worth the reader's time. Magdalena was a sister to Maria Apollonia Hartman Rice, who is a fascinating subject in her own right, as she was an accomplished lady and the mother of twenty-one children.

Samuel moved to Ohio, where he found a wife in 1857. The couple settled in Columbiana County. Ohio sent thousands of men into the Union Army, including the 76th, which was mustered in Newark, Ohio. Samuel joined them in 1862. This regiment fought mainly in Tennessee, Kentucky, and Georgia, and traveled nearly ten thousand miles during their service, which included Sherman's March to the Sea. After the Grand Review in Washington at war's end, the regiment mustered out and the soldiers were traveling home when disaster struck. The steamer *Argosy* ran aground in a storm, which caused its boilers to explode. Many jumped overboard to escape the flames. Ten men drowned, and though Samuel was never officially identified as one of them, it is presumed he drowned in the Ohio River.

THOMAS GILLESPIE

Today, fifteen-year-old boys have their minds on sports and girls, not necessarily in that order. Thomas Gillespie had much more than that on his plate in 1861. His father had just passed away, leaving his mother, Margaret Armstrong Gillespie, alone with Thomas; Anna, who was thirteen; Charles, seven; and Joel, three. The 1860 census shows the then-fourteen-year-old as a laborer trying to support the family.

He enrolled with the Bucktails on June 4, 1861, but did not muster in until March 3, 1862, due to his age. At muster in, he gave his age as eighteen. He was light-complexioned, with light hair and blue eyes, standing 5'7". Who knows what his motivation was to enlist: seeking adventure or just a regular paycheck to help his mother?

Whatever the reason, Thomas joined the rest of Company B in Virginia. The war was raging in earnest in the spring and summer of 1862 as the Confederates tried to build upon their early successes and the Union tried to find leaders who would utilize its superior numbers and materials. Charles City Crossroads was the site of a deadly confrontation that was part of the Seven Days Campaign. This battle is sometimes referred to as Frayser's Farm or Glendale, and it was the next-to-last battle of the campaign that saw a total of about forty thousand casualties. Thomas Gillespie, sometimes spelled Galespie, was killed in action on June 30, 1862, just under four months after entering the service. He was buried on the field of battle. No record of a reinterment at a national cemetery has been found.

Recordkeeping was substandard, to say the least, as is evidenced in Thomas's case. An examination of Margaret Gillespie's struggle to obtain a widow's pension reveals much about the government's failures. It took much back-and-forth dialogue from those trying to help Margaret until a pension came her way more than three years after her application. At one point, a letter from the file shows that the application could not be approved because no report of Thomas's death had reached the adjutant's office. Affidavits from his superior officers were required to support her claim while, in the interim, Margaret had no means of support.

WILLIAM H. JOHNSON

Despite limited information on the next subject, it was important to include him in this book due to the segment of the population he represents: a segment often ignored, barely understood, often shunned, rarely acknowledged. That man was William H. Johnson. That population segment was mental illness.

The Bates index card for William shows that he was thirty-two at his enrollment on June 4, 1861, at Duncannon. He was 5'8", with dark hair, a dark complexion, and hazel eyes. William's residence was listed as Perry County, where he was employed as a farmer.

The muster files for Company B of the 42nd reveal little. But reading between the lines tells us about society's reaction to this illness then, and that not much has changed over the past century and a half. The comments on the muster-out file categorized Private William H. Johnson as a "lunatic." This terse statement follows: "sent to U. S. Insane Asylum by order of Genl. McClellan (time unknown)." By the close of 1861, the Bucktails of Company B had only served about six months but had already seen hard fighting, the discharge of nine of their number via surgeon's certificates, the deaths of Samuel Galbraith and George Raub at Dranesville, and the ousting of Private William H. Johnson.

Post-traumatic stress would remain undiagnosed for more than a century, but there is no doubt about its existence during the Civil War. That is when a term for its effects first surfaced—"soldier's heart." This term was initially used as an explanation for the changes perceived in men who served in the war and returned to try to pick up the pieces of their lives. We are left to ponder William's fate.

CONRAD JUMPER

Jacob Jumper farmed in Cumberland County's Frankford Township before he and wife Elizabeth crossed the mountain and set up shop on a farm in Perry's Centre Township. Jacob died in 1844, leaving sons Jacob and Conrad to till the land.

When the war broke out, twenty-six-year-old Conrad was quick to answer the call. Henry Woodruff of New Bloomfield was recruiting a company of men for the 2nd PA Regiment and Conrad raised his hand to join. The regiment mustered out after ninety days in the summer of 1861. Conrad must have taken a liking to the military because he volunteered again in March 1862. He became a member of the Bucktails on March 6. When he mustered into Company B at Duncannon, he stood 5'6" tall, with dark hair, gray eyes, and a light complexion. All was well until Lee's first foray toward the North in September. A fierce battle occurred at South Mountain on September 14. Though this was but a preliminary to the events two days later at Antietam, it was deadly. Conrad was one of the Bucktails killed in action that day. A record of his interment at the National Cemetery at Antietam has not been found. It is quite likely he was buried where he fell and may still be there today.

PETER LEHMAN

The Peter Lehman family emigrated to America in 1852, arriving aboard the ship *Leila* in Baltimore on September 14. Peter had in tow his wife, Christiana, and six children ranging in age from Elizabeth, fifteen, to Sarah, three. Peter the younger was nine. Like many before them, they came from Prussia and possessed a strong work ethic and a desire to have a better life in the United States. The elder Peter was listed as a laborer on the ship's manifest, but he no doubt had iron-making experience as well as friends and relatives who had come before him. The family quickly settled in Penn Township, where he continued as a laborer.

The younger Peter was born in Württemberg in 1843. He was working at the Iron Works as a catcher when he enlisted on May 27, 1861. Like the others, he mustered on June 4. He was described as 5'6" tall, with dark hair, a light complexion, and blue eyes. A catcher in the iron industry "caught," or transferred, the iron to and from the presses. A younger brother, Jacob, later worked as a puddler after he finished a hitch in the army.

The Bucktails almost always led the way for the other reserve units and suffered because of it. Their activity at Antietam was near Dunkard Church and a strip of woods close by that they successfully charged and took from the Rebels with their customary vigor. Over the course of the two-day fight, their loss in killed and wounded was 110 men. Peter received a mortal wound at Antietam on September 17, 1862, almost ten years to the day after landing in America. He died three days later and rests in Duncannon Union Cemetery.

AMBROSE MAGEE

Richard Lowery Magee moved from Adams County to Perry when he was a teen. Here he met and married Margaretta Black and settled in Carroll Township. The couple's oldest child, Ambrose, was born on June 18, 1842. Brothers William, Henry, Lafayette, Stephen, and John, as well as sisters Sarah, Margaret, and Harriett, followed. Richard was a carpenter and a teacher; Ambrose became a butcher. When he enlisted on May 27, 1861, Ambrose was described as 5'6" tall, with light hair, a light complexion, and dark eyes. He fought in all the battles and skirmishes in which the Bucktails were engaged until he was wounded in the right thigh at Fredericksburg on December 13, 1862.

Ambrose was taken to Patent Office Hospital in Washington, D.C., where the leg was amputated on February 27, 1863. Complications arose and he died on March 1. He was buried in the Soldiers' and Airmen's Home National Cemetery in Washington, then reinterred at New Bloomfield Union Cemetery among relatives. Brother William traveled to Harrisburg at the age of fourteen and tried to enlist but was turned away, though he managed to sign on as a teamster and served out the war in that capacity.

Grave marker for Ambrose Magee in the old New Bloomfield Cemetery near Carson Long. Note that the descriptor for this Bucktail cites service with the Kane Rifles. The Bucktails were known by many names.

JOHN O'BRIEN

Another mystery man is Sergeant John O'Brien. He emigrated to the U.S. from Ireland, and, in the 1860 census, was living in Penn Township with Pierce Power, Catharine O'Brien, and sixteen-year-old Mary O'Brien. All listed their birthplaces as Ireland.

John was a catcher at the Iron Works when he enlisted. He was tall, at a quarter inch under six feet, with red hair, blue eyes, and a florid complexion. His age was listed as twenty-two, so he probably was born in 1839. John enlisted as a private but had been promoted to sergeant by the time the Bucktails fought at Gettysburg. John continued to serve admirably until he was wounded on May 9, 1864, at Spotsylvania Court House in Virginia. He was taken to the hospital in Baltimore but died there of his wounds on June 4, 1864, three years to the day after he had mustered in.

THEODORE A. PARSONS

A latecomer to Company B was Theodore A. Parsons, sometimes spelled Parson. Theodore was born in 1846 and mustered into the Bucktails on March 6, 1862, nine months after most of the others. This may have been due to his age. In the 1850 census, he was listed as three, and his age was shown as fourteen in 1860. So he probably was barely seventeen at most when he enlisted. His parents were George W. and Mary M. Swords Parsons. George had died on January 12, 1860, "from fall of tree," according to mortality records. Theodore was listed as being 5'5" tall, with brown hair, dark eyes, and a dark complexion.

His military career was tragically cut short when he was killed in action at the Battle of Charles City Crossroads in Virginia. This battle occurred on June 30, 1862. A younger brother, William, born in 1848, also enlisted quite young into Company A of the 201st PA Regiment in 1864.

GEORGE RAUB

George Raub's family has had a lot of surnames attached to it. Most of George's military information is under the name Raup. Census data from Wheatfield Township shows the family name at various times as Roup or Raub. Charles and Catharine Raub emigrated to the U.S. from Prussia with children George, Mary, and Michael, and like most who were recent arrivals, tried to Americanize the name and fit in. Often speaking broken English made it difficult for census takers and recruiters, but one constant was the desire to defend their adopted country. George, like thousands of others, volunteered.

Census data shows he was born in 1844. He enlisted with the Bucktails on May 27, 1861, and mustered on June 4. George listed his occupation as laborer without designating the industry. He was likely employed at the Iron Works since so many recent arrivals from the Württemberg area of Prussia had iron-making experience. George was described as 5'6¼" tall, with a light complexion, light hair, and blue eyes. Unfortunately for George, his army career was short. He was the other Bucktail killed at Dranesville on December 20, 1861. He rests in Duncannon Presbyterian Cemetery.

JOHN SAYERS

The Bucktails of Company B had three men killed in action on June 30, 1862, at Charles City Crossroads. All were very young. All were Perry Countians. Along with Privates Gillespie and Parsons, Private John Sayers also gave his life that fateful last day of June. John Sayers is also sometimes shown as John Sear, John Sayer, or John Sears. In the 1860 census for Wheatfield Township, John Sears resided with and worked for Lewis and Melinda McNeal on their farm.

At his enlistment on June 4, 1861, John was a nineteen-year-old farmer with a light complexion, light hair, and blue eyes. At a quarter inch under six feet in height, he would have been the all-American male figure. He also would have been a big target for the Confederate muskets. No burial information has been located for any of these brave young men from Perry. That is a shame today, but even more distressing for the loved ones who waited at home for these men to return. Chances are good that their families had no idea where their boys perished.

GEORGE HALBERT SPAHR

The Spahr family of Duncannon was another that sent four sons off to war. Enos was a member of the 54th PA Regiment, John was a member of the 194th. George and Joel were Bucktails. Joel enlisted on May 27, 1861, as did most of the others; George did not enlist until five months later on October 10, 1861. George Halbert Spahr (sometimes spelled Sparr) gave his occupation as farmer at enlistment, while the 1860 census lists him as a day laborer living at home with parents John and Margaretta. Born in 1840, he was the second son and third of nine children. He stood 5'7" tall, with dark hair, a light complexion, and gray eyes.

George served through the first two years of the war without incident but became sick over the winter of 1862–1863 and entered the hospital where he passed away. A note on the muster-out file reads, "Feb 7, 1863, of smallpox at Chesapeake Genl Hospital." George returned to

Duncannon and was laid to rest with many other Bucktails in Duncannon Union Cemetery.

JACOB E. STUCKEY

John Jacob and Mary Stuckey raised a family in and around Duncannon on a carpenter's wage. The 1850 census shows them residing in Watts Township with daughters Margaret and Lydia, as well as Jacob and Ira. Oldest son John Jacob was born in 1828 and does not appear; he may have been an apprentice at that stage of his life. Zachariah, another son, arrived in 1852, but he does not appear in the 1860 census, neither does Mary's husband, John. In 1860 the family was living in Duncannon, where Mary lists an occupation of nurse, and twenty-year-old Jacob was a heater. A heater in an iron foundry was the man who placed the hot iron in a press or drop hammer for forging. Depending upon the nature of the part being manufactured, he may have had to reheat the iron midway through the forging process, a hot and physically demanding occupation.

By nature, census data is basic, but one can surmise that by this time Mary had her share of heartache; more would follow. Three Stuckey sons volunteered: John J. was with Company H of the 133rd, Ira was with Company A of the 201st, and Jacob became a Bucktail. Jacob E. Stuckey was born in 1839, so his stated age at enlistment was twenty-two on May 27, 1861. He stood 5'4½" tall, with sandy hair, a florid complexion, and gray eyes. His stated occupation was boatman. He mustered in as a private but received a promotion to corporal at an unspecified time. At Fredericksburg he was in that role and no doubt leading his men in what was an ill-fated and ill-conceived attack. On December 13, 1862, he suffered a wound to his right leg and was hospitalized. Some deaths are quick, and some are not. Jacob lingered for nearly a year. He died on November 17, 1863, at home. A notation in the U.S. Registers of Deaths of Volunteers states the following: "While on furlough from W and Vine Sts G H Phila Pa. Ampu rt thigh." Jacob was interred at Duncannon Presbyterian Cemetery. Brothers John and Ira were reunited with him there later. All three brothers are together now in a small hillside location under some trees, a peaceful spot far removed from the chaos they witnessed during the war.

VII.

The Early Artillery

THE 14th PA Reserve Regiment was mustered in as the 43rd of the line and became the 1st PA Light Artillery. At the outset, there were only four companies or batteries, but by war's end, eight batteries formed the regiment. Normally, four to eight cannons were in a battery. Company G was originally equipped with four smooth bore guns. By the time it was engaged at Gaines Mills, those had been replaced by six 12-pound howitzers.

This regiment fought with the Reserves, occasionally equipped with muskets. The infantry was sometimes referred to as "cannon fodder," so being a cannoneer held the attraction of delivering rather than receiving artillery fire. However, that also made gunners a target. Three Perry County men were members of Battery G, fighting in the spring of 1862 at Manassas and Mechanicsville before the engagement at Gaines Mills on June 27, 1862. Gaines Mills was a small engagement when compared to Antietam or Gettysburg, but it was deadly—nearly nine hundred Union soldiers lost their lives there, including four Perry County artillerymen.

AMOS BARGE

We know more about Elizabeth Ellen Miller, who married Amos Barge on June 4, 1854, in Carroll Township, than we know about Amos. Private Barge enrolled on July 24, 1861, at Harrisburg and mustered in two days later. He was a twenty-six-year-old laborer living in Perry County. At 5'10", he was tall, with black hair, hazel eyes, and a fair complexion. At the time, they had two children, Harvey, who was born in 1856, and Charles, who was slightly more than a year old.

Gaines Mills was an especially deadly affair for Battery G. Included in Elizabeth's application for a widow's pension is a declaration of facts that recounts the events of Amos's death, citing "musket ball from the enemy which entered his breast and killed him almost instantly."

After her husband's death, Elizabeth relocated to Rock Island, Illinois, where young Charles died on May 15, 1864. Elizabeth later remarried and stayed in the Midwest for the balance of her days.

STINSON P. EVERILL

Robert Everill was born in Huntingdon County in 1796, but by 1820, when Perry County was formed from part of Cumberland, he was in the Blain area. There, he wed Jane McKee, and the couple began raising a family. John was born in 1823 and was followed by Sara, Samuel, Stewart, and Stinson, who was born in 1841. Like his father, Stinson was a laborer. When he enlisted on July 24, 1861, he was described as 5'7", with a ruddy complexion, brown hair, and hazel eyes.

Stinson became part of Battery G two days after he enlisted and headed off to war. Eleven months later, he was at Gaines Mills, pulling the lanyard of a howitzer. Stinson received a severe wound on June 27 and was taken to a nearby farmhouse for treatment. The Adams house was the scene of desperation as doctors frantically tried to save their patients. One would not use the term "lucky" when referring to a soldier who was killed instantly, but Private Everill was decidedly unlucky in that regard. His wound became infected, as many did due to the lead content of Minié balls and the less than sanitary conditions. He lingered for a few days, finally dying of what the doctor recorded as "phightrismus fever." Today, we commonly refer to it as "lockjaw."

Though no confirmation has been found, Private Stinson P. Everill was probably buried in Gaines Mills and later reinterred at Cold Harbor National Cemetery. Approximately two years after Gaines Mills, another major battle was fought on the same turf, this time called Cold Harbor.

SAMUEL S. LONG

Certainly, most county residents who fought in the war did so with Pennsylvania's Volunteer Regiments; however, some opted for the traditional army. Samuel S. Long, of the Donnally Mills area, enlisted with

Company E of the 5th U.S. Regular Army Heavy Artillery. In late 1863 to early 1864, this unit was assigned to the Department of the Susquehanna, where Samuel enlisted in Harrisburg as a twenty-three-year-old.

The son of Henry and Bernhardina (Bandina) Flickinger Long, Samuel had an older brother, William, and sisters Margaretta and Sarah. The Longs farmed in Tuscarora Township east of Eshcol. Samuel listed his occupation as farmer both when he registered for the draft in 1863 and when he enlisted. Perhaps he chose the regular army as a career.

At that time, the regular army regiments were sent to quell riots and otherwise peace-keeping missions as often as they were in the battlefield. From the Harrisburg area, the 5th Artillery's Battery E was deployed to the Washington vicinity. There, in the summer of 1864, Samuel was one of hundreds who became ill. The D.C. region was known for swamps, mosquitoes, and disease—then and now.

There is conflicting information as to the malady that brought down young Private Samuel S. Long. The Register of Deaths in the Regular Army shows three entries for Samuel Long, and all note him as being with Battery B of the 5th Artillery. One lists him as dying of typho-malarial fever on August 11, 1864. On that same page, two other listings show a date of death of September 28. They both show death "near Petersburg" and "acute diarrhea" as the cause.

WILLIAM ROUSE

Another Saville Township man enrolled in Company K of the 41st Regiment in Chambersburg along with the Hench brothers, the Fry brothers, and others. He also was transported to Harrisburg, where he transferred not to another company within the regiment, but to another regiment. William Rouse joined Battery G on August 10, 1861. Private Rouse had been a miller prior to the war and had a wife, the former Mary Jane Kirkpatrick, and two sons, Charles and George. The couple had married on November 3, 1853.

William had been born to George and Catharine Jane Hench Rouse in 1833. He had sisters Susannah, Mary, Isabelle, and Nancy, as well as brothers Samuel and John. William was described as having light hair, a fair complexion, blue eyes, and standing 5'9". He also was hit with a deadly Minié ball on June 27, 1862, at Gaines Mills.

Mary Jane never remarried. Charles and George were educated in the Soldiers Orphan School in McAlisterville, learning the trade of cabinet-making. They returned to Perry, residing in New Bloomfield with their mother. The boys operated a cabinet-making shop and undertaker business there.

VIII.

More Perry County Artillerymen

IT appears Perry Countians in the ranks of the artillery were uncommon; still, some served and some died. The 152nd PA Volunteer Regiment became an artillery unit known as the 3rd PA Heavy Artillery. The differentiation between light and heavy artillery often was slight, but typically heavy artillery batteries were stationed at forts, while light artillery generally accompanied and supported infantry. Of course, as with everything else, this was not always the case.

A typical Union battery consisted of six guns divided into three two-gun sections. The battery would have 100 to 140 men who were cross-trained and thus could do a variety of the jobs required to staff the guns. When in battle, each man was assigned a specific task to achieve maximum efficiency.

The 2nd PA Heavy Artillery, which was the 112th PA Regiment, was organized in early 1862 and spent most of its time over the next two years in the Washington, D.C., and Maryland areas. There, it participated in many of the battles in northern Virginia. Later, new recruits were added in such large numbers that the extra men were organized into the 2nd Provisional Artillery and sent to the Petersburg battlegrounds. The two entities were reunited there and fought at the Crater and in virtually every engagement in that sector, losing heavily. It mustered out in January 1866.

The 3rd PA Heavy Artillery was garrisoned at Fortress Monroe. Then, when needed, parts of the regiment were detached and sent by ship or overland to the scene of the action. This regiment saw action at most of the battles in the Eastern Theater of the war, as well as serving on gunboats at Plymouth, North Carolina. It was a regiment skilled in many facets of warfare, serving at times as light artillery supporting infantry. A detachment that included Batteries F and G was sent to Gettysburg, where they fought and died as part of Captain Ricketts's battery. This unit served throughout the war and was mustered out on November 9, 1865.

IX.

The Men

It speaks volumes about the men who volunteered to put themselves in harm's way not once, not twice, but three times! Many Perry Countians held that distinction; two of whom were George W. Topley and Eli W. Orris.

GEORGE W. TOPLEY

George Washington Topley was born on his namesake's birthday in 1836. He was the son of Alexander F. and Susannah Zeigler Topley of Landisburg and then later New Bloomfield. George was fourth-oldest of eight children. His brother Lemuel volunteered with the 133rd PA Regiment. Their cousin Samuel Topley later became a Bucktail with the 1st PA Rifles.

George was listed as a tinner when he enlisted in 1861. First, he was a member of the 2nd PA Regiment from April 1861 until July 1861. He then enrolled on August 20, 1861, and mustered in as a sergeant eleven days later into Company D of the 47th PA, both times under New Bloomfield's Captain Henry Woodruff. George was reduced in rank to private almost immediately and then discharged on a surgeon's certificate on December 7, 1862. The reason cited was "deafness."

Deafness was not enough of a reason to keep George from a third hitch. This time he enrolled as a private in Battery K of the 2nd PA Heavy Artillery. No doubt service in a battery of cannons eventually made everybody deaf. At this enlistment on February 17, 1864, George was described as having a light complexion, brown hair, and blue eyes. He was a farmer now and stood 5'8½" tall. He was part of the 2nd Provisional Artillery in the fighting in and around Petersburg, Virginia.

George was killed in action on June 14, 1864, near Petersburg and is buried in Poplar Grove National Cemetery.

ELI W. ORRIS

Though sparsely populated, Ickesburg and surrounding Saville Township provided scores of men for the Union Army. Patriotism ran deep there. Eli W. Orris served with three different units. He first was as a member of the 133rd PA Infantry, serving from August 11, 1862, through May 26, 1863. Shortly after his honorable discharge from that regiment, he again answered the call when fear gripped Perry Countians as Lee's Army of Northern Virginia moved toward the mid-state. Eli joined the dozens of county residents who formed the 36th PA Militia in July 1863 during the Gettysburg crisis. Lastly, he became a member of Battery G of the 3rd PA Heavy Artillery on February 16, 1864.

Eli was born to Saville Township farmers Samuel and Elizabeth Rice Orris on June 26, 1841. He was the oldest of five, with brothers Charles, Samuel, and Henry, as well as a sister, Mary Ellen. When he enlisted with the 3rd Artillery, he was described as having a fair complexion, light hair, and gray eyes. He was a carpenter who stood 5'5¼" tall.

Eli would have seen desperate combat at Fredericksburg and again at Chancellorsville with the 133rd. With the 3rd Artillery, he would have been engaged in battle in eastern Virginia. He escaped the battlefields unscathed but could not escape illness. Confined to a hospital in Baltimore, Eli passed away on October 6, 1864, from a condition described in The U.S. Registers of Deaths of Volunteers as "chronic diarrhea," a condition that may have brought down nearly as many soldiers as Rebel musket fire. Eli rests now with most of his family members in Buffalo Cemetery at Saville.

SAMUEL PECK

Three Peck families farmed in close proximity in the areas of New Germantown, Blain, Horse Valley, and the far western reaches of Saville Township, as well as in southwestern Juniata County. They were all related and arrived in the area from Fulton County. Samuel, David, James, and John were names prevalent in each family, so some intermingling of records may have occurred. Our subject here is Samuel Peck, whose father was also named Samuel. The elder Samuel and wife, Rachel, appear in census data for Madison Township beginning in 1840, at which time Samuel was warranting tracts of land in northern Perry and across the Tuscarora Mountain near Honey Grove. The 1860 census shows his land valued at $5,000 and individual property appraised at $1,000—substantial sums for the time. Their male children were shown as farm laborers and carpenters. The children, from oldest to youngest, were Morrison, Matilda, David, Samuel, James, and John. Morrison served briefly in the 18th PA Militia, while David cast his lot with the 49th Pennsylvania. This hard-fighting regiment had dozens of young men from the far western regions of Perry and Juniata Counties, many of whom fought and shed blood on the fields of Gettysburg.

Samuel enlisted in Company L of the 2nd PA Heavy Artillery in Chambersburg on November 20, 1862. He was mustered in on December 6. The 2nd PA Heavy Artillery spent the majority of its time in defense of the U.S. capital. Samuel's time with the unit was brief. As happened to so many others, the combination of unhealthy conditions in the marshy area of 1860s Washington and being exposed to germs from the assemblage of men from all levels of society brought down this nineteen-year-old farm boy. Samuel died of "Typhoid Pneumonia" according to the U.S. Registers of Deaths of Volunteers on December 17, 1863, in the regimental hospital in Washington. He lies in the Soldiers' and Airmen's Home National Cemetery in the capital he defended.

JOHN F. KLECKNER

Another of Saville Township's young men would join the ranks of the 2nd PA Heavy Artillery. John F. Kleckner became a member of Company G. He enlisted in Carlisle on March 30, 1864, and gave his age as eighteen, which may have been overstating it since the 1860 census listed him as thirteen. The 1850 census showed his age as three, so it would seem that John was probably seventeen when he enlisted. In March 1864, a plethora of available artillery soldiers forced the army to create the 2nd PA Provisional Heavy Artillery. John was transferred there on April 20. These soldiers were heavily engaged at the Battle of the Crater and at the Battle of Deep Bottom, where a great many soldiers were killed and wounded. Though we don't know precisely where

John suffered a wound, chances are high it was at one of these battles in late July or early August.

John's parents were Michael and Mary A. Smith Kleckner, who farmed in Saville Township. John's brothers also fought for the Union. Jacob was in Company I of the 53rd, Daniel was in Company I of the 17th Cavalry, and Henry later enlisted in Company B of the 202nd PA. The Registry of Deaths of Volunteers shows that John died of a gunshot wound while being treated at the General Hospital at Broad and Cherry Streets in Philadelphia on August 11, 1864. He was interred at Philadelphia National Cemetery on West Oak Avenue.

CASPER ROBINSON

We first encounter Casper Robinson in the 1860 census for Penn Township. He is listed with the John Greek household, employed as a farmhand. Other than a working relationship, it is unknown if Casper was related to that family. Casper enlisted on February 18, 1864, in Harrisburg and mustered in the following day. He became a member of Battery K of the 3rd PA Heavy Artillery. Casper had a ruddy complexion, light hair, and gray eyes. He was 5'3½" tall and listed his occupation as farmer. His index card not only shows his residence as Perry County but also states that he was born in the county.

Casper's service was incredibly short. The 3rd Heavy Artillery was garrisoned at Fortress Monroe, and just six weeks after his assignment, Casper perished in the camp hospital on March 23, 1864, from what the U.S. Registers of Deaths of Volunteers states was "pneumonia." He is listed as being buried in Hampton National Cemetery, but interestingly, no dates of birth or death are noted. He does have a grave marker there. He also has a gravestone in Duncannon Union Cemetery that does have information. However, his date of death on the tombstone is March 24, 1864, which conflicts with the date supplied by the registry. His calculated birthdate, based upon information on the stone, would have been August 31, 1844, making Casper just nineteen at his death. His marker at Duncannon is beside those of John and Ann Greek, which may suggest that Casper had no family in the area. That may be a lingering question with no answer. It is, however, certain that Private Casper Robinson was another young man gone too soon.

STEPHEN D. WILLIAMS

Stephen D. Williams grew up in Lancaster County on the family farm. His parents were Caleb and Lydia Dean Williams. Stephen, who also went by Stevenson Williams, was born on January 13, 1837. His family moved to a farm near Newport in the 1850s. Though Stephen helped on the farm, he was also a shoemaker. The 1860 census shows Stephen living in Newport in the home of Levi Clouser. The bustling town was a place where Stephen's shoemaking skills were more in demand than on the farm. The town was also a place where one could meet young women. Stephen was attracted to a neighbor by the name of Mahala Barrick. Mahala also sometimes answered to a different name—Matilda. The pair were united in marriage on Christmas Day 1860. A daughter, Virginia Sarah, was born in 1863.

Stephen served two tours in the army. First, he enlisted in the 133rd PA Regiment, where he served nine months. Then, he and Mahala's brother John enlisted in Pennsylvania's 3rd Heavy Artillery Battery G in February 1864. Stephen was described as being one-quarter inch short of 5'7". He had a fair complexion and gray eyes to go with dark hair.

Stephen's second tour of duty was both brief and tragic. He was captured on the skirmish line at Deep Bottom along the James River on May 18, 1864. John Barrick was captured the same day. Both were sent to Andersonville Prison, where living conditions were made worse by severe overcrowding. Confederate officials knew something had to be done. Their solution was to quickly establish another prison not far away in Millen, Georgia. Stephen and John were among the first prisoners to arrive at the new facility in October. By then, both men were ill. Stephen had chronic diarrhea that ultimately led to his death on November 5, 1864, just before other prisoners were paroled due to the advancement of General Sherman, whose army was marching toward Savannah.

Stephen was buried in a mass grave. George Barrick, Stephen's father-in-law, died in 1899. His obituary contains this heart-breaking entry concerning Stephen's death: "his brother-in-law, John M. Barrick, also a prisoner of war, was standing by the young man's side when his life went out."

Mahala remarried a man named George Free. This marriage also ended in tragedy while the Free family lived in Duncannon. George died during the Johnstown Flood of 1889. With his body lying in the house, the river rose so rapidly that the family had to escape to high ground. After the water receded, Mahala returned to their house, reclaimed her husband's body, and had him interred at Newport Cemetery.

X.

The 46th Pennsylvania Regiment

THE 46th PA Infantry contained some of the earliest recruits to respond to the call for volunteers. Among others, the Logan Guards of Lewistown had been drilling prior to the war in anticipation of the coming wave of secession and were the first Pennsylvania troops who reported to Washington in mid-April. After their three-month terms were up, most reenlisted for three years and formed the nucleus of a highly effective fighting unit that included men from Perry.

JOHN GEORGE BAIR

A relative latecomer to the 46th was Private John George Bair of Buffalo Township. He enrolled on February 19, 1864, in Harrisburg and mustered into Company F on February 20. John was 5'4" tall, with black hair and eyes. He lived with his large family and was a farmhand. The Bair clan was a tight-knit group living and farming together, with cousins close by who also were farmers. The Bairs were well represented in the Union Army with John, J. Peter, and Samuel all serving, as well as cousins Jesse and Jeremiah. J. Peter, Samuel, and Jeremiah were with Company I of the 208th, and Jesse served in Company C of the 149th.

John George Bair was born to Jacob and Sarah (Clay) Bair in 1840. He was one of at least nine children. Right before entering the service, John wed Susannah Knouse Peters, fully anticipating a return to raise a family of his own. Alas, his military career was brief. He was captured near Marietta, Georgia, later that summer on June 22. Incarcerated at Andersonville, he, like so many others, did not last long. He died from chronic diarrhea on August 24, 1864, and was buried there in the National Cemetery. A marker for him, as well as many members of his family, stands in Bucks Valley Church Cemetery.

DANIEL B. SINGER

Daniel B. Singer was born to Christian and Mary Ann Danner Singer in 1843. The Singers resided in Buffalo Township, where the 1850 census shows that Christian was a "boot and shoemaker." Others in the household were daughters Lydia, Mary, and Louisa, and sons John, William, and Christian. The elder Christian died in 1856, which put the family in a bit of turmoil. The 1860 census shows their household in Buffalo Township as Mary E. Singer, a self-described "Lady"; William, a farmhand; Louisa; Christian Jr; and David. There is a puzzling entry beside David's name: "House of Refuge." Though the ages match for Mary A. in 1850 and Mary E. in 1860, it is uncertain they are the same person.

At enlistment, David was described as 5'5" tall, with a ruddy complexion, sandy hair, and brown eyes. David married Margaret Bostdorff in Duncannon on October 15, 1863, and became a father one year later but may not have known it.

David B. Singer became Private Singer in Company I of the 46th PA Regiment on February 28, 1864. His tenure with the 46th was short, as he was hospitalized in June at No. 3 U.S. Hospital in Nashville, Tennessee, and died there of inflammation of the brain. David rests in Nashville National Cemetery.

SAMUEL THOMAN

Samuel Thoman didn't spend much time in Perry County. Records indicate he was born on May 13, 1813, in York County, to Johan and Magdalena Thoman. It is difficult to determine exactly when the Thoman family settled in Perry County, but it was prior to 1835. That was the year Johan passed away and was interred at New Bloomfield Union Cemetery. Magdalena joined him in 1856. Samuel's brother John also rests there.

After marrying Sarah (Novinger) Thoman, Samuel moved to the Millersburg area, where he was employed as a miller. Their children were Sarah and Emanuel. Samuel enlisted on September 2, 1861, in Harrisburg at the age of forty-eight, according to the muster files for Company D of the 46th PA Regiment. He was described as being six feet tall, with a light complexion, gray eyes, and brown hair. His age didn't slow him apparently, as he could keep up with his younger brethren. Samuel's time in the army was brief. There were several battles fought for the control of Winchester, Virginia, each more deadly than the last. The first one proved deadly to Samuel on May 25, 1862. He died as a result of "wound in arm," according to the Register of Deaths of Volunteers and is buried in Winchester National Cemetery. Sarah continued to move north, settling in the Richfield area, where she died in 1893.

SAMUEL WOLF

It was quite common for trades to be passed down through the generations in mid-nineteenth-century America. Most men earned their living by the sweat of their brows. The advent of iron-making facilities, such as the huge complex in Duncannon, was new to Perry County. Prior to that, many families were known by their association with a trade. Blacksmithing at that time was a much-needed skill in any community, not only for shoeing horses and keeping wagons rolling, but also because the local smith was often the man people turned to for repairs or creating items for the home and farm. Such a blacksmithing family was the Wolf clan of Duncannon. The 1850 census reveals that Samuel, as well as sons John and Samuel, all plied that trade in Duncannon.

The elder Samuel wed Elizabeth Spicer in Baltimore on August 21, 1817. They had children John, Elizabeth, Samuel, Sarah, Maria, Hezekiah, and Mary Ann before Elizabeth's premature death in 1837. Later remarried, Samuel fathered Henry and Hiram. Hiram was a member of the original Bucktails from their beginning to their mustering-out in 1864.

Son Samuel enlisted on September 2, 1861, with Company D of the 46th Regiment. He was born in 1828, making him an elder statesman. He mustered in on the last day of October as a corporal at the age of thirty-three. Samuel was elevated to sergeant on September 14, 1862, and further promoted to first sergeant before earning a commission as second lieutenant at Kelly's Ford, Virginia, on August 4, 1863. His description at the time of his enlistment shows him to have been exactly what one would picture in a blacksmith. He stood 6'2½", tall with a dark complexion, black hair, and hazel eyes.

In a veteran furlough home, he married Catherine (Kate) Bird in Harrisburg on March 17, 1864. The couple had little time together, and the union produced no children. According to her pension application filed only months later, Kate was seventeen. Her husband, Second

Lieutenant Samuel S. Wolf, was "shot through his right breast while leading his men into action" at the battle of Peach Tree Creek near Atlanta on July 20, 1864. Lieutenant Wolf was originally buried there before being reinterred at Marietta National Cemetery in Cobb County, Georgia.

WILLIAM WRIGHT

A notable example of how everyone's lives were intertwined with this war is the story of the William J. Wright family of Watts Township. The 1860 census shows William farming in the New Buffalo area with wife Anna Jane and children Thomas and Margaret. Jane, as she most often was known, was the daughter of Margaret and Robert Fox, who also farmed in the area. Jane would not be able to keep the horrors of war from repeatedly casting its shadow over her doorstep.

In July 1863, William Wright, as did all able-bodied residents, registered for the draft. He continued to be a married farmer in Watts Township. At the time he was registering for the potential of serving in the war, Jane's brother, Robert, was marching with the second coming of the Bucktails—the 149th Pennsylvania—as they approached the hamlet of Gettysburg. Sadly, Robert became a victim of the bloodbath that devastated that small Adams County community.

William enlisted in Harrisburg at the age of thirty on February 24, 1864. By that time, the couple, who had wed in November 1855, had three children, as Thomas and Margaret had been joined by brother William. Private William J. Wright was now a member of Company I in the 46th PA Infantry, heading for the farm fields of Virginia to fight. At Kulp's Farm on June 22, William was reported as missing in action. He had been captured and sent to Andersonville Prison in Georgia, an overcrowded, mosquito-infested facility with no shelter from the stifling summer heat. Food, when available, was barely life-sustaining, not to mention of inferior quality. William was one of hundreds who perished from scurvy. He died on October 14, 1864, and was buried in what is now a national cemetery.

Jane remained a widow for a year. She married another Watts Township soldier, William Liddick. William had served with Company H of the 47th. William survived the war but died young, like so many other veterans, in 1886, leaving Jane a widow for the second time.

XI.

The Deadliest Assignment

MY research, though far from perfect, indicates that the deadliest assignment for Perry County soldiers was as a member of the 47th PA Regiment. Company D was recruited in New Bloomfield, Company H in Newport, and there was a sprinkling of county men in other companies. They had truly little activity in the Eastern Theater of the war, spending much of their time in the Deep South. Though their battles were just as ferocious as those fought in Virginia, the names of these contests may not be as familiar. Pocotaligo, South Carolina; Pleasant Hill, Louisiana; Sabine Crossroads, Louisiana; and Cedar Creek, Virginia were battlegrounds that proved costly to Perry County families. No doubt when the grim message arrived announcing the fate of these brave souls, the survivors had no clue where their loved ones met their doom. As noted earlier, Rebel muskets were not the only instruments of death. When young men were taken so far from home for the first time, disease ravaged many, and areas of Louisiana, Key West, and South Carolina were breeding grounds for malaria, typhoid, and other infections that thrive in sultry weather and swampy conditions.

History lessons in school often give the false impression that the Civil War was fought primarily in Virginia except for the battles in Antietam and Gettysburg; of course, I may not have been paying attention. Nevertheless, the fighting in Tennessee, Georgia, and the states of the Deep South was savage and deadly. The 47th PA Regiment has a history of unparalleled success amid some of the most desperate fighting seen by any regiment anywhere. As testament to the severity of their involvement, 16% of this book is devoted to the valiant dead of the 47th.

GEORGE WASHINGTON ALBERT

George Washington Albert came into this world on May 15, 1827. His parents, Jacob and Catharine Albert, farmed in Spring Township and, in addition to George, had James Elliott and Susannah. Though there was a nine-year age difference, George and James enlisted together in Company H of the 47th. James later transferred to Company D. George married Elizabeth Foose and together they had a son, Henry, and daughter, Mary Catharine, by the time he enlisted. His index card lists him as a tinsmith who stood 5'6" tall, with black hair, a sandy complexion, and hazel eyes. He mustered on September 19, 1861, and along the way gained a promotion to corporal. While the regiment was in Louisiana, George contracted dysentery and was hospitalized in the Barracks Hospital in New Orleans. He was discharged on a surgeon's certificate and put on the USS *Yazoo* for the trip home. Unfortunately, his condition deteriorated aboard ship. George died on April 29, 1864, and was buried at sea. There is a monument to George and his wife in Ludolph's Cemetery in Little Germany.

As was the case with so many young boys at this time, Henry was assigned to an orphanage where he received his education. Later he joined the migration westward and settled in San Bernardino County, California, where he bought land, planted orange trees, and became one of the prominent citrus farmers of the area.

JOSEPH ACKER

Joseph Acker grew up on a farm in Greenwood Township with a Mennonite heritage. That upbringing is normally not associated with being a warrior, but in the 1860s, a revolution occurred that went beyond the "sectional war," as some referred to the conflict. Industry was exploding, travel was becoming easier, life would never be the same, so young men from all social classes went off to war. Sometimes spelled Auker, Joseph was born to Joseph and Catharine in 1841. Theirs was the typical large farm family of the period, with five boys and three girls. In addition to helping on the farm, Joseph was a carpenter when he enlisted on October 6, 1862. The 1860 census lists him as a shoemaker, but information may have been confused with other Joseph Aukers. At any rate, he was mustered into Company D of the 47th on November 6, 1862, from a recruiting depot in Allentown.

After serving in Louisiana in the Red River Campaign, the regiment was reassigned and fought closer to home with General Sheridan in the Shenandoah Valley, where it heavily engaged the enemy in several major battles. Cedar Creek, the culminating battle for control in that vital part of Virginia, was a Union victory, albeit a costly one. Joseph was killed in action on October 19, 1864, along with several of his Perry County comrades. His remains are in Winchester National Cemetery.

DANIEL BISTLINE

Some young men were spared the horrors of the battlefield because disease struck them down first. Such was the case for Spring Township's Daniel Bistline. Daniel's name often appears as Beistline in military records. He was the youngest of ten children, born to farmers George and Jane (Laser) Bistline in 1841. Listing an occupation of laborer at enrollment, Daniel stood 5'7" tall, with a light complexion, light hair, and gray eyes. He enlisted in Elliottsburg on August 20, 1861, and was mustered into Company H of the 47th on September 19.

Daniel served, albeit briefly, with friends and neighbors, and was well liked by them as evidenced by their resolution upon his death. He was buried beside a fellow Spring Township recruit after he died at a training camp near Washington, D.C., only about six weeks after mustering in. The muster files contain this memorandum: "Died 11/5/61 at Camp Griffin, Va. of fever." This is further evidence that when these young men, who were never away from home before, first exposed their immune systems to new germs and new environments, often a deadly outcome followed.

WILLIAM CLOUSE

The Landisburg, Spring Township, and Tyrone Township areas of Western Perry were a hotbed of pro-Union sentiment in the aftermath of the firing on Fort Sumter. One can imagine the news hitting the far reaches of Henry's Valley and Sheaffer's Valley very slowly, but obviously that was not the case. Dozens of volunteers flowed down Shermans Valley like the creek from which it gets its name; or did the creek take its name from the valley?

George Clouse met and married a Henry's Valley girl by the name of Elizabeth Henry. John, was born in 1835; Susannah, in 1837; William, in 1840; and Sarah, three years later.

When William enlisted for three years in Company D of the 47th in New Bloomfield, he was described as 5'8" tall, with sandy hair, blue eyes, and a florid complexion. He mustered on August 31, 1861, so theoretically, he would be discharged on September 1, 1864—or would he? The end of Private William Clouse's term is anything but clear-cut. The muster files for his company contain the message "discharged at Berryville Va. at expiration of term September 14, 1864." Unfortunately, that is not accurate. Admitted to the field hospital at Sandy Hook, Maryland, on September 8, 1864, he was discharged by a surgeon's certificate three days later. The Register of Deaths of Volunteers notes his death from typhoid fever on September 12, which is the date listed in the records of Antietam National Cemetery, where Private Clouse was laid to rest.

To further muddy the waters, in the paperwork associated with his mother's application for a pension, twice it is written that William died on December 20, 1864. Elizabeth was entitled to the pension since William had no wife, nor children under the age of sixteen, and since her husband, George, could not work. Here is a recap of Elizabeth's quest to receive a mother's pension that serves as an example of the thousands of cases similar to hers.

She, like dozens of other Perry Countians, relied upon New Bloomfield attorney Lewis Potter to assist in that process. Her pension file is typical in that it consists of twenty-seven pages of testimony and other correspondence. First, Mr. Potter had to secure two witnesses who were approved by the court as being "respectable and entitled to credit" to affirm that they saw Elizabeth "make her mark" on the application. The two men, Abraham Henry and George W. Sheaffer, further had to avow that they knew William to be the son of George and Elizabeth Clouse, and that they knew George Clouse was unable to work to sustain the family.

A local storekeeper had to provide a declaration of facts that he sold items such as coffee, molasses, and other goods to William for use in the Clouse household prior to William's enlistment. Landisburg physician D. B. Milliken swore that George Clouse was under his care and that George was unable to work due to physical limitations.

Discrepancies in muster file information also contributed to delays and the need to have William's commanding officer provide statements to prove William had died while on duty. Two items in the muster files were particularly confusing. One stated that William was "discharged on surgeon's certificate of disability September 11, 1864." Another entry claimed, "previous file reports for September, October list him absent sick."

Obviously, mail was the only avenue for corresponding between New Bloomfield and Washington, D.C. in the 1860s; a painfully slow process that was only exacerbated by the involvement of government agencies. After months of back-and-forth correspondences, Elizabeth was granted an eight dollar per month pension.

WILLIAM F. DUM

William F. Dum's story gets very blurry as the names became Americanized. There were at least three William Dums in Spring Township at the same time: William F., William H., and William R. Our William F. was the son of Frederick Dumm, or Dum, or Thommen. Frederick was of the third generation of the Thommen family in America. Fredeirich I arrived from Switzerland in 1805, Frederich II was born in Switzerland, and William's father, Frederick, was born in the United States. The third Frederick lived a short life, as did his first wife. In total, he fathered two girls and two boys, one of whom died at age one. Frederick had been married twice, with the second marriage also of a short duration.

William F. was a carpenter when he enlisted on August 21, 1861. He mustered in a month later and became a member of Company H of the 47th. He was described as 5'6" tall, with a light complexion, black hair, and gray eyes, and gave a residence of Elliottsburg. He reenlisted along with many others in the regiment on October 19, 1863. About two months later, citing military service and the "uncertainty of life," he filed his last will and testament in the Perry County Courthouse on December 14. In that document, he bequeathed all his possessions to a half-sister, Elizabeth Dum. His stated reasoning was that his other half-sister had married and "has enough without getting anything from me."

Perhaps William had a premonition. In any case, he was one of many who were slain at Pleasant Hill, Louisiana, on April 9, 1864, and presumably was buried there.

JOHN F. EGOLF

Pvt. John F. Egolf served almost from day one. He first enlisted with Company D of the 2nd PA Regiment under Captain Henry Woodruff in New Bloomfield on April 20, 1861. This was a ninety-day regiment mustered out on July 26. On January 8, 1862, John re-enrolled in Company D of the 47th, again under Captain Woodruff. Patriotism ran deep in the Egolf family, as younger brothers also served: David in the 173rd and 149th; Joseph in the 36th. Their parents were Joseph and Susannah (Mickey) Egolf of Spring Township.

When John enlisted, he was a blacksmith. He served without incident through 1862 and '63 in the Red River Campaign and the early battles in the Sheridan's Valley Campaign but was killed in action at Cedar Creek. John rests in Winchester National Cemetery, close to the remains of several comrades of the 47th.

JOHN EVANS

Private John Evans was one of a large contingent of farm boys from Miller Township to swell the ranks of Company H of the 47th. John was the son of Abraham and Sarah (Smith) Evans. He gave his age as twenty at enrollment on the last day of July 1862, but he was born in 1844. He was a farm laborer and the oldest of a family of seven sons and one daughter. He was 5'6" tall, with dark hair and gray eyes.

John enlisted a little later than most of his friends from Miller Township. He mustered on August 2. At that time, the 47th was moving into South Carolina, and it's unknown where he caught up with the regiment after some basic training. However, he moved west with them to the Red River area and served in Louisiana, where he was sickened. Confined to the regimental hospital, his condition deteriorated, and on June 11, 1864, he died there in New Orleans. According to the U.S. Registers of Deaths of Volunteers, his diagnosis was "Chronic diarrhea and pneumonia." John is interred at Chalmette National Cemetery in Louisiana.

GEORGE FOLEY

Martin and Elizabeth (Keeny) Foley operated an apparel store in Liverpool. Martin was a tailor and son George followed him in the profession.

The 1850 census shows the family included daughters Catharine and Ann, as well as another son, James, who was a boatman. George was born in 1829. By 1860, Martin was not listed in the household. George now resided with wife Matilda (Sweger) Foley, son Martin, and mother Elizabeth.

George enlisted with Company B of the 36th on May 4, 1861, in Liverpool and served until discharged on a surgeon's certificate on December 7, 1862, at Fortress Monroe, Virginia. At enrollment he stood 5'5" tall, with black hair and blue eyes. He, like all other male residents of age, registered for the draft in July 1863. A note on that registration acknowledges that George had "18 months in service Penn Reserves V.C." While the muster-in date on the records for Company D of the 47th is blank, the muster-out information is clear—George is listed as having died in Convalescent Hospital in Philadelphia on April 23, 1864. His diagnosis was "Phthisis Pulmonarias," which is normally used as a synonym for pulmonary tuberculosis. He was buried in Glenwood Cemetery. There is also a government-issued headstone in Liverpool Cemetery for George that observes his service in Company B of the 36th, a happier outcome than that of his days in the 47th.

DANIEL FOOSE

Michael Foose was one of dozens of Pennsylvania Dutch who moved from Berks County to Perry in the early nineteenth century. His life often entwined with the military. He was a member of the Landisburg Infantry, recruited in 1814 at the height of the second British invasion. He served about six weeks in that unit without seeing action. His youngest son, Daniel, who enlisted with Company H of the 47th on August 25, 1861, in Elliottsburg, saw no action as well, but that did not save him. One of thirteen children, young Daniel was born late in life, 1842, to Michael and Susannah (Schober) Foose on the family farm in Little Germany. His sister Elizabeth had wed George Albert, also in Company H, who did not return from the war either.

Daniel mustered on September 19 and no doubt was eager to be off on an adventure that would take him away from home for what probably was the first time. He was 5'4" tall, with a sandy complexion, light hair, and blue eyes. Only thirty-three days later, his military career and his life were over. Daniel died in the regimental hospital on October 22, 1861, at Camp Griffin in Virginia of what was described as "congestive fever." His comrades buried him under a big chestnut tree, where Daniel Bistline joined him two weeks later.

JAMES ELISHA GALBRAITH

Miller Township near Newport sent many young men off to war, none younger than James Galbraith. James gave his age as nineteen and his occupation as a farmer when he enlisted on September 14, 1861, but census data indicates he was sixteen at most. When he mustered into Company H of the 47th five days later, James was described as having a light complexion, light hair, and blue eyes. He was 5'6" tall.

James's parents, originally from Dauphin County, were Elijah and Elmira (Rhue) Galbraith or Galbreath. The 1860 census shows the Galbraith family living in Miller Township and engaged in farming. This extended family shows another son, Samuel, who resided on a neighboring farm with his son, Charles. Samuel enlisted with the Bucktails and was killed at Dranesville in December 1861. Young James followed his brother into service and only outlived him by about six weeks. James Elisha Galbraith contracted disease in January 1862 while in our nation's capital. Succumbing to this malady on February 1, he was laid to rest in the Soldiers' and Airmen's Home National Cemetery there.

JACOB GARDNER

John K. and Elizabeth (Shatto) Gardner also farmed in Miller Township. According to the 1860 census, they raised six sons—Reuben, John, Jacob, William, Ephraim, and Charles—along with daughter Catharine. Four of the boys were soldiers. Ephraim, born in 1846, enlisted in the 208th in 1864. Reuben, John, and Jacob enrolled in Company H of the 47th on August 20, 1861, and mustered in a month later. Reuben had served at the outset of the war in Company D of the 2nd Regiment, and by virtue of his prior experience and an obvious aptitude for the job, he entered as a sergeant. John and Jacob mustered in as privates.

It was apparent that all the boys had intelligence and could handle increased responsibilities. It did not take long for John to be promoted to corporal and then to sergeant. Reuben rose all the way through the ranks to be a captain at discharge in 1865. Jacob never got the chance for promotion.

At enlistment Jacob was a 5'6"-tall farm laborer, with a light complexion, light hair, and brown eyes. The regiment moved to the Washington, D.C., area to train and become accustomed to army life. But as we have seen, many young men succumbed to disease in quick order. Jacob R. Gardner had been born on January 15, 1841. He would not see his twenty-first birthday, passing away in the regimental hospital at Camp Griffin of typhoid fever on January 8, 1862.

MARTIN HARPER

The small town of Landisburg was well represented in the ranks of the Union Army. The Edward Harper family had three sons in the war, all with the same regiment—the 47th. Edward was a weaver born in Ireland. He emigrated to America and somehow wound up in western Perry County. He and wife Mary Ann raised sons John, Thomas, Edward, Martin, and George, with George, Edward, and Martin all serving in Company D of the 47th, commanded by their brother-in-law Henry Woodruff. Edward was wounded at Cedar Creek but survived the war, as did George. Martin was not so fortunate. He enrolled on August 20, 1861, in New Bloomfield and mustered in eleven days later. In '61 and '62, the 47th spent much time in Florida and South Carolina; while there, Martin developed tuberculosis and was discharged on a surgeon's certificate on July 28, 1862, from Beaufort, South Carolina, and was sent home. He arrived barely ahead of the Grim Reaper. He passed away on August 16, 1862, and was laid to rest in Landisburg Cemetery. Government-issued stones mark his and George's graves. Brother Edward lies in Chestnut Grove Cemetery in Marysville.

JOHN W. HOLMES

According to census records, William Holmes was born in Maryland, while his wife, Elizabeth, was a native Pennsylvanian whose maiden name was Pee. In 1850 William was shown to be employed in "coaling," which would indicate mining. Ten years later, he was a lime burner. He and Elizabeth had a large family that included Emanual, John, Abraham, Zachariah, Albert, Edward, Westley, Jacob, and Emery. Sadly, Elizabeth passed away three days after Christmas in 1857. Interestingly, William owned property near Pine Grove, and part of his land is where Pine Grove Church of God now stands, and where he, Elizabeth, and many other family members are interred. Both censuses show John W. listed. It seems he always used his middle initial. On September 20, 1861, he enrolled into Company H of the 47th. He was eighteen and stood 5'3" tall, with brown hair, blue eyes, and a light complexion.

Corporal John W. Holmes had a remarkable journey through various infantry regiments. It was difficult to determine with which regiment to associate the Miller Township lad, but the 47th was his first assignment, where he likely contracted the disease that would eventually put him in a grave. John was sick when he was left behind by the 47th as they marched south to wage war. After he recovered sufficiently, he was transferred on January 8, 1862, into Company B of the 36th, which contained many Perry Countians. The sickness plagued John throughout his military career to such an extent that he didn't muster out with his regiment. Instead, he was transferred again. This time, on May 31, 1864, he became part of the newly formed 190th. However, his time with that unit was also brief. John was among the many soldiers of the 190th to be captured near Petersburg. John had been promoted to corporal by the time he was hospitalized in Division One U.S. Hospital at Camp Parole in Annapolis, Maryland. He passed away on October 8, 1864, with what was officially labeled "phthisis pulmonalis" (tuberculosis), and is buried in Annapolis National Cemetery, much closer to where his father had been born and where his father would die in 1900.

FRANK M. HOLT

Sergeant Frank M. Holt spent little time in Perry County, but he enlisted from New Bloomfield twice. He first enrolled in Captain Henry Woodruff's Company D of the 2nd PA on April 20, 1861, and mustered out on July 26. Instead of returning to his native New Hampshire, Frank stayed in New Bloomfield and mustered in again under Woodruff in Company D of the 47th on August 31, 1861, at the rank of sergeant, no doubt due to his prior service and abilities.

Frank was born to farmers Edwin and Susan (Marden) Holt in 1838. In both the 1850 and 1860 censuses, the family resided in Amherst, New

Hampshire. Frank appears in the 1860 census in a New Jersey hotel as a "Map Agent;" perhaps that business brought him to Perry in the early spring of '61. Nevertheless, Frank chose to stay in Perry County after his service in the 2nd.

The early part of the 47th Regiment's service was spent training in the Washington, D.C., area, known for swamps (of differing kinds) and prone to steamy summer and fall weather. Many soldiers were sickened; Frank had the dubious distinction of being the first casualty in the ranks of Company D, though sadly, the first casualty in the regiment was Sunbury's thirteen-year-old drummer boy, Boulton Young. "Boltie" and Frank each died from smallpox; Young on October 17, Frank on October 28 in a Washington hospital. Both were buried in Washington due to fear of spreading the disease by sending the bodies home.

The *Perry County Democrat* published a "tribute of respect to the memory of Frank M. Holt" by saying, "Never has the death of a comparative stranger called forth more heart felt sorrow in this borough." Frank was only twenty-three.

SAMUEL HUGGINS

Samuel Huggins of Greenwood Township was a little older than most of his comrades in Company H of the 47th. He was born in either 1824 or '25 depending upon the source. When he enlisted on September 20, 1861, in Newport, Samuel was already married with three children. He had wed Mary Ann Strausser, and the couple had Sarah, William, and Samuel by the 1860 census, which showed him toiling as a laborer. However, at enlistment, Samuel gave an occupation of blacksmith. He was 5'9" tall, with a light complexion, light hair, and blue eyes.

He mustered in as a private on September 29 with the 47th. As we know, the 47th was in the Deep South for most of '61 and '62 and fought in a major battle near Pocotaligo, South Carolina, on October 22, 1862. This was the second battle of Pocotaligo; the first one had been waged about five months earlier. Samuel was wounded in the leg during the battle, then hospitalized in Hilton Head and treated for nearly two months. He succumbed to complications of the gunshot wound on December 15, 1862, and rests in Beaufort National Cemetery in South Carolina.

COMLEY IDALL

Some family names can easily be associated with certain geographical locations. Common surnames found over the years in Perry County are Bower, Reisinger, Hench, Foose, Lightner, Stambaugh, Smith, and Jones. However, one advantage of an uncommon name is that it is easier for researchers to trace over the generations. That is a long-winded way to introduce Comley Idall. His parents were William and Mary (Streeper) Idall. The family lived mostly in Lancaster County, but the 1860 census shows William with son Comley and daughter Merilla engaged in farming in Miller Township. Mary had died earlier that year, while son Lewis and another daughter, Regina, were on their own. It appears Perry County may have been a midway point in William's westward migration, because the 1870 census finds him in Minnesota.

Comley enlisted with Company D of the 2nd PA and then reenlisted with the 47th. Comley joined Company H on September 30, 1861, and went down to Dixie. His brother, Lewis, who by then was in Illinois, served with the 17th Illinois Infantry Regiment. Another victim of the battle at Pocotaligo, Comley was wounded on October 22, 1862, and hospitalized in Hilton Head, South Carolina. One week later he died from his wounds and sleeps in Beaufort National Cemetery along with other Perry Countians.

GEORGE STEIN ISETT

Little is known about the early years of George Stein Isett of Liverpool. He was born to Henry, a Liverpool carpenter, and Sarah (Rogers) Isett on July 16, 1835. The 1850 census shows George and Henry living alone in the borough of Liverpool. George had sisters Mary, Elizabeth, Rebecca, and Rosanna. Henry passed away in 1860, as had two of the sisters.

George's listed occupation at enrollment was boatman. He was twenty-five years old when he mustered into Company D of the 47th on the last day of August 1861. After training in the Washington, D.C., area, they headed south to Key West in February 1862 and garrisoned at Fort Taylor there. The conditions were terrible, as the weather was hot and sultry. Many soldiers were sickened by typhoid, yellow fever, sunstroke, and camp maladies such as dysentery. George contracted "acute dysentery" and was hospitalized. He died on May 17. He was buried along with many others in Key West Post Cemetery. That post was abandoned in 1927 and the bodies were relocated to Barrancas National Cemetery. Many of these gallant men suffered the ultimate indignity of having their remains mishandled. George was one. He lies in an unmarked grave with over two hundred others.

HARRISON JONES

Robert and Jane (Hart) Jones farmed in the Shermans Dale area and raised a typically large farm family of seven girls and four sons. They sent two of their sons off to war: Theodore enlisted with the 208th in 1864, and Harrison signed on with Company D of the 47th on September 2, 1861. Harrison was listed as a farm laborer in the 1860 Carroll Township census and on the enlistment file.

He served when the regiment was stationed in Florida and South Carolina, and when asked to reenlist, he did so in Key West on October 10, 1863. He moved westward with the regiment and survived the sweltering climate of Louisiana and Mississippi and was no doubt relieved when they headed back to Washington. Assigned to march with Sheridan up the Shenandoah Valley, the 47th helped lay waste to the so-called "breadbasket of the Confederacy," as they were in constant skirmishes with Jubal Early's troops. The regiment was heavily engaged at Cedar Creek as first the Rebels routed the Union Army, then were in turn routed themselves. Harrison was one of many casualties that day, killed in battle on October 19, 1864. He rests in Winchester National Cemetery.

URIAH WILLIAM KEIZER

A splendid example of how much this war wrapped itself around the lives of virtually every family is the case of Uriah William Keizer. Often going by Urie or William, Keizer was born on June 10, 1818, making him forty-six at muster on February 20, 1864. His surname was often spelled Keiser, Kiser, or even Kaizer. Urie wed Margaret Saylor on May 22, 1844, and farmed in Saville Township according to the 1850 census. By that time, the couple had welcomed Emanuel, Sarah, and Margaret Ann to the family. Joseph arrived a year later. They resided in the Spruce Hill area of Juniata County in 1860 before moving back to Perry, settling around Sandy Hill. Margaret's family had moved there from Juniata in 1839.

Emanuel joined Company C of the 47th about two months before his father enlisted. Uriah was never assigned to a company; nevertheless, he marched and fought with the regiment in the Red River Campaign during the spring of '64.

In addition to the Keizers, the Saylor family was well represented in the Union Army. Margaret's brothers, Henry and Peter, served in the 16th PA Cavalry. A nephew, Ellis, later served with the 208th.

Emanuel saw ferocious battles in Louisiana as well as the Shenandoah Campaign, serving for twenty-five months. He mustered out with the balance of the regiment on Christmas Day 1865. His father's term of service was tragically much shorter.

Private Uriah William Keizer developed what was commonly referred to as camp fever. He was admitted to the medical center near New Orleans before being transferred to Marine General Hospital in May, just three months after mustering in. After lingering for two months, Urie succumbed to the disease on July 29, 1864. He was buried in Chalmette National Cemetery in St. Bernard's Parish, Louisiana.

Margaret Keizer only outlived her husband by a little more than one year, passing away on September 5, 1866. The two youngest children, Joseph and Margaret Ann, were now orphans of the court. A Madison Township man, Andrew Loy, was appointed their guardian and handled their affairs, including the administration of the government pensions while they were minors.

SAMUEL KERN

Michael and Catharine (March) Kern farmed in Madison Township near Blain in the middle of the nineteenth century. They had children Anna, David, Hannah, William, Henry, George, and Samuel. Both the 1850 and 1860 censuses show the Kern family there, but by 1860 Catharine had died. Michael later moved west and resided with son-in-law Samuel Kessler in Shelby County, Illinois. David also moved and was a member of the 180th Ohio Regiment. Samuel by then was in the army as well.

Born in 1840, Samuel enlisted in the 47th PA in New Bloomfield on August 20, 1861, and was mustered into Company D by August 31. He was a farmer like his father. Like many of his comrades, he reenlisted on October 10, 1863, while in Key West, Florida. He headed west like his father, but with the army instead of a Conestoga wagon. In the defeat suffered at Pleasant Hill, Louisiana, on April 9, Samuel was one of many who were captured and imprisoned in Camp Tyler, Texas. Private Samuel M. Kern died a prisoner there on June 12, 1864.

THE KOSIER BROTHERS

John and Mary (Rice) Kosier farmed in Centre Township. The name is spelled variously as Coser, Koser, Krosier, and Kosier depending upon the source. Perhaps, it should be "Patriots." The Kosiers had a dozen children, five girls and seven boys. Several of the boys moved to the Midwest both before and after the Civil War. One of those boys heading west prior to the outbreak of war was Henry Rice Kosier.

Henry settled in Pope County, Illinois. There he enlisted on September 1, 1861, and mustered in a week later into Company A of the 48th Illinois Regiment. He was described as 5'5" tall, with dark hair, dark eyes, and a dark complexion. Henry was a twenty-three-year-old unmarried carpenter.

The following spring saw the regiment heavily engaged in the initial stages of the battle of Shiloh, also known as Pittsburg Landing, where the regiment lost half its number. The battle was an early success for the Confederate Army, but the timely arrival of more Union troops turned the tide. Nevertheless, it was an extremely costly affair. More than thirteen thousand Union troops became casualties over the two days—Henry Rice Kosier was one. Severely wounded, he along with hundreds of others were placed aboard steamships in the Tennessee River. There he succumbed to his wounds and died on April 10, 1862.

Henry's brothers, William, George, and Jesse, all enlisted on August 31, 1861, in New Bloomfield and were mustered into Company D of the 47th. By virtue of his prior service under Captain Woodruff in Company D of the 2nd Regiment, George entered as a sergeant and eventually rose to the rank of first lieutenant. All three reenlisted in Key West in October of '63.

Jesse was born on December 4, 1842, and had been an apprentice tanner to Peter Swartz when the 1860 census was taken. At enlistment, he showed an occupation of tanner. Jesse managed to avoid the sicknesses so rampant within the ranks of the regiment while in the Deep South, but back up North, it caught up with him. He was diagnosed with pleurisy while in the field hospital at Sandy Hook, Maryland, and died on August 30, 1864. Initially buried at Weverton, Maryland, Jesse's remains were reinterred on October 31 at Antietam National Cemetery nearby in Sharpsburg. Jesse was only twenty-two years old.

JOHN W. LIDDICK

There would have been confusion in the ranks of Company H when anyone shouted for John Liddick. Three men would have answered: John W., John F., and John H. All were from the eastern part of Perry as well as another John W., who enlisted in Company A of the 9th PA Cavalry. Our John was born on November 19, 1838, to David and Catherine Gamber Liddick, who farmed in Watts Township where they raised a large family. John's siblings were Elizabeth, Jacob, George, Isaiah, Sarah, Mary, Susannah, Benjamin (who enlisted in the 36th PA), Cyrus (who enlisted in the 46th PA), and David (who enlisted in the 83rd PA).

John was 5'6" tall, with brown hair and blue eyes. He listed his occupation as laborer. According to the muster file, John enlisted in Newport but "joined co. from recruiting depot 18 Sept '64 at Berryville, VA." His time was brief. The regiment was heavily involved at Cedar Creek, Virginia, incurring hundreds of casualties. John was wounded on October 19, 1864, and sent to a Baltimore hospital. John lingered for three weeks, succumbing to his wounds on November 8, 1864. Burial information has not been located. Since John was unmarried, his parents were eligible to apply for his pension. Curiously, both David's and Catherine's names appear on the pension index card, which also contains two different pension application numbers.

STERRETT LIGHTNER

Sterrett Lightner was in his late forties when the war broke out. He was a married farmer with a large family consisting of wife Elizabeth (Sheibley) and thirteen children, most of whom were still at home. Tucked away in Sheaffer's Valley, he could have easily sat back and watched while younger men made war. But he did not. Sterrett enlisted in Landisburg on August

20, 1861, and mustered into the 47th on September 29. He was assigned to Company H and headed south with his regiment. He was described as 5'6" tall, with light hair and gray eyes. He has the distinction of serving in the Civil War at the same time as two of his sons. William served in Company C of the 9th PA Cavalry, and David served with Company H of the 133rd. Sterrett's brothers also served in the war.

It did not take long for the changes that army life entails to prove harmful. As so many others, these men were suddenly exposed to sicknesses, the elements, and substandard and often meager rations that were so different from what their bodies had become accustomed to. Sterrett was hospitalized in Beaufort, South Carolina, in March 1862. It took him about six months to recover sufficiently to rejoin the regiment, but he did so in late September. He served for two years before coming down with another sickness: this time typhoid. He was admitted to a Philadelphia hospital but did not recover. Fifty-year-old Sterrett Lightner died in November 1864 and was buried at Mount Moriah Cemetery in Philadelphia. His army records may be confused with other Lightners, and his date of death is questionable but probably was November 3.

MICHAEL LUPFER

The Lupfer and Loy surnames are two of the oldest in the storied history of Perry County. The families were united when Casper Lupfer wed Maria Barbara Elizabeth Loy on August 11, 1789. The newlyweds had much in common, as each had a connection to the Revolutionary War: both Casper and Maria's father served in militia battalions. Both families had emigrated to America in the early 1700s. Both families came to Perry from Berks County. By the end of the War of 1812, Maria had become a mother of fourteen. Michael was born to the couple on March 22, 1807.

Michael and Eliza were married on May 24, 1836. Their children were Mary, William, George, Josephine, Jacob, and an infant who died shortly after birth in 1851. Eliza also passed away that year, possibly due to complications of childbirth. Michael and sons William and George all enlisted. William and George became members of the 133rd PA; Michael cast his lot with Company H of the 47th at an age when most men were pondering retirement.

Michael Lupfer enlisted on September 13, 1861, and mustered in five days later. His age on the muster roll is thirty-five, nineteen years lower than his actual age. He stood 5'9" tall, with a sandy complexion, dark hair, and blue eyes. The 1850 census shows him residing in New Bloomfield, employed as a stonemason. Ten years later, he was living with a brother in Centre Township, employed as a brickmaker. However, he gave an occupation of butcher upon enlistment.

Despite his advanced age, it appears Private Michael Lupfer kept pace with the rest of the company until they moved to Louisiana. On March 14, 1864, Michael was transferred to what was initially called the "invalid corps," then later termed the "Veteran Reserve Corps." This transfer to the 164th Regiment's 2nd Battalion was designed to keep soldiers in the service even if they could no longer wage war. The men in this classification were used as hospital stewards, drivers, nurses, and other non-combat duties. Michael was admitted to U.S. University Hospital in New Orleans in a weakened conditioned. He eventually was discharged on a surgeon's certificate on August 5, 1864, and sent home. Alas, he could not recover and soon joined his wife in New Bloomfield Union Cemetery on September 16, 1864.

WILLIAM MAYES

Private William Mayes is a mystery man. He listed New Bloomfield as his address upon enlistment with Company D of the 47th PA on August 20, 1861. At twenty-three, he enrolled at New Bloomfield and mustered in eleven days later in Harrisburg. By trade, he was a cooper. William reenlisted with the 47th at Key West, Florida, on October 10, 1863, before moving west with his unit. He, like so many others, became ill. "Chronic diarrhea" is listed as the cause of death on March 30, 1864, while William was in the hospital in New Orleans. He was first buried in Monument Cemetery there. Later disinterred, William rests far from home in the Chalmette National Cemetery in St. Bernard Parish, Louisiana.

ALEXANDER MUSSER

Benjamin and Isabella (Topley) Musser had a tailor shop in Newport. Benjamin and son Oliver were tailors, and another son, Alexander, was listed as a shoemaker on his enlistment card. They also had sons Isaiah and William along with daughters Isabella and Elizabeth.

Alexander enlisted on August 20, 1861, with the 47th. Mustered in on the thirty-first, Alexander was assigned to Company D. His cousin George Washington Topley was in that company as well. Perry County communities are tight-knit today and were even more so in the mid-nineteenth century as evidenced by muster rolls that show neighbors serving with neighbors, and relatives serving with relatives.

Alexander and George's time together was relatively brief. George was discharged on a surgeon's certificate on December 7, 1862, but by then, Alexander had already become one of the many casualties at Pocotaligo. He was killed in action on October 22 of that year.

NICHOLAS I. ORRIS

Nicholas I. Orris was born in Saville Township to farmers George and Sarah (Shull) Orris on December 16, 1840. He was the eighth child born to the couple. A younger brother, David, was born on July 5, 1848, which may have led to Sarah's death, as she passed away on August 16, 1848. Nicholas had a brother, Samuel, who was wounded at Chancellorsville while serving with the 148th PA. One of Nicholas's sisters, Elizabeth, had a husband who served with Samuel in the 148th.

At enlistment, Nicholas was described as twenty-one years old, with light hair and light complexion. He was a blue-eyed, 5'7"-tall farmer. Nicholas served with Company H of the 47th and reenlisted with them while in Florida on October 19, 1863. Then came the move west and the Red River Campaign that proved so costly to the 47th. Nicholas was killed in action at Pleasant Hill, Louisiana, on April 9, 1864.

THE POWELL FAMILY

John W. Powell Sr. was born in Scotland in 1786. He emigrated to America and settled down in Saville Township. Sons Daniel and John were born near Ickesburg shortly after the turn of the nineteenth century, and each later moved down the valley where they raised children and farm crops in Tuscarora Township. Daniel and wife, Mary (Bouseman) Powell, had children Daniel, Maria, George, Nancy, Franklin, Alexander, Emeline, and Jacob. John and his wife, Anne (Clouser) Powell, had children

David, John, Andrew, William, Solomon, Peter, and Caroline. Words that could describe the Powells would be hardworking, patriotic, and ill-fated.

Daniel Jr. enlisted on August 20, 1861, in New Bloomfield. He was born in 1841 and listed his occupation as farmer. His cousins, John Jr., William, Andrew, and Solomon, also enlisted the same day. All five Powells became members of Company D of the 47th.

After spending time in the Washington, D.C., area, the 47th was sent south to Key West, Florida. There they spent several months preparing and guarding Fort Taylor. The heat and humidity, as well as the mosquitoes, exacted a toll upon these boys from up North. Dozens were sickened. When the regiment was ordered to South Carolina, seven soldiers were too sick for the journey. John Powell was kept behind as their nurse. All seven men died, but John did all that could be done for them, falling ill himself. He was the final man to die on August 29, 1862, not a year after mustering in. He was buried at Key West Post Cemetery and later relocated to Barrancas National Cemetery.

Solomon was the youngest of the four brothers. He was a nineteen-year-old farm laborer when he enlisted, and despite all that had transpired with John, he elected to reenlist in Company D of the 47th when in Key West on October 12, 1863. The regiment headed west this time and fought several engagements in the Red River Campaign. At Pleasant Hill, Solomon was captured on April 9, 1864. He was imprisoned in the POW camp at Pleasant Hill but did not fare well. He died on June 7, 1864, and was buried there.

Andrew was born on August 3, 1841, and was one of the sick who made the trip to South Carolina, but he was discharged on a surgeon's certificate and sent home in November 1862. He then enlisted in Carlisle on October 5, 1863, into Company C of the 149th. That unit moved with the Army of the Potomac and dogged Lee's army in Virginia. At the battle of the Wilderness, many lives were lost and many soldiers were taken prisoner on both sides. Andrew was captured on May 5, 1864, and taken to the infamous Andersonville Prison. He, like many others, did not last long. In less than four months, on September 6, Andrew became the third brother to perish. His condition was described as chronic diarrhea. He is buried in Andersonville National Cemetery.

That brings us to the fourth brother, William. He also reenlisted at Key West and went on the Red River Campaign as well as the Sheridans Valley Campaign. Along the way, he earned a promotion to corporal on September 19, just three months after Solomon's death. He was mustered out with his regiment on Christmas Day 1865 and became the only son of John Powell Sr. to return from the war.

Grave marker for Corporal William Powell in the Wila Cemetery. William was the only one of four brothers to survive the war. A cousin also perished.

And what of cousin Daniel? Daniel reenlisted and participated in the Red River Campaign and the Valley Campaign, the culmination of which was the battle at Cedar Creek on October 19, 1864. Daniel fell that day and thus became the fourth to die from the Powell clan. In just over three years, four of the five who had left their Tuscarora Township farms were gone. This cruel war had taken all they had to offer and left bereaved families behind.

THE ROBINSON BROTHERS

John and Margaret (Miller) Robinson appear in the Newport census data for 1840, but from there the trail goes cold. They had the following children, whose birth years are estimates taken from the 1850 census: Sarah A.K. in 1836, Elvenia in 1838, Amos in 1840, Jason in 1842, and William H. in 1844. That 1850 census shows all five children living with William Miller, twenty-seven; Elizabeth Miller, twenty-four; and George W. Miller, eighteen. The Millers were Margaret's siblings. The 1860 census shows Elizabeth married to Charles Boyles with George W., William H. Robinson, and Amos Robinson residing with them in New Bloomfield. Meanwhile, Jason Robinson lived with printer John Sheibley in New Bloomfield, where Jason was Sheibley's apprentice.

From there, Amos served with Company C, as did William, who enrolled on August 20, 1861, then was transferred to Company D. His stated occupation at enlistment was farmer. His stated age was eighteen but it was seventeen at most, possibly younger. He was described as having black hair and gray eyes. William was one of the early casualties at Key West only two months after the regiment arrived there. He contracted typhoid fever and died of that disease on April 4, 1862. He was buried in Key West Post Cemetery and then later reinterred at Barrancas National Cemetery in Pensacola.

Jason enlisted one day before William, but he stayed with Company H. It is unclear why William was transferred but Jason was not. Records indicate that William was ordered to transfer. Jason's stated occupation at enrollment was printer. His stated age was nineteen. Jason would have been at Key West while William was battling disease. He went to South Carolina later with the regiment and participated in their battles in that state. As we have already seen, the second battle of Pocotaligo was costly to the 47th; Jason was another recruit killed in action on October 22, 1862.

JOSEPH SHELLEY

John and Catharine (Dissinger) Shelley raised a baker's dozen children in Rye Township from the 1830s to the 1850s. Joseph was born in August 1834. He enrolled on December 1, 1863, at Newport and was mustered into Company H of the 47th nine days later. At enrollment, he was a laborer who was tall for his day at 6'1". He had brown hair, a sandy complexion, and hazel eyes. He had married Margaret Carlin in 1860 and was father to William Harrison Shelley, born on February 26, 1862.

Joseph's career with the 47th was brief, and he served the bulk of his term in the Valley Campaign with Sheridan. There, in the final struggle at

Cedar Creek, he was killed in action on October 19, 1864. His remains lie in Winchester National Cemetery.

HENRY SHEPLEY

Henry Shepley was born around 1840 in the Landisburg area where his parents farmed. His father, Benjamin, was originally from Delaware while his mother, Susannah, was a native of Pennsylvania. Others in the family were Catharine, George, Lewis, Margaret, and Parkinson, who was two years younger than Henry. The 1860 census shows the Shepley family farming in Toboyne Township near New Germantown. Henry was not shown with the family in 1860 and probably lived in or near Harrisburg since that is the residence he gave at enlistment into Company H of the 47th on September 19, 1861. Interestingly, Parkinson also enlisted in Company H but at Elliottsburg. Henry described himself as a laborer. He was about 5'7" tall, with a light complexion, sandy hair, and gray eyes.

Both brothers reenlisted while in South Florida in October 1863. The 47th then moved west, where the fighting was severe and diseases were rampant. Henry was captured and sent to the prisoner of war camp at Salisbury, North Carolina. He passed away there on December 10, 1864, and was interred at the prison graveyard but is not listed there now, which probably indicates that he rests among the many unknowns. Parkinson was more fortunate and mustered out at war's end. He was able to pick up where he left off with his life. Henry, like hundreds of thousands of others, was not.

JEROME Y. SMALL

Centre Township farmers Adam and Elizabeth (Yockey) Small appear to have been the typical mid-nineteenth-century farm couple. They raised sons John, Jerome, Hezekiah, Benjamin, and Sylvester, and daughters Mary, Melinda, and Charlotte. John and Jerome served in Company H of the 133rd for nine months from August '62 through May '63. Then in June '63, they were listed in the draft ledger for Centre Township. Both were unmarried: John was still farming, while Jerome was listed as a lawyer. No record of further service is evident for John, but Jerome reenlisted in November 1863, and his index card indicates he joined Company D of the 47th from a recruiting depot on December 10, 1863.

Jerome's service with the 47th was not much longer than his tenure with the 133rd, and it certainly did not have the same result. Private Jerome Y. Small was another of the many casualties suffered at Cedar Creek, Virginia, on October 19, 1864. Jerome received a mortal wound that day. While it is unclear how long he lingered, indications are that it was thankfully brief. Burial records show he was initially buried in New Town Lutheran Church Cemetery and then later reinterred at Winchester National Cemetery along with comrades from the 47th as well as other hard-hit regiments.

GEORGE H. SMITH

Centre Township delivered large numbers of its sons to the Union Army, including Private George H. Smith, son of Samuel C. and Matilda Smith. The 1860 census shows the family engaged in farming. George had siblings William, Mary, Samuel, and Catharine. Upon enlistment on August 20, 1861, George was 5'8" tall, with light hair and gray eyes. His occupation, like his father's, was farmer. He had been born in 1842.

George was mustered into Company H of the 47th on September 19 and moved south with the unit. He served through the campaigns in Florida and South Carolina, and the beginning of the Red River Campaign. He, like thousands of others, developed a chronic case of dysentery. This disease incapacitated some for brief periods, stayed with some throughout their lifetime, and killed many, including George. He was hospitalized in Natchez, Mississippi, where he suffered and eventually succumbed to the disease on July 9, 1864. The U.S. Registers of Deaths of Volunteers lists his death as chronic diarrhea, but it could be the same. George is buried in Natchez National Cemetery.

JEREMIAH SMITH

Little information is available on Jeremiah Smith prior to 1850. His index card shows an age of thirty-four at enrollment, so his birth should have been in 1827. He was married on New Year's Day 1852 in Ickesburg to Mary Martin. They had a son, Lewis, in 1854.

Jeremiah was 5'10" at enlistment on September 18, 1861. He had a sandy complexion, brown hair, and gray eyes and mustered into Company H of the 47th the following day in Harrisburg. Jeremiah survived

Key West but was sickened there or soon after because he was admitted to Hospital No. 3 in Beaufort, South Carolina, on August 6, 1862, with dysentery. He lasted only two days in the hospital. The entry after his name in the U.S. Registers of Deaths of Volunteers lists his cause of death as "chronic diarrhea." Jeremiah was laid to rest in Beaufort National Cemetery.

EMANUEL SNYDER

One must wonder at the motivation to enlist. Was it patriotism? Was it to get a regular paycheck? Was it to escape tragedies or conditions at home? Was it just because it was the right thing to do? Emanuel Snyder of Buffalo Township would not have had to enlist on September 2, 1861, but he did. He was a thirty-eight-year-old farmer with three young children at home and no wife. Jacob was twelve, Mary was ten, and Margaret was almost seven. Emanuel's wife, the former Caroline Charles, had died on March 22, 1855, after a marriage of just under nine years. Some information suggests that more children had been born to the couple but had died in infancy.

Whatever the reason, Emanuel, born on August 25, 1823, joined others, most of whom were younger, in Company D of the 47th. He moved south with the regiment to Key West and then up to South Carolina. We have already seen how the conditions in the Deep South at the time wreaked havoc upon the men. While in South Carolina around June 1, 1862, Emanuel first became ill. Confined to the army's hospital on Hilton Head, he fell gravely ill, and it was determined to send him home on a sick furlough to recuperate and see his children. Once back home, the chronic dysentery only worsened until he eventually died on January 8, 1863. Private Emanuel Snyder was one of a handful of these Perry County men who returned home only to die. Perhaps though it was too brief, the time he spent with his children was cherished by all. He was buried in Hunter's Valley Cemetery.

HENRY STAMBAUGH

David and Elizabeth (Kell) Stambaugh raised fourteen children, eight girls and six boys, on their farm in Spring Township. Henry, born in 1838, enlisted on August 20, 1861, in Elliottsburg and was mustered into

Company H of the 47th thirty days later in Harrisburg. He was a 5'9"-tall farmer, with a sandy complexion, light hair, and blue eyes. The family was well-to-do, so Henry certainly did not need the security of army pay. Therefore, one must think that duty called the twenty-three-year-old.

Henry was with the regiment at Key West and in their movement to South Carolina. During the battle of Pocotaligo, Henry was killed in action at Frampton's Plantation. His final resting place's location, like that of quite a few other soldiers who fell there, has not been identified.

JEFFERSON WAGGONER

Having ancestors who fought in the Revolutionary War would make anyone proud. It could also place additional pressure upon a descendent to measure up. Perhaps that had some bearing on why Jefferson Waggoner enlisted at such an early age. Grandfather John had distinguished himself as a sergeant in 1780. Jefferson, born in 1845 to Benjamin and Elizabeth (Weibley) Waggoner, enlisted at sixteen, though his stated age was nineteen, on August 20, 1861. He mustered in on September 19 and was assigned to Company H of the 47th. He was described as 5'4" tall, with a light complexion, light hair, and gray eyes. His occupation was carpenter, and he gave his residence as Elliottsburg, though he was born and spent most of his life in Madison Township according to census data.

Jefferson's service term was eerily like that of Henry Stambaugh's. During the battle of Pocotaligo, he, too, was killed in action at Frampton's Plantation. And, like Henry, his remains have not been specifically located. It must be devastating to a family to get the news that their young son has perished, and perhaps more heartbreaking to have his body mishandled in such a way.

SAMUEL WAGNER

Many immigrants from Germany gravitated to Shermans Valley. Johann and Katharina (Trostle) Wagner arrived, like so many others, from Württemberg. They raised a family that included several blacksmiths, among them Samuel and George. George moved to northern Pennsylvania and enlisted there in Company E of the 7th PA Cavalry. Samuel enlisted in New Bloomfield and mustered into Company D of the 47th on the last day of August 1861.

Though Samuel's residence is New Bloomfield on his index card, the family lived in Saville Township. He was just seventeen at enlistment. Samuel survived the ordeals at Key West, Pocotaligo, and even Pleasant Hill, though he was wounded there on April 9, 1864. He was one of the soldiers put aboard the steamship *Pocahontas*, which set sail from New Orleans on May 24, bound for New York. The anticipation of going home and leaving the war behind likely gave Samuel and the other soldiers a huge boost of morale despite their wounds. Alas, as this cruel war has shown repeatedly, there are myriad ways to take lives. Late on the night of June 1, the ship *City of Bath* accidentally rammed the *Pocahontas* off the coast of Cape May. Heroic acts saved many passengers and crew, but not Samuel. He was lost at sea along with forty others. The body was never recovered. No monument was erected to his name. Just when it appeared he would return to Perry County and pick up the pieces of his life, the long arms of the war snatched him back.

JONATHAN WANTZ

Information on Jonathan Wantz is woefully lacking. His index card shows him to be a twenty-two-year-old farmer upon his enlistment with Captain Woodruff's Company D of the 47th PA Regiment on August 20, 1861, in New Bloomfield. While "Bloomfield" is listed as his residence at enlistment, he is not listed on the 1860 census.

Private Wantz survived the rampant diseases men encountered throughout the Deep South, as well as the many battles the 47th fought, until he was wounded and captured at Pleasant Hill, Louisiana. He and Solomon Powell died of their wounds on April 8 or 9 and, in the words of a comrade, "were probably buried together in a cemetery at Pleasant Hill behind a brick building being used as a hospital." Jonathan's mother, Elizabeth, applied for and received a mother's pension, which would indicate Jonathan was unmarried.

FREDERICK WATTS

With a name like Frederick Watts, living up to the heritage of the famed Brigadier General Frederick Watts would be a challenge. It appears that Private Watts, sometimes spelled without the "S" in army records, was a relative but not of direct lineage. His father, David, was a farmer who first tilled the land in Wheatfield Township before moving to Miller Township, where the 1860 census shows him with wife Rachel and children Johnathan, Frederick, Nancy, and Rebecca. Daughters Jane and Rachel, as well as another son, James, are not with the family in 1860. Johnathan later enlisted with the 201st and James with the 7th PA Cavalry before both moved to Iowa.

Frederick, born in 1842, enrolled on September 14, 1861, at Newport, then mustered into Company H of the 47th five days later in Harrisburg. He gave farm laborer as his occupation. Tall at six feet, he had a sandy complexion, light hair, and gray eyes. After training in the Washington, D.C., area, he sailed south with his regiment and landed at Key West, where he, like so many others, suffered from a climate different from anything he had experienced before. In short order he became sick and was admitted to the regimental hospital at Fort Taylor. Frederick perished from pneumonia at the hospital on February 13, 1862, just five months after enlistment. He is another of the many Perry County soldiers to be buried at Barrancas National Cemetery in Pensacola.

JAMES THOMAS WILLIAMSON

Information on James Thomas Williamson is scarce. When he enlisted with Company D of the 47th Regiment in New Bloomfield on August 20, 1861, James listed Landisburg as his address. Employed as a currier, he was thirty-five, with dark hair and dark eyes. Tall for that era, he stood 6'2". He mustered in as a corporal, no doubt a tribute to his age. James was wed to Catherine, and information on her is scarce. A James Thomas Williamson and wife arrived in New York City from Britain on March 12, 1849, aboard the ship *Ivanhoe*, however, there is no verification that couple is the one of this narrative. After James's sudden death, Catherine remarried and was the Catherine McClure residing in Shippensburg in the 1870 census. The pension application Catherine filed in 1888 shows her name at that time as McClure.

It is frustrating to secure such little information on an American patriot who gave his life for his country. Corporal Williamson was discharged on a surgeon's certificate on August 5, 1862, while serving at Beaufort, South Carolina. He was sent home but barely made it before dying. He is buried at Landisburg Cemetery and lies beneath a government-issued headstone. The grave marker lists the date of death as August 1862. He is the lone Williamson buried there.

ANDREW AND WASHINGTON A. WORK

The Work family history, as far their Perry County connection, is slight. On the surface, it appears that Andrew and Washington Work were related, possibly even brothers, but that connection remains to be made. The Work family history outside of Perry County is extensive. They arrived in Lancaster County in the mid-1700s and gradually moved west, where they were large landowners both in Pennsylvania and in the Midwestern states. Here information is harder to find.

Andrew and Washington each listed a home residence of Duncannon upon enlistment. They each were masons, and each in his early to mid-forties. Each became privates in Company D of the 47th. Census data indicates Washington may have been forty-six, but his given age at enrollment was forty-three, the same as Andrew. Each signed up in New Bloomfield on August 20, 1861, and each mustered in on the thirty-first. Washington's census information from 1860 shows him married to Rebecca Bierbower Milliken Work, but both Andrew and Washington had been married previously and their spouses were deceased. Washington and Rachel's children were Mary, Alfred, Martha, Samuel, Washington A., Thomas, Edward, Emma, and John. Washington A. Work moved westward and ended up serving in the Civil War in the 1st West Virginia Light Artillery.

Andrew Work is more of a mystery man. He was left behind in Washington when the 47th sailed south. He was hospitalized in Union Hotel General Hospital and died there on February 27, 1862. He was buried in Soldiers' and Airmen's Home National Cemetery.

Washington sailed south with the regiment but, being unaccustomed to the climate in Key West, he quickly became ill. Discharged on a surgeon's certificate on July 12, 1862, Washington was sent home with chronic dysentery. He never rid himself of the malady and passed away at home on September 21, 1862. He is buried in Duncannon Union Cemetery.

The 47th PA arrived in our nation's capital on September 21, 1861, and began a tenure unparalleled in Civil War history. In the next four years and four months, they marched over 1,200 miles (about the distance from Florida to New York City), made a dozen sea voyages, and fought in most of the southern states as they gained a legacy as one of the most stalwart regiments in the Union Army. The Iron Brigade, the Bucktails, and others gained more notoriety, in part because the 47th fought hundreds of miles from home, but their record speaks for itself. During their term of service, 8 officers and 287 men in the ranks lost their lives, the majority dying from disease. We have listed 46 men from Perry County who perished during the war while serving in that regiment, far more than the total from any other regiment.

XII.

The 49th Pennsylvania Regiment

THE 49th PA Regiment had a tour of duty closer to home, as they fought primarily in the Eastern Theater of the Civil War. They were present at Antietam, Chancellorsville, Fredericksburg, Gettysburg, Winchester, and Petersburg. Even though they were not heavily engaged in every battle, the 49th saw plenty of action, and its men paid a heavy price. The regiment was recruited primarily in the central part of the state, with many men coming from Center, Mifflin, Huntingdon, and Juniata Counties. Company I was recruited in Juniata County, and many men were transferred to Company A. Some Perry Countians enrolled in Port Royal and fought with Company A; not all returned. Here are sketches of these men.

WILLIAM ATTIG

Private William Attig of Millerstown was the son of George and Susan (Gable) Attig, born in 1833. Two older siblings died young, but four brothers lived to adulthood and all four fought in the Civil War. Peter, Levi, and Henry H. G. fought together in Company I of the 133rd PA after William enlisted in the 49th. William was twenty-seven when he enlisted in Juniata County on September 9, 1861. He was 5'9" tall, with dark hair, a dark complexion, and brown eyes, and listed his occupation as laborer. While information is incomplete, the 1850 census shows him living with his parents and three brothers in Millerstown.

His service was interrupted a year later when he was confined to a convalescent camp in Alexandria, Virginia, on September 2, 1862. He rejoined the 49th and fought with them at Gettysburg and as they chased Lee's army south afterward. At the battle of Rappahannock Station on

November 7, 1863, William received a gunshot wound to the head during a valiant and successful charge on enemy breastworks. He was taken to Soldiers' Home in Washington, D.C., where he succumbed to his wounds on November 24, 1863. Buried two days later, he was then exhumed on the twenty-eighth when older brother Levi arrived to claim the body.

GEORGE WASHINGTON BEATTY

George Washington Beatty resided in Juniata County when he enlisted on September 3, 1861. His family spent time in Saville Township prior to moving across the Tuscarora Mountain. The 1850 census shows George living in Saville Township at home with parents Joseph and Permelia (Axe) Beatty. Joseph supported his large family as a carpenter. George's siblings were Martha, Robert, Samuel, Margaret, Sara, Permelia, Joseph Samuel, and Hannah. Robert enlisted with the 107th PA, Samuel served in Company H of the 36th Militia, and Joseph Samuel joined Company C of the 3rd PA Artillery Regiment.

Mustered into the 49th on October 24, George was described as 5'9" tall, with dark hair, a fair complexion, and blue eyes. His occupation was laborer. He soon was detached to the regimental commissary department as a clerk. Then George had a lengthy stay in a Philadelphia hospital from June '62 to January '63. He rejoined his regiment and then reenlisted on February 28, 1864, at Brandy Station. He, along with many of his comrades, fell in the fierce fighting in the Wilderness and Spotsylvania areas of Virginia. George was killed at Spotsylvania Court House on May 12, 1864, and was buried there. One government report lists him as reinterred at Fredericksburg, but as yet, cemetery records do not show his name.

SAMUEL CLAY EBRIGHT

John Hunter and Sophia (Clay) Ebright farmed in Penn Township. In addition to daughters Mary, Catharine, Isabella, Caroline, and Amelia, they had three sons: George, Samuel, and Henry. Henry was born in 1848 and thus missed the war. Alas, George and Samuel did not. Bucktail George (mentioned on page 30) died in '62.

Samuel was a farmhand, according to the 1860 census, and lived with his parents. He was born on May 23, 1839. At enlistment in Carlisle, he was described as 5'5½" tall, with dark hair, a dark complexion, and gray eyes. His listed occupation was laborer.

Samuel mustered in to Company E of the 49th on June 9, 1864. At that point, the regiment was preparing to head west for the Shenandoah Valley Campaign. His service time was brief, as he soon developed a case of typhoid fever. He was hospitalized in Sheridan Field Hospital near Winchester and succumbed to the dreaded disease on November 26, 1864, according to the U.S. Registers of Deaths of Volunteers. Samuel was laid to rest in Winchester National Cemetery.

JAMES ENDSLOW

Corporal James Endslow taught school before entering the service. He was born to Samuel S. Endslow and wife Maria McNeal Endslow in 1840. Sometimes spelled without the "D," Samuel was a miller by trade. He operated a mill on Shermans Creek about a mile southeast of Blain, and his name still graces the covered bridge on Adams Grove Road near the beautiful old red brick house he built. James had siblings Alice, Jane, Martha, and William. He also had cousins Samuel and John, who lived in neighboring Juniata County, and all three enlisted there on September 5, 1861. They became members of Company I of the 49th Regiment. Samuel survived the war. John died of chronic diarrhea on November 24, 1863.

James had dark hair and gray eyes and stood 5'9" tall when he mustered in. He earned a quick promotion to corporal but would not fulfill those duties for long. He contracted typhoid and died on January 13, 1862, at the general hospital in Alexandria, Virginia. James was returned to Blain, where he was buried in Toboyne Presbyterian Church Cemetery, which appropriately lies adjacent to a former grist mill.

GEORGE P. HARTMAN

It is uncertain when George P. Hartman left his native York County for the Shermans Dale area of Perry; certainly prior to August 11, 1859. On that date George wed Mary Corman in Carroll Township. He was a farmer in Carroll, 5'5" tall according to his muster-in date of June 5, 1864. He was drafted and entered the service at Carlisle as a twenty-eight-year-old with dark hair, a dark complexion, and gray eyes. George and Mary had sons Johnathan and Jacob by the time Uncle Sam called.

George became a private in Company E of the 49th and went to Virginia to fight for his country. His term of service was short, as he was admitted to Sixth Corps Hospital at City Point, Virginia. George's name was sometimes incorrectly spelled as Hortman. There is also a discrepancy as to his cause of death on December 30. One source lists his demise as a case of "chronic diarrhea." The U.S. Registers of Deaths of Volunteers notes it as due to "inflammation of the lungs, pleura." One wonders, what difference does it make?

Though recordkeeping was not a governmental strength during the war, scrutinizing pension applications afterward was taken seriously. Widows and qualifying parents had to jump through hoops and fight for months or years to prove worthy of an eight-dollar-per-month allowance.

Mary's pension file, a typical example, includes thirty-four pages of documentation with letters and testimony of witnesses attesting to the marriage, the births of her sons, and the cause of death. If today's government was as frugal, taxes would be substantially lower than the current rates. Mary persisted through an attorney, Lewis Potter, and eventually received the much-needed pension long after George was laid to rest in the national cemetery at City Point.

GEORGE E. HELLER

George E. Heller was born to John and Sarah Warren Heller on October 20, 1830, in Menallen Township, Adams County. He, as well as several of his brothers, moved north with George, settling in Millerstown according to the 1860 census. That census lists George living with his wife, Margaret Kinser Fry Heller, and children, Hulda and Wilbert. Later in 1860, Laura joined the family. George was recorded as a laborer. When he enlisted on September 9, 1861, he was 5'6" tall, with dark hair, a dark complexion, and blue eyes. He mustered into Company I of the 49th on October 24. On March 30 of the following year, George was promoted to corporal.

One report has him dying of wounds near Petersburg, Virginia; however, the U.S. Registers of Deaths of Volunteers shows he died on August 25, 1862, of "diarrhoea acute" while a patient in Satterlee General Hospital in Philadelphia. George was returned to Millerstown and interred at Millerstown Memorial Cemetery.

Margaret, like so many other women, was left alone to care for her small children. She married Peter Longacre in 1866.

JACOB REESE

It is disheartening when information is limited about a soldier who gave his life for his country. Such is the case with Jacob Reese of Greenwood Township near Millerstown. He appears in the 1860 census living with and working as a farm laborer for the John Acker family of Greenwood Township. His stated age was twenty-one, though at enrollment one year later, he gave an age of twenty-four. His index card shows him to be 5'5" tall, with dark hair, a dark complexion, and blue eyes when he enlisted in Juniata County on September 9, 1861.

Jacob mustered into Company I of the 49th PA on October 24, 1861. One year later, on October 22, he was discharged due to illness, though he is not listed on the muster-out rolls. Jacob died just eighteen days later and was buried in the Acker family cemetery near Millerstown. This and the fact that he is not found in other census data suggests that he may not have had family in the area.

WARREN STAHL

Born on October 12, 1844, Warren Stahl was only sixteen when he enrolled in Juniata County on September 16, 1861. He mustered into the Federal Army with Company I of the 49th Regiment just twelve days after turning seventeen. He was the oldest son born to William and Anna Stahl and had brothers William and Frank, as well as sisters Ellen, Sarah, Josephine, Alice, Melinda, and Mary. Father William made a living as a tailor, but enlisted and served with Company I of the 133rd PA in 1862.

Warren began his term of service, like thousands of others, at Camp Griffin in Virginia. It is unclear what Warren contracted, but it was deadly. Shortly after his eighteenth birthday, Warren died on November 27, 1862, in the camp hospital at Hagerstown, Maryland. Warren was returned to his home and buried in Millerstown Memorial Cemetery, another in a tragically extensive line of young men who would not live to fulfill lives that held so much promise at the outbreak of the war.

XIII.

The 51st Pennsylvania Regiment

THE name James A. Beaver is well known to Pennsylvanians. Beaver was a Union general, a great politician who could have held high national offices had he so desired, and a Pennsylvania governor for whom Beaver Stadium is named. His brother Jacob is less well known, possibly because his life was cut short by war. Both were born in Millerstown and spent their early childhoods there. Their parents were Jacob and Anna Eliza (Addams) Beaver. The elder Jacob died tragically young in 1840. Anna later married clergyman S. H. McDonald and the family relocated to Bellefonte.

Jacob was born on March 6 in the year his father died. Just ten years later, Jacob was part of the McDonald family in Bellefonte, according to the 1850 census. By the time of the 1860 census, Jacob had moved to Lewisburg, where he was a clerk.

The Beaver family had, even then, a long and distinguished history of military service, with Revolutionary War generals on both sides of the family. Images of the Beaver brothers show rugged good looks and indicate a demeanor that would command respect, even without a uniform. Those reasons are why both James and Jacob entered the service as officers.

Jacob enlisted in Lewisburg on June 6, 1862, as a second lieutenant and quickly was promoted to first lieutenant in Company H. He served only three months and was in that capacity when the 51st stormed the famous Rohrbach Bridge at Antietam. This bridge has been unofficially renamed for General Burnside; however, renaming it in honor of the 51st PA would be more appropriate. In a doomed effort to secure the bridge, wave after wave of Union soldiers shed their blood on that bridge, their broken bodies piled up like cordwood. The 51st has its monument beside the bridge and lists twenty-three men killed there, including Lieutenant Jacob Gilbert Beaver. Another eighty-four men were wounded in action on September 17, 1862. Jacob Beaver would be returned to Millerstown, where he rests in Millerstown Memorial Cemetery.

XIV.

The 53rd Pennsylvania Regiment

THE 53rd PA Regiment was engaged in nearly every battle and skirmish in the Eastern Theater of the war from beginning to end. They were cut to pieces at Fredericksburg, losing 158 killed and wounded out of 287 engaged. As part of Hancock's corps at Gettysburg, they fought in the Rose Woods near the Wheatfield. With some of its companies on detached duty, the regiment had only 124 men present for duty in the epic struggle for possession of 20 acres of grain. Their loss that day was staggering as 6 were killed, 67 wounded, and 6 listed as missing in action. This 65% casualty rate was one of the highest endured during the battle and attests to the fierceness of the fighting in this area and to the mettle of the men. Several Perry Countians were in their ranks, though no companies were recruited in Perry.

JOHN HEISER

Company I was recruited in Perryville (Port Royal), Juniata County, on September 19, 1861. With its proximity to Port Royal, the Millerstown area provided quite a few recruits for the 53rd. Brothers Henry, John, and Philip Heiser were quick to answer the call and entered the service on October 10, 1861.

John William Heiser was born to Daniel and Mary Hoffman Heiser on January 2, 1837. The 1860 census lists John as a laborer living in Greenwood Township. He was married to the former Matilda Spade. They welcomed their first child, Hannah Rebecca, on December 2, 1860, about ten months before John went off to war.

The service records of the three brothers, as well as those of another John Heiser, are likely intermingled. John received two promotions during his term of service. He is shown as a corporal on the 53rd's plaque at the Pennsylvania Memorial at Gettysburg. He is listed as a sergeant on his interment records. John was wounded near Dinwiddie, Virginia, and died of his wounds in Emory General Hospital in Washington, D.C. His marker in the cemetery shows a date of August 29, however the U.S. Registers of Deaths of Volunteers shows it as August 30, 1864. He was laid to rest in the national cemetery in Alexandria, Virginia.

WILLIAM HARTLEY HUTTON

William Hartley Hutton and his wife, Margaret Long Hutton, moved from Lancaster County to Miller Township near Newport in the 1850s. The 1860 census shows the farm couple with William's mother, Sarah, and two daughters, Lucinda and Delphina. Born on July 5, 1826, William was one of eight sons and one daughter born to Joel Hutton and the former Sarah Hartley. According to information given in his registration for the draft in July 1863, William still farmed in Miller Township and was thirty-eight years old. However, his enlistment information from February 4, 1864, indicates an age of thirty-seven at that time, which is more accurate. William was 5'8" tall, with dark hair, a dark complexion, and blue eyes.

William moved with his company to the Petersburg area in the spring of '64, but his military career took a tragic turn upon his capture on June 16. He was taken to Andersonville Prison, where he contracted scurvy shortly after his arrival. In a declaration of facts contained in William's pension file, given by First Lieutenant Elliott Brown, also an Andersonville prisoner until mid-September of that year, William "was much reduced in health and strength when I saw him last at Andersonville." Brown further testified "he was so feeble it was evident he could not survive." There is conflicting information as to his death, but that pension file indicates his date of death as November 15, 1864. Though he was afflicted at Andersonville, his death was reported in Florence, South Carolina. He has a memorial on his wife's monument in Newport Cemetery.

A neighboring farmer, James Thompson Toland Sr., was appointed as guardian for William's minor children. Toland's wife had died in 1863, and in October 1865, Toland wed Margaret Hutton. After Toland's death in 1878, Margaret married a third time. It is that name, Rutter, under which you will find the memorial to Private William H. Hutton.

We have and will continue to note many times the intertwining of the lives of these Civil War era families. In another example, James Thompson Toland Jr., serving with the 102nd PA Regiment, died in Gettysburg of disease on the same day William Hutton passed.

XV.

The 60th Pennsylvania Regiment (3rd Cavalry)

THE 3rd PA Cavalry was recruited in the eastern part of the state except for Company H, which was primarily stocked with men from the Newville area. The unit was attached to the Army of the Potomac, fighting mostly with the Third Corps. They were engaged in all of the battles in the Eastern Theater, including Fredericksburg, Antietam, and Gettysburg, losing 169 men during their term of service. Two Newville-area men with Perry roots enlisted.

Jonathan Koser, a Berks County native, moved to Perry County sometime prior to 1818. In that year, and for seven years afterward, he was a member of a militia group called the Landisburg Guards. He wed another Berks County native who also had relocated to Perry, Mary Ann Culbertson, at her home in New Germantown on October 18, 1830. Sons Culbertson and Alexander were probably born in Perry, but that's uncertain. Eight more children followed, including David, Mary, George, Jonathan, Samuel, Susannah, Nancy, and Martha. It is certain that these later siblings were all born after the farmers moved to the Newburg area. George enlisted with Battery B of the PA light artillery.

Both Alexander and Culbertson were single when they mustered into Company H of the 60th PA Regiment (3rd PA Cavalry) on August 17, 1861. Neither survived. Corporal Alexander Koser (sometimes spelled Kosier) died on May 22, 1862, in a hospital in Brooklyn, New York. He is buried in Cypress Hills National Cemetery there.

Private Culbertson Koser was discharged on November 22, 1862, "on account of disability." He was sent home but never recovered from his wounds and died on August 16, 1864. Culbertson was laid to rest alongside his parents and several siblings in the Zion Reformed Church Yard in Mifflin Township.

XVI.

The 65th Pennsylvania Regiment (5th Cavalry)

THE 65th Regiment was a cavalry regiment recruited in various parts of the state in the fall of 1861, at a time when Union troops, especially cavalry, were sorely needed. They spent time in the Washington area before rushing into service in eastern Virginia. It was during this period of the conflict that Jeb Stuart's Rebel Cavalry rode roughshod over Union cavalry forces. Stuart's men were better equipped, better trained, and better commanded than the horsemen in blue. In an effort to demonstrate that Union horse soldiers were up to the job, they were often thrown headlong into desperate situations.

Daniel Charles O'Donnell farmed in the New Germantown area before the war. He was the son of Henry and Mary Bernheisel O'Donnell, born on New Year's Day 1834. Daniel had brothers, William, John, and Alexander, and sisters, Elizabeth and Priscilla. Alexander would later enlist with Company G of the 21st PA Cavalry.

Daniel was married to Nancy Raymond O'Donnell and had four children: Rebecca, who died at age three, Margaret, Ephraim, and Emma. He enlisted on September 22, 1862, into Company M. Some information lists him as unassigned. In fact, much of his information is mysterious. The muster file shows he was captured on February 7, 1863, and then was "held prisoner," but the location isn't listed. Two companies of the 5th PA Cavalry, L and M, were sent to Williamsburg Road on that date. They encountered a Confederate cavalry force estimated to be ten times their scant one hundred men. After many charges and countercharges, thirty-five members of the 5th PA were killed, wounded, or captured. Certainly Daniel was one of those captured. From there, the trail runs cold. His muster file contains the notation "captured February 7, 1863 not on muster out role."

Daniel has a veteran's burial card that shows a death date of June 5, 1865. His tombstone in Fairview Methodist Cemetery along Route 274 west of New Germantown has this information: "died June 5, 1865, aged 31 years, 5 months, 4 days." Whether Daniel rests there or if the stone is a cenotaph is unknown.

XVII.

Another from the 77th Pennsylvania Regiment

THE next man is included in this book due to his unusual service record. Although he was out of the service at the time, he died while the matter of the war remained unsettled. Furthermore, the disease that claimed his life was most assuredly contracted while in the service. Daniel Nagle was a young farm lad from Liverpool Township. Born on January 30, 1841, his parents were Daniel and Elizabeth Stailey Nagle. Daniel was described as 5'10" tall, with a fair complexion and blue eyes. He had older brothers, John and William, and sisters, Elizabeth, Mary, Sarah, and Jane. John served with the 47th Regiment. William did not get the opportunity to serve as he died in 1851.

Daniel enlisted at Chambersburg on September 14, 1861, and was mustered into Company C of the 77th thirty-two days later. After only about two weeks, Private Nagle was transferred to the regimental band on November 1. Most regiments had a band in the early part of the war. They served a valuable purpose in boosting morale, often playing while on the march and at night after a grueling day. However, they soon became superfluous, as it was deemed necessary to keep the fighting men supplied with food and the accoutrements of war rather than non-combatants. The band was discharged on January 31, 1862. Some men were transferred into the ranks, while others were released. After a military career that spanned little more than three months, Daniel was sent home. He barely made it back before dying on February 13. He was laid to rest in Liverpool Cemetery, where he has been supplied with a government-issued headstone that reads "Band 77th Pa. Infantry."

XVIII.

United States Cavalry

MANY Perry Countians served and died with the regular army or a U.S. Cavalry unit. They are more difficult to find than soldiers who were in the volunteer army, but occasionally I have stumbled across one when researching another soldier.

Such was the case with Sylvester Morton. His older brother, Lemuel, born in 1842, served with Company B of the Bucktails. In researching Lemuel, I happened across his younger brother, Sylvester. It is staggering when you see a boy listed in the 1860 census as being twelve and then later see his name listed as a Civil War casualty.

Lemuel and Sylvester were sons of a farm family in Carroll Township. Their parents were Martin and Dosia Eagler Morton. October 26, 1862, was the day Sylvester crossed the mountain and enlisted in Carlisle. He mustered into Company A of the 158th PA Regiment on November 1, 1862. He could not have been more than fifteen, if he was that. At 5'9" tall, perhaps he looked much older.

Sylvester was hospitalized with an undisclosed illness in Washington a short time later, and he did not rejoin the regiment until August 11, 1863. The following day, he and the rest of the regiment mustered out. On February 19, 1864, Sylvester enrolled in Company K of the 3rd U.S. Cavalry. This unit saw service in the Western Theater of the war, but Sylvester saw little of it. He contracted typhoid fever and died on July 27, 1864, in Little Rock, Arkansas. He was probably only seventeen, and now he lies in Little Rock National Cemetery.

XIX.

Jones's Independent Cavalry

MANY independent companies arose in Pennsylvania with the reports of the northern advancement of Lee's Army of Northern Virginia. Many soldiers who had previously served in other early regiments enlisted. One of these units was Jones's Independent Cavalry, which John Jones recruited in Juniata and Perry Counties. Dozens of men from Perry offered their services in the event that Lee might be successful in routing Meade's Army of the Potomac and thereby threaten life beyond Gettysburg. Though they saw no action, they were at the ready, and at least one man perished as a result of his service during the two months this unit was mustered in. The company began service in Harrisburg on June 24, 1863, and mustered out on August 12 of '63.

Samuel Tudor was born in Baltimore in 1808. He wed Emeline McComas in Baltimore County, Maryland, on March 13, 1833. It is unclear when Dr. Samuel Tudor began practicing medicine in Madison Township, but he and Emeline first appear in the 1850 census. In addition to giving a rural community desperately needed medical treatment, they were a giving family who routinely provided safe harbor for orphaned children and others in need. They had a son, John, who was born on July 20, 1834. Much about John is unknown other than that he was a teacher in Madison Township when he registered for the draft and when he enlisted with Jones's Independent Cavalry.

These independent companies were fighters, not recordkeepers, so we are unsure what disease may have afflicted John. When he returned to his family, John was ill, and despite having a doctor in the house, he passed away on October 18, 1863. His mother died in 1874, and Samuel passed on December 1, 1890. All rest in Emory Chapel Cemetery, midway between Green Gates and Kistler along Route 850. Samuel applied for John's pension, indicating that John had no wife or children.

As an interesting side note that illustrates who the Tudors were, an excerpt from Samuel's will leaves his entire estate, except for a dozen silver spoons that went to his "beloved niece Fanny Nicholson," to his "faithful housekeeper Ellen Snyder." He went on to write "these bequests are intended as a partial remuneration to her for over twenty years of service (without compensation) to myself and family."

XX.

The 7th Pennsylvania Cavalry

NO more famous cavalry unit existed than the vaunted U.S. 7th Cavalry, infamously led after the Civil War by George Armstrong Custer. While not as famous, Pennsylvania had a 7th Cavalry, 80th PA Regiment. The 7th PA Cavalry Regiment fought mainly in Alabama, Georgia, Kentucky, and Tennessee, earning many accolades and the sobriquet, "The Saber Regiment." Wielding sabers, the 7th gained a reputation for fearlessly charging opposing infantry, artillery, and cavalry, often cutting their way through and sending Rebel soldiers fleeing. It is credited with opening and closing the bloody battle of Chickamauga. These men scouted, foraged, and fought on foot and in the saddle, often riding day and night until either their horses gave out or they did. They covered thousands of miles and fought numerous engagements with little sleep and meager rations.

JOHN WESLEY CROOKS

The unit included numerous Perry County men, one of whom was a doctor named John Wesley Crooks. John was not born in Perry County and did not spend that much time there, but he married a Carroll Township girl, Rachel White, practiced medicine there, and was buried there. The 1850 census shows that Rachel was living with her family on a Shermans Dale-area farm, and another roll shows John as a physician in Carlisle. By 1860, the couple had moved to Indiana County, where they stayed briefly before returning to Perry County. John was a Carroll Township resident when he registered for the draft in July 1863. The couple had four daughters, Margaret Anne, Mary Helen, Jean E., and Priscilla Elizabeth, between 1855 and 1863.

John, born on January 29, 1826, had a long history of military service. He first served in the 5th Infantry in the Mexican War, then in Company C of the 9th PA Cavalry, before finally serving in Company M of the 7th PA Cavalry. His stint in the 9th was brief. He mustered in on October 11, 1861, but was discharged for a medical disability in August 1862. Then he enlisted with the 7th on February 22, 1864. However, this term of service was also brief. Near Shelbyville, North Carolina, on June 20, 1864, John was mortally wounded and died there. He is interred in Youngs Church Cemetery in Shermans Dale alongside Rachel.

The couple's four girls received their education in the Perry County Orphans of Soldiers System and were active participants in the alumni association for former orphans. Known as "sixteeners" due to the requirement that these students leave the program upon turning sixteen, this association held annual meetings for many years where former orphans could catch up with old classmates and friends. These alumni gatherings were held all over the state, and records show the girls traveled to many of them.

JOHN DURHAM

Many people in the nineteenth century were born, were raised, married, and died in the same small geographic locale, like Perry County. Not so with John Durham. In census data, he listed his place of birth as Delaware. He made his home in West Fallowfield, Chester County, in 1850. Ten years later, John, with wife Mary Stone Durham and eleven children, were in Carroll Township, Perry County. Their oldest, William Henry, was born in 1838. Frances, John, Mary Ellen, Anna Elizabeth, David, Rachel, Lewis, Sarah, Clara, and Jacob followed. The 1850 census showed John was unemployed. In 1860, he was a laborer. Although we can only speculate as to the reasons, the regular pay of army life may have been an incentive for him to enlist on August 23, 1861. Eleven days later, John was a private in Company I of the 7th PA Cavalry. Several men from Carroll enrolled with him; none approached John's age. His son, John Alex Durham, served with Company H of the 47th and happily survived the war.

The elder John was born on April 19, 1813, just thirty-eight years to the day after Paul Revere completed his famous ride. At the age of forty-eight, though he understated his age by four years when he enlisted,

John began his own ride. He served with honor and had no trouble keeping up with the young bucks in the regiment. The 7th saw fierce fighting in Tennessee. While there, according to a letter he sent home, he suffered a leg injury due to a puncture wound from a nail.

There exists conflicting information as to his cause and date of death. The muster file states he died in 1862, while a letter from Lieutenant McAllister, announcing his death, indicates it was March 21, 1863. The U.S. Registers of Deaths of Volunteers also indicates the March date and states a cause of "pyemia," which is consistent with blood poisoning from a wound such as John described.

In his last letter home, dated January 4, 1863, John expressed to Mary that he thought he was getting better and hoped to be discharged soon. Also included in the letter, written while hospitalized, were these words that detailed the ferocity of the fighting near Murfreesboro: "a man that came in last night told me that the battle of Shiloh was as nothing compared to this. He said he believed he could walk for 7 miles on the bodies of dead men." Also included in the letter was the sad news that a comrade and neighbor, Henry Fry, had been killed.

Lieutenant McAllister sent a letter to Mary just three months later, announcing John's demise. Mary, like many others, struggled to obtain the pension she so richly deserved. At John's death, Mary had five children under the age of sixteen. That pension would be a lifesaver if she could obtain it. After months of back-and-forth letters, Mary was awarded an eight-dollar-per-month pension in April 1864. Initially buried near Tullahoma, John was among the hundreds reinterred in Stones River National Cemetery. He rests there today among scores of comrades.

HENRY S. FRY

Pennsylvania and its counties were much less populated in mid-1800s America than today, so national events like this war impacted families in many ways. The war wove its way in and around not only the soldier's lives, but also their families. Henry S. Fry, of Carroll Township near Shermans Dale, is a case in point.

Henry was born to Daniel and Anna Sunday Fry in 1838 in Carroll Township. Daniel died noticeably young in 1849; only forty-seven years old. Henry's siblings were Mary Ann, Catharine, and Samuel.

Henry wed Victoria Morton, a fellow Carroll Township resident, on December 22, 1859. Alas, the couple had no children. The following year, the newlyweds resided with and worked for the Lawrence Hipple family, who farmed in the township. Lawrence and wife, Sarah, had two sons go off to war, John and William. William A. Hipple and Henry S. Fry shared the same fate: neither returned alive to Carroll Township.

Henry was promoted at an undetermined time as the entry in the muster files states, "Corporal Henry Fry was killed at Stones River Tennessee 12/31/62." Henry was laid to rest in Stones River National Cemetery in Murfreesboro. Victoria later married Reverend Simon Wolf a year after the war's end and had children with him.

DANIEL S. SHATTO

A relative latecomer to the 7th was Daniel S. Shatto of Tyrone Township. Daniel was the son of John and Mary A. Sheaffer Shatto, born around 1840. Daniel's siblings were Johnathan, Caroline, Samuel, and John Jr. There were many Shatto families in Perry in the mid-nineteenth century and unfortunately the sons seemed to all be named Daniel, David, John, or Samuel; therefore, there may be some intermingling of records. The 1850 census shows the family residing in Tyrone Township, where the elder John was a laborer.

At enlistment on February 20, 1864, Daniel stated he was twenty-two. He mustered into Company M of the 7th PA Regiment. Daniel was captured around October 1 later that year in southern Tennessee and taken to Cahaba Prison Camp near Selma, Alabama. That prisoner of war camp was a paradox due to the two men in charge. Captain Henderson was a Methodist minister and was known to treat the Union prisoners with decency. In fact, the camp had one of the lowest prisoner death rates of all Confederate prisons. However, the other man in charge, Colonel Samuel Jones, was the opposite and was accused of brutality and even of having some prisoners murdered.

Private Daniel Shatto received no decency at Cahaba Prison. He was apparently hospitalized toward the end of his life because there exists a record of Daniel and several others being "buried from Hospital." He died on April 21, 1865, and was initially buried in Montgomery, Alabama. He was later reinterred at Georgia National Cemetery in Marietta.

XXI.

The 83rd Pennsylvania Regiment

LATE in the war, several regiments were reconstructed: Their original organization's ranks had been depleted to such an extent that new companies were added. Two examples are the 83rd and the 104th, both of which had men from Perry's eastern region. Though these two regiments were engaged heavily in the war's first three years, the men who became part of these regiments in March 1865 did not see much of the war.

The men who became soldiers in March didn't know it, but the war only lasted about another month in the east. Nevertheless, as we've seen repeatedly, Rebel Minié balls weren't the only instruments of death. Sometimes the lust for pageantry and recognition by the hierarchy put the enlisted men in peril.

Cornelius Buffington was shown to be an "ambrotypist" when he registered for the draft in 1863. Prior to that, and also when he enlisted, he supplied blacksmith as his occupation. Cornelius was born to Solomon and Elizabeth Romberger Buffington on September 7, 1830, in Lykens.

He moved across the river and settled in the Montgomery's Ferry area sometime in the 1850s. He had been married previously to Elizabeth Crum. Together they had a son, John, and a daughter, Amelia. Elizabeth likely died in the 1850s because Cornelius remarried. The 1860 census shows his new wife as Sarah (Riggleman), who was now in the home with Cornelius, John, and Amelia. When Amelia died, her death certificate revealed that her mother was indeed Elizabeth Crum.

Cornelius Buffington enlisted on March 7, 1865, as a sergeant in the new Company K of the 83rd PA Regiment. He was one of many who collapsed under the sweltering sun near Washington during a dress parade at war's end. He recuperated at Campbell U.S. Hospital after being admitted on May 5. On June 2, Cornelius was discharged on a surgeon's certificate and sent home. He died suddenly on August 9, 1865, and was interred at Liverpool Union Cemetery.

XXII.

The 9th Pennsylvania Cavalry

THE 92nd PA Regiment was formed as a cavalry unit and therefore is known as the 9th PA Cavalry. Company A was recruited in Perry County. Many soldiers from Perry dotted the ranks of other companies, including Company C, which had a large contingent of county men. Infantrymen were fond of making jokes about the cavalry, such as, "never saw a dead cavalryman." That may have been true in some regiments, but not the 9th PA. This unit rode thousands of miles and fought in dozens of battles in Kentucky, Tennessee, Georgia, and the Carolinas.

Twenty-one Perry Countians were counted among this regiment's fallen. It participated in Sherman's March to the Sea and was instrumental in achieving victory in North Carolina. Along the way, it was commended for bravery numerous times. The 9th has the distinction of being selected as an escort for General Sherman to accompany him when he received the surrender of General Johnston on April 26, 1865. In fact, it was a company of the 9th that received the flag of truce sent by Johnston, requesting to meet with Sherman to discuss surrender terms. Here are some sketches of Perry County men who made the supreme sacrifice while serving in the ranks of that remarkable regiment. You will note that several members lost their lives in the waning days of the war. We often forget that Lee's surrender did not end the war. There was still more killing to be done after April 9, 1865.

SAMUEL BAKER

Pennsylvania Route 17 courses through nearly all of Perry County on a scenic thirty-six-mile trip from Liverpool westward. It meanders past farms, small towns, churches, and general stores on its trip to Blain, where it ends at what would be the town square if Blain were large enough to have a town square. Where that road ends, the story of Samuel Baker begins. Samuel, born on October 29, 1836, was the oldest son and second child born to Cornelius and Mary (Mumper) Baker. The Bakers farmed about a mile east of Blain, where they raised the typical crops and a large family that included nine sons. In addition to Samuel, his brothers helped to swell the ranks of the Union Army. When the youngest to enlist, Jeremiah, did so in 1865, he became the sixth son to volunteer. A seventh, David, tried to enlist but was turned away because he was too young. A stone monument to this family of patriots sits along Route 17 in front of the family homestead. The Baker home is on a ridge some two hundred yards away, standing in silent testimony to the history that transpired there more than a century-and-a-half earlier. Perry Countians should be proud of the record forged by its residents during the Civil War, particularly of a family so devoted to the cause that six sons fought not for glory but for their beliefs.

The Bakers served in both infantry and cavalry regiments. Three Baker brothers served in Company C of the 9th PA Cavalry: Samuel, Henry, and Cornelius. John served two terms, one with the 133rd and then later with the 93rd. Fred served in the 20th PA Cavalry, and Jeremiah was with Company F of the 149th.

At enlistment with the 9th PA, Samuel was a carpenter, as were Henry and Cornelius, skills taught by their father, who, with his sons, built their farm home. Twenty-seven years old, Samuel was 5'5" tall, with brown hair, brown eyes, and a florid complexion. Samuel had previously served in the 133rd with John. He had been mustered out in May 1863, and then a year later was back in the army. This time, in the 9th Cavalry, enlisting on September 12, 1864, in Harrisburg. Cornelius and Henry had enlisted three years earlier and were both corporals by that time.

Although the Army of Northern Virginia had surrendered on April 9, action in North Carolina was still fierce. Three days after Lee's surrender, in action near Raleigh, Samuel received a mortal wound and died the following day. His body was returned to Perry County, where he rests in Blain Union Cemetery near his parents. Brother Cornelius Baker kept a diary in which he noted prominent events of his days in army life. That journal reveals not only the life of a soldier but also how one can become numb to the near constant fighting and bloodletting. His entry for September 12, 1865, merely states that his brother Samuel had received a mortal wound and had been left on the field.

JOHN R. BOYD

The 1860 census shows John R. Boyd living at home with parents Hugh and Hannah (Kinnel) Boyd in Jackson Township. Hugh was a farmer, while his two sons, William and John, were master carpenters. Brothers David and Dennison, as well as sister Martha, were also in the home. Another sister, Eliza, had moved away. John was a big man at 6'2" tall, with a dark complexion, brown hair, and gray eyes. He enlisted on September 4, 1861, and was mustered into Company C of the 9th Cavalry on October 11. There is also information that he married Rebecca Shoemaker on October 27 of that year. Though the date is in question, the marriage is not. A little girl, Anna, was born in 1861. It is also in question whether John ever saw her.

In the battles and skirmishes that were continual that summer, John was killed at Triune, Tennessee, near Franklin, on June 11, 1863. Burial information has not been found. Chances are that he was buried where he fell. The nearby Stones River National Cemetery was created in 1865 to honor the men from that battle. Soldiers were also exhumed from area burials and reinterred there. Over 2,300 unknowns are included in that burial ground. It is possible John is one of those.

JAMES BUCKWALTER

Henry and Emily (Wynn) Buckwalter moved to Perry County from Chester County sometime in the 1850s. They settled in Juniata Township near Wila, which was known formerly as Milford. There, in the 1860 census, Henry was a miller as was son James. James had been born to the couple on January 16, 1841. Another son, Henry, had just passed away from typhoid fever in March about the time daughter Ida Emily was born. The youngest Buckwalter, Joseph, was ten.

James volunteered with the 9th PA Cavalry on September 9, 1861, and mustered in a month later. Assigned to Company C, he was promoted to company bugler almost immediately. While television and movies show buglers sounding the signal to charge, they were much more important than that. Infantry moved to the sound of drums in the Civil War. Artillery and cavalry did everything by bugle calls: from waking in the morning to going to bed at night, and everything in between. The lead bugler was stationed beside the commander during times of conflict so he could relay orders. Assignment as a bugler was an extremely important and respected position in a cavalry company, but it was also very dangerous. Just as infantry tried to take out the opposing color guard to create confusion, so too did opposing cavalry try to eliminate the bugler.

James was 5'3" tall, with a light complexion, brown hair, and blue eyes. The 9th PA moved to the Western Theater of the war and was stationed for a time near Jeffersonville, Indiana. There, James came down with a sickness that was not identified in the hospital records. He was hospitalized there and died on February 2, 1862. He rests in the Wila cemetery.

GEORGE L. DENTLER

Learning a trade in the mid-nineteenth century was just as important then as it is now. Often the instructor was the patriarch of the family. Such was the case with George L. Dentler. George's father was Jacob Dentler, a blacksmith in Spring Township. The 1860 census shows both men plying that trade. Parents were sometimes the only teachers, as it was still haphazard as far as attending school was concerned. George's mother, Margaret, likely also taught her daughter, Eliza, everything she could about being a homemaker, wife, and mother. Blacksmithing was an extremely necessary and important vocation at the time. It required knowledge of the properties of iron, how hot to make a proper fire, and the ability to take a plain piece of metal and shape it into tools, horseshoes, and, sometimes, art. It took a strong man with endurance and attention to detail. A good blacksmith was always in demand.

The army also needed blacksmiths. Their skills were required for keeping wagons, cannons, caissons, and horses moving. George L. Dentler enlisted in Landisburg on October 4, 1861, and mustered in a week later. At enrollment he was described as 5'9" tall, with a dark complexion, brown hair, and blue eyes. He was born in 1837 and had wed Catharine Dunkleberger in September 1860, but the couple had no children. George was assigned to Company C of the 9th Cavalry and was certainly instrumental in keeping the regiment moving as they headed to war.

We have already seen how many men became sick after being exposed to new surroundings and unfamiliar faces. Men from differing areas of the state and country were suddenly assembled in a concentrated area. Even men as tough as blacksmiths could not withstand the onslaught of disease. The government's recordkeeping early in the war was lax, so the nature of his affliction is uncertain, but George perished on April 18, 1862, while stationed in Nashville. George L. Dentler was buried in the national cemetery in Nashville, Tennessee.

DAVID TRESSLER DUM

Many members of the Dum family still reside in Spring Township, which sent dozens of its sons off to war. Among those was David Tressler Dum. His father's family settled in the Markelsville area before moving westward to the Green Park vicinity. After coming to America, the Thommen name gradually became Thumma and then Dum. Frederick Thommen sired Johannes, who altered his name to John Dum. John's wife was the former Maria Catharina Tressler, who sometimes appears in records as Mary Catherine Dum. According to the 1860 census for Spring Township, they raised a large family that included Catherine, Frederick, Elizabeth, David, William, Mary, John, Hannah, Susannah, Samuel, George, and Margaret. Frederick became a member of the 208th in 1864. David enlisted with Company C of the 9th Cavalry.

David's index card shows that he enlisted in Muncy on September 24, 1864, and was mustered in the same day. He listed Williamsport as his residence. That may have been true, however government records from that era contain an inordinate number of mistakes. That card shows him to be a 5'9"-tall farmer with dark hair, a dark complexion, and gray eyes. David's term of service mirrored that of Samuel Baker, even to the point of receiving a mortal wound on April 12, 1865, in the same cavalry fight. Like Samuel, he passed away the following day near Raleigh, North Carolina. The two privates were interred temporarily outside the house where they succumbed to their wounds. Cornelius Baker mentions in his diary how he and a fellow soldier returned to that house, found the graves of the two fallen heroes, and marked them with boards from a bed's headboard. David is now buried in Mount Zion Cemetery in Elliottsburg beside his parents.

BENJAMIN EBRIGHT

William Ebright met and married Anna Shannon while both resided in the western part of Cumberland County. They later moved to East Pennsboro Township and raised a family, including daughters Mary Jane, Sarah Ann, Elizabeth, and Susannah. Benjamin was born to the couple in 1841 or 1842, and Harvey arrived about thirty years later. By that time, the family had relocated to Penn Township, where William's brother John lived. By 1860 Benjamin had already moved there and was working as a fieldhand for the John Houser family.

Benjamin had two cousins who were in the army. We unfortunately already met both George (page 30) and Samuel (page 89). Benjamin enrolled at Duncannon on September 23, 1861, and was mustered in ten days later into Company A of the 9th Cavalry. At enlistment, Benjamin was a farmer standing 5'4" tall, with a fair complexion, brown hair, and gray eyes. His given age was twenty.

Private Benjamin C. Ebright was reported missing on November 24, 1863, at Dandridge, Tennessee. In reality, he had been captured and sent to a Richmond prison. He was transferred to Andersonville Prison in February '64. He was admitted to the hospital there on July 23, but it was too late. His diagnosis was scorbutus, more commonly known as scurvy. This killer deteriorates the body to the point that standing is impossible, sores are present all over the body, and usually teeth fall out. George died the day he was hospitalized.

To add insult to injury, his name sometimes appears as Elright, as did both George's and Samuel's. In fact, his name is spelled Elright on his tombstone in Andersonville National Cemetery.

CORNELIUS FOOSE

John Foose and wife Phebe (Blain) lived for a time in Landisburg before relocating to Duncannon, where John was an innkeeper. They raised ten sons and one daughter and sent three of those boys off to war: all at young ages. The oldest was Thomas Jefferson Foose, who enlisted and mustered into Company A of the 9th Cavalry at twenty. Michael would enroll in the 16th PA Cavalry as a fifteen-year-old, and Cornelius joined Thomas on October 9, 1861, just after turning seventeen. Thomas was a schoolteacher, and even though he was only seventeen, Cornelius gave that as his occupation as well. Cornelius had a light complexion, sandy hair, and hazel eyes and was 5'5½" tall.

Thomas and Michael served long terms without incident. Cornelius was not so fortunate. He was wounded at Stones River. The U.S. Registers of Deaths of Volunteers lists his death as April 3, 1863, from wounds received. His burial information in Stones River National Cemetery carries a date of March 19. Since interment at that cemetery was several years after the fact, it would seem logical that the death occurred April 3, as was recorded in the register.

ISAAC GLADDEN

One of the few certainties about Isaac Gladden is that he was a Perry County resident in 1850. He appears in the census for Wheatfield Township as a five-year-old member of the John Varley family. John's son Phillip and daughter Elizabeth join John, Isaac, and an eight-year-old girl named Rachel Knour on the farm. It is interesting to note the neighbors of this farm family. Isaac Wilson resided close by, as did Moses Gladden. Moses's brother, William Gladden, later relocated to Wheatfield Township as well, noteworthy due to the rarity of the surname Gladden in Perry County. In fact, a subsequent search for that surname in county cemeteries turned up only six: Moses, William; his wife, Mary; son Joshua; Joshua's wife, Elizabeth; and Cillinda Gladden Wilson, Isaac's wife.

Isaac Gladden's father has not been identified, but as it turns out, Elizabeth Varley was his mother as verified by her application for a mother's pension, after she had wed a man named Jones, and by her death certificate.

Isaac Gladden enlisted in Company M of the 9th PA Cavalry on August 10, 1864, in Harrisburg at the stated age of twenty. He described himself as a farmer. He had a fair complexion, light hair, and blue eyes. He stood 5'3" tall.

Isaac's death is no clearer than his life. The muster file for Company M states that he "died Feb 5, 1865 in Rebel Prison at Florence, S.C." His veterans card file states, "held at Andersonville and survived." If he truly had survived, no pension would have come the way of Elizabeth Varlet Jones, so the muster file is likely correct, which it usually is.

DAVIDSON U. HENCH

To say that I, as the author/researcher for this book, have learned much on this journey would be an understatement. Sometimes you learn things in life that were right under your nose all the time. Such is the case with our next hero. In a search like this one, you often start at the end and work forward. Working from a list of cemeteries that honor these Civil War veterans, I saw that Davidson U. Hench was buried in Emory Chapel Cemetery. My immediate response was "Where in the world is that?" It's less than two miles from where I have lived for seventy years, and a place I have passed thousands of times. No chapel exists there anymore, and the cemetery, though right along Fort Robinson Road, is in a quiet little spot beside a pasture where the cows are just across the fence and love to watch you as you investigate the tombstones.

Davidson was born to Conrad R. and Elizabeth (Hall) Hench on August 8, 1838. Elizabeth died in 1852, and Conrad married twice more and had well over a dozen children. Davidson was the second-oldest. Conrad made a living as a brick mason; Davidson was a teacher before enrolling on September 16, 1861. He was twenty-three but gave his age as twenty at enlistment. At any rate, he mustered in as a corporal on October 17. He was 5'11" tall, with light hair, a light complexion, and light eyes. Assigned to Company E of the 9th Cavalry, he headed for the Western Theater of the war.

A brisk battle was waged at Tompkinsville, Kentucky, on July 9, 1862. It was a costly affair for the 9th, and Davidson was one of many casualties. He sustained an undisclosed wound and was sent home on sick furlough. Davidson's condition grew worse. He died on December 2, 1863. Though Emory Chapel Cemetery contains only about one hundred graves, it is populated by Davidson and ten other Civil War veterans.

JOHN JONES JR.

John Jones Jr. enlisted in the 133rd PA Infantry on August 11, 1862. This was a nine-month regiment that included three companies mostly comprised of residents from Perry County. They were one of the hardest hit regiments at Fredericksburg and gained a reputation for discipline and courage under fire. In just six months, John was promoted twice: first to corporal on January 4, 1863, and then to sergeant a month later. Clearly, he was a soldier's soldier. He mustered out with the company on May 26 of that year, but one term of enlistment was not enough for John Jones.

John's parents were farmers in Juniata Township. His mother, the former Esther (Hetty) Meredith Jones, had passed away in 1856. John's youngest brother, William, was born that year. Quite possibly those two events were connected, as many mothers died in childbirth in the nineteenth century. John had sisters Rebecca, Martha, Mary, and Jane to go with brothers Daniel Meredith, Alfred, and William.

Like so many others who served a term in the infantry earlier in the war, John enlisted this time in the cavalry. He enrolled on September 25, 1864, and mustered into Company G of the 9th PA Cavalry as a private. This was one of the many cavalry regiments involved in the pursuit of Johnston's Confederate Army during the final stages of the war. In one of the last cavalry engagements, known as the Battle of Monroe's Crossroads in North Carolina, the 9th fought dismounted near Solemn Grove. John was killed in battle on March 10, 1865. There is a monument to John in Middle Ridge Cemetery.

JACOB KEIM

Scores of Swiss and German immigrants moved into Perry County in the early to mid-1800s. George Keim was among the many who settled in the Duncannon area. He farmed a tract of land in Wheatfield Township with wife Christena Long Keim and children Christena, Aaron, Susannah, William, Sarah, Eliza, and Jacob. In the 1850 census, Jacob listed his birthplace as Pennsylvania. In 1860, he was listed as being born in Germany. In that 1860 census, Christena was noted as a farmer and Jacob was an apprentice carpenter. George had died in 1857.

The index card for Jacob describes him as a 5'5"-tall carpenter living in Duncannon. He had a fair complexion, light hair, and blue eyes. Depending upon the source, Jacob's name appears as Keim, Keime, and Kime. He enlisted on September 26, 1861, in Duncannon and mustered in eight days later in Harrisburg. He joined many other county men in Company A of the 9th PA Cavalry and headed off to war in the Midwest.

It was not long before the young man from Wheatfield Township came down with sickness. The U.S. Registers of Deaths of Volunteers does not have a diagnosis for Jacob. It dates his death as March 29, 1862, in the regimental hospital in Bowling Green, Kentucky. Many soldiers were exhumed from this and surrounding areas and then reinterred at Stones River National Cemetery, but Jacob's name does not appear in those records. He may be one of the 2,307 unknowns who rest there.

WILLIAM KUHN

Samuel and Elizabeth Kunkel Kuhn began married life in Saville Township. They appear there in the 1850 census. The census ten years later lists them as being in Madison Township near Andersonburg. Their first child, Mary Ann, was born in 1832. She was followed by George, Eliza, Sara Ann, William, Samuel, Catharine, Isabella, and Daniel. By 1860, the elder Samuel was already suffering from an illness that would claim his life by July 19, 1864.

William was born in 1840. According to the pension application filed by his mother in 1864, he had helped to support the family for a number of years by working on neighboring farms.

William enrolled on the first day of September 1861 and was mustered into Company E of the 9th PA Cavalry on October 17. He was described as a twenty-one-year-old farmer who stood 5'10" tall, with a light complexion, light hair, and dark eyes. Just nine months later, on July 9, 1862, he was wounded at Tompkinsville, Kentucky, where he was hospitalized. In a statement of facts filed during the lengthy process Elizabeth endured while striving to get a pension, William's commanding officer indicated that Private Kuhn was suffering from typhoid. William died of his battle wounds on August 5, 1862. He is buried in Nashville National Cemetery in neighboring Tennessee.

JOHN W. LIDDICK

No matter the cause for which they fought, nor the circumstances involved, every death in this cruel war was tragic. Some historians believe that as many as three quarters of a million lives were lost in just over four years. But the circumstances surrounding John W. Liddick's death make his loss one of the most gut-wrenching of all.

John W. was born to Frederick and Elizabeth (Louden) Liddick in 1832 in Watts Township. His brothers were Jacob, John F., Amos, Thomas, and William, and his sisters were Sarah and Louisa. John F. and William served in the 47th, while Jacob was a blacksmith in Company D of the 9th Cavalry. Jacob had earlier been a member of the 133rd. The name Liddick dots many regiments, as they were a stalwart family.

John W. was married to Lydia Ann Louden and had children Christian, Elizabeth, and John by the time he enlisted in Duncannon on September 27, 1861. He was mustered in just six days later in Harrisburg and joined Company A of the 9th PA Cavalry. At twenty-nine, John W. was 5'7" tall, with brown hair, a light complexion, and gray eyes. He, like his father, farmed in Watts Township.

John W. served through the battles in Kentucky and Tennessee and elected to reenlist as a veteran volunteer on January 1, 1864, at Mossy Creek, Tennessee. As an enticement, veterans who reenlisted were granted furloughs. John W. was making his way home on furlough by train and was nearly there when tragedy struck. Here is the entry from the U.S. Registers of Deaths of Volunteers: "having reenlisted & while on his way home on furlough with regt, he being intoxicated fell off the train, at or near Black Log Station Juniata County Pa. about 4 AM April 25, His rt leg & arm was mashed together with other injuries from which he died the same day." John W. Liddick was buried in Hill Church Cemetery in Watts Township. So close to a well-deserved thirty-day furlough, John succumbed to a temptation that took his life and devastated his family.

ISAAC MCCLINTOCK

Isaac McClintock was born in 1838 to William and Mary A. McAllister McClintock of Carroll Township. Isaac was a laborer according to the 1860 census and his enlistment information. His father, William, died in 1852, and his sister Mary Ellen passed in 1859. His mother remarried in 1853 to John Cleland, a Carroll Township farmer. In light of those developments, it was no wonder that a census showed Isaac residing with a different family, John and Elizabeth Fair, also of Carroll Township.

Isaac enlisted in Shermans Dale in 1861 on the last day of September. A month later, he joined Company I of the 9th PA Cavalry in Harrisburg. He was described as being 5'8" tall, with dark hair, a light complexion, and gray eyes. Isaac brought his mother more sadness when he was killed in action on July 9, 1862, at Tompkinsville, Kentucky. By that time, Isaac had been promoted to corporal. On July 31 of that year, the *Perry County Democrat* ran a brief obituary noting that he had been "shot in three places." Further, the paper said this about Isaac: "He was a brave and worthy young man and his early death is deplored by all who knew him." According to that obituary, "his body was recovered and interred by his comrades in arms."

ALEXANDER MCCOY

Information on Alexander McCoy is scarce. We know he was born to Elijah and Margaret (Barnett) McCoy of Wheatfield Township, by some reckoning, in 1827; others suggest the year is 1829 or 1830. The 1850 census shows the family engaged in farming and lists Alexander as twenty-three. Others in the family include Sarah, John, Frederick, Mary, Keziah, Margaret, Henry, and Liza. In the census ten years later, Alexander is shown as being thirty. His father had died and so had brothers John and Frederick. His mother, Margaret, was in the household as well as Sarah, Keziah, Margaret, Henry, and Joseph.

Alexander enrolled on September 28, 1861, in Duncannon and mustered in five days later in Harrisburg. At enlistment he was described as 5'6" tall, with a dark complexion, brown hair, and blue eyes. He was listed as a thirty-four-year-old farmer from Duncannon.

Alexander is listed in the muster-out files for Company A of the 9th PA Cavalry as a "vet," meaning he was a veteran volunteer who reenlisted. The men of the 9th reenlisted in January 1864 at Mossy Creek, Tennessee, so we can assume all was well at that time. After the following April and for the next year, the 9th was part of the cavalry charged with defeating the rebels in Tennessee, Georgia, and the Carolinas. They rode with General Sherman, and after reaching Savannah, they turned north and fought their way to North Carolina. They were involved in battles and skirmishes near Goldsboro in March and April 1865. The only information contained in those muster files about Alexander is that he was captured and died in prison at Goldsboro, North Carolina. The army does not know much about Alexander McCoy, which is a shame because he gave all he had to them and their cause.

THE RICEDORFF BROTHERS

The Ricedorff family of Juniata Township was one of dozens of Perry County families who moved to the Midwest to take advantage of cheap farmland and wide-open spaces. While they were here, Samuel and Lydia (Foulk) Ricedorff raised a typical large farm family that included sons Daniel, John, Samuel, Ezra, Frederick, and Jeremiah. Daughters were Mary, Catharine, and Lydia. The 1860 census shows the Ricedorff clan had moved to the Des Moines, Iowa, area, where they were farming. Daniel had wed Sarah Barnett Linn on December 28, 1854, and stayed behind in Perry County. The couple had three children by 1860: Mary, John, and Lydia.

At enlistment in Newport, Daniel Webster Ricedorff (sometimes spelled with one f) was a thirty-one-year-old laborer who stood 5'10½" tall, with a light complexion, brown hair, and blue eyes. He mustered in as a wagoner on October 11, 1861, and was assigned to Company C of the 9th PA Cavalry, though muster files note him as a private in the ranks.

After its initial training, the 9th moved into the Tennessee and Kentucky areas. There, many soldiers became ill; one of them was Daniel. He was confined to the regimental hospital in Lebanon, Kentucky, where he passed away on November 9, 1862. He was buried in Lebanon National Cemetery there.

Living in Iowa since 1856, the Ricedorffs left Pennsylvania behind but not the war. Iowa sent a fair share of its young men off to war, and three of the Ricedorffs went also. All had been born in Pennsylvania but fought representing Iowa. Samuel G. Ricedorff joined the 46th Iowa Infantry, John W. enrolled in Company H of the 29th Iowa Infantry, and when Ezra enrolled in the 47th Iowa Infantry in 1864, he became the fourth brother to serve.

John had wed Georgia Hastel after arriving in Iowa. They had a daughter, Mary T. Ricedorff, and resided in Afton, Iowa, when John enlisted on August 12, 1862. The 29th Iowa Regiment was mustered in at

Council Bluffs, Iowa, on November 8, 1862, one day before Daniel died in Lebanon, Kentucky. The 29th saw most of its activity in its first year in Arkansas and in the White River Campaign. The weather was severe throughout the winter months of this campaign. Many soldiers were sickened and many perished. John W. Ricedorff died of an undisclosed disease on September 1, 1863. He was buried in the national cemetery in Little Rock, Arkansas, which is 450 miles from where Daniel lies in Kentucky.

SAMUEL SNYDER

The small town of Blain was well represented in the 9th PA, with at least ten enlistees from the town and surrounding area. Three did not return alive. The 1850 census shows Samuel Snyder resided with the Daniel Roush family in the Blain area of Madison Township. The household consisted of Daniel and wife Mary, her father Johnathan Seager, and fourteen-year-old Lydia Seager. Johnathan and Daniel were shoemakers. Samuel was also with the Roush family in the 1860 census. That year, Daniel Roush is listed as a farmer. Samuel was a shoemaker, and the Seagers were not shown. It is unclear if Samuel was a relative of the Seagers or Roushes. Perhaps he was there simply to learn a trade.

When Samuel enrolled in the 9th Cavalry on September 11, 1861, he was 5'3" tall, with a light complexion, red hair, and gray eyes. He was a twenty-three-year-old shoemaker. Samuel mustered into Company C of the 9th, so he would have been serving with many others from Blain, as well as men from other areas of western Perry County. There were quite a number from the Landisburg area in that regiment in Companies A and C. The 9th was assigned to the border states of Kentucky and Tennessee for its first two years. One small but hotly contested battle occurred at Thompson's Station, Tennessee, on March 5, 1863. In that fight, Samuel Snyder was mortally wounded. Hospital notes indicate it was a wound to the left lung. He died that day and is buried in Stones River National Cemetery in Murfreesboro, Tennessee.

MATTHEW BOYD PATTERSON STEWART

Matthew Boyd Patterson Stewart was born in Duncannon sometime in 1834 to parents Richard and Mary (Fry) Stewart. Siblings William,

Eliza, Sarah, John, and Alfred were already in the household; Thomas and Isaac were born before Mary died in 1839, not reaching her fortieth birthday. Richard passed away in 1854. Matthew stayed in Duncannon while many of his brothers moved westward to settle in the Pittsburgh area. The census of 1860 reveals that M. B. P. Stewart, as he is often listed in army files, was a nailer. He had wed Ellen Ashton and the couple had children Mary, William, and Charles. Life was good for the Stewarts before the war intervened. Another daughter, Sarah, was welcomed into the family in March 1861.

At enlistment, M. B. P. stood 5'5" tall and had a dark complexion to match his dark hair and hazel eyes. By September 11, he was employed as a wheelwright. Stewart mustered into Company A of the 9th PA Cavalry on October 3, 1861. Exhibiting a propensity for command, he was promoted to corporal. Then, when he reenlisted at Mossy Creek, Tennessee, on January 1, 1864, he was promoted to sergeant. Meanwhile, brother Isaac Fry Stewart had enlisted in the 102nd Infantry and later became a member of the 6th PA Heavy Artillery.

Although being a sergeant was a major advancement in the ranks, it often put the man out front and made him a target. At the battle of Griswoldville in Georgia on November 22, 1864, Stewart was one of a sizable number of casualties within the ranks of 9th Cavalry. He was killed in action that day and subsequently buried on the battlefield. He was reinterred at Andersonville National Cemetery.

JOHN A. STOTLER

Private John A. Stotler is the second 9th Cavalry bugler to make this unenviable list. In all, four 9th PA Regiment buglers perished during the war. Little is known about John's life and death. The 1860 census shows John resided in Duncannon with his father, John, and two much younger brothers, Ebert and William. The elder John was a weigh master. No occupation for John A. was listed. Between that census and his enlistment on September 11, 1861, John married Mary Waite. No records of any children have been found.

John mustered in as a musician on October 3, 1861, with Company A, and left to learn the myriad bugle calls that would signal the regiment to get up in the morning, go to bed at night, and all the calls used in battle. John died in Leitchfield, Kentucky, on April 9, 1862, one year from the beginning of this cruel war and three years before it would end. John rests in Duncannon Union Cemetery.

EDMUND WEBSTER

In its storied four-year existence in the Union Army, the 9th Cavalry had well over one hundred Perry Countians in its ranks. Some served from beginning to end, others mustered in later in the war. One who joined from Carlisle on the final day of August 1864, was Private Edmund Webster of Greenwood Township. Edmund, born in Juniata County on September 11, 1837, had lived in Delaware Township on the family farm according to census records from 1850. His parents were Jacob and Martha (Durst) Webster.

Edmund married Susannah Catherine Rouch in Liverpool on November 26, 1857, and moved to Greenwood Township, where he was employed as a laborer. In the 1860 census, the Edmund Webster family included Sarah, Daniel, and Wellington. Edmund joined Company M of the 9th PA, and once in the Federal Service, it did not take long for disease to attack him. Confined to U.S. General Hospital in Wilmington, North Carolina, Private Edmund Webster died on March 10, 1865, little more than six months after enlistment. He was buried in Wilmington National Cemetery.

ROBERT WILSON

Another man whose service in the army was tragically cut short was Robert Wilson of Wheatfield Township. Robert appears in the 1850 census for Wheatfield as a member of the Isaac Wilson family, who farmed for a living. His mother was the former Cillinda Gladden. And even though Cillinda is a name rarely seen, it seems her personal information is confused. That census lists her age as thirty, but her tombstone in Evergreen Cemetery indicates she would have been thirty-three: a more realistic age since she had a son, John, who was fifteen. Furthermore, the biography information in Evergreen's website indicates she passed in 1837.

For that matter, Robert's information is confusing. The index card lists a date of death as April 12, 1862, but the tombstone in Evergreen lists March 1863. What is known is that Robert enlisted on September

17, 1861, at Duncannon and mustered on October 3 in Harrisburg. He was a private in Company A of the 9th Cavalry. He was described as having a medium complexion, brown hair, and gray eyes. He was a 5'10" farmer who was twenty-one at enrollment. Robert was one of six children. A younger brother, William, later became a member of Company A of the 20th PA Cavalry.

As we know, the 9th moved to Tennessee that first winter, where many new recruits fell ill. Robert was one of them. He died of disease in Springfield, Tennessee, on April 12, 1862, according to army records, just seven months after enlisting.

XXIII.

The 93rd Drafted Infantry

THE first national military draft was established when President Lincoln signed the bill into law on March 3, 1863. Volunteer numbers were dwindling, but the need for soldiers was not. A stipulation in the act was that men could buy an exemption or find a substitute willing to stand in for them.

An eighteen-year-old from Shermans Dale, Levi Owen Young, volunteered as a substitute. Levi's parents were Joseph and Esther Emiline Owen Young. Joseph was a millwright in Carroll Township. The family included, from oldest to youngest, Margaret Ann, Levi, John Henry, Amos, Fanny, Amelia, Enos, and Mary. Levi was born on April 5, 1846.

He enlisted and mustered in at Carlisle on November 29, 1864, when he was just eighteen and became a member of Company C of the 93rd Infantry. Sadly, he would not see his nineteenth birthday.

In the spring of 1865, the 93rd Regiment was skirmishing and fighting nearly every day as the army tried to capture the Confederate rail center at Petersburg. It was imperative that Petersburg be taken because its capture would effectively mean the demise of the capital in Richmond. Many casualties resulted, but in the end, Petersburg fell to Union forces. But not before Levi Owen Young also fell. He was killed in action on March 25, 1865, just fifteen days before Lee's surrender. Levi was returned to Carroll Township and rests in Young's Church Cemetery.

XXIV.

The 99th Pennsylvania Infantry

THE 99th PA Infantry Regiment was recruited and organized at Philadelphia between late July 1861 and late January 1862. Philadelphia was a recruiting depot much like West Chester and Harrisburg, where men gathered to await assignments to regiments; therefore, though most men in the 99th were from the Philly region, there were many from other parts of the state as well. The 99th was part of the force that defended our nation's capital until assigned to the Army of the Potomac in late summer 1862. It was engaged at Bull Run and in nearly all battles in the Eastern Theater, including Gettysburg, where it lost one third of its men.

Most men who grace these pages spent most or all of their pre-war years in Perry County. But some, like Edwin Eshelman, used Perry as a brief stopover on his way to glory. Edwin Madison Eshelman was born in Lancaster to Benjamin and Martha Frank Eshelman on April 2, 1822. He grew to adulthood there and took a wife, Fianna Hostetter, on February 19, 1852. Shortly thereafter, he relocated to the Montgomery's Ferry area near Liverpool. Their daughters were Mary Ann, Lydia Ann, and Sue Ella. They also had sons Abraham and Hagar. The 1860 census lists Edwin as a distiller and miller at Montgomery's Ferry. It also shows Edwin lived next door to his brother Justus, who served with the Biddle Rifles, the precursor to a large portion of Company B of the 36th PA.

At enlistment on August 21, 1861, Edwin was 5'6" tall, with dark hair and gray eyes. He was assigned to Company E. Edwin reenlisted at Brandy Station on January 4, 1864, and received a promotion to corporal. He became quite ill and was sent to the Mt. Pleasant Hospital in Washington, where he passed away on October 3, 1864. Edwin was returned to Lancaster County, where he lies in Lancaster Cemetery.

XXV.

The 101st Pennsylvania Infantry

THE 101st PA Regiment is not usually associated with Perry County for two reasons. First, it was recruited primarily in the western part of the state, and second, because most of its action was in the Carolinas. But with that said, some recruits were gleaned from Cumberland County and from Dauphin County, which border Perry.

This regiment was organized in late summer 1861 and departed for Washington, D.C., the following February. From there, it participated in the Peninsula Campaign and spent time in Suffolk and Newport News. New Bern, North Carolina, was the next stop before garrisoning at Plymouth, North Carolina, from July 1863 through April 1864. There, most members reenlisted. It was reported to be a mostly pleasant duty until the regiment went to Roanoke Island for a short stay. Upon return to Plymouth, the fort was attacked by an overwhelming force. They held as long as possible but finally surrendered en masse on April 20. The captive officers were sent to Macon, Georgia; the enlisted men were shipped to Andersonville Prison, where, by June 1865, half their number had perished. When freed in May, the survivors were mustered out and finally sent home.

WILLIAM A. DILE

Private William A. Dile was one of the men who enlisted in Harrisburg. He was shown to be a 5'11"-tall farmer with blue eyes, a dark complexion, and light hair, born to Johannes and Catharine (Smith) Diehl in 1844. The Diehl family name is seen a variety of ways, including Deal and Dile. Most often it is spelled Dile from William's generation on. Johannes, or John, was a weaver by trade, who died quite young in 1847, leaving Catharine with children Sarah, Rachel, Josiah, Henry, George, Abraham, Samuel, and William. Interestingly, the 1850 census shows Catherine with Samuel and William, but the other children were apparently with friends and relatives. In 1860, only Abraham is shown with her. Abraham went to war with the 208th in 1864, Samuel enlisted in the 101st in November 1861, and William joined him on January 5, 1862. Samuel's story had a better outcome than William's, however it is interesting, nonetheless. Samuel was wounded in the right leg during the battle at Williamsburg, North Carolina, on May 5, 1862. He recovered and returned to action, but that wound troubled him for decades. Finally, in October 1912, he felt something hard under the skin and the Rebel bullet was extracted!

Both men reenlisted while the regiment was stationed in the Plymouth area. William even found a wife while there. He married Elizabeth Anne Dough, of Roanoke Island, on February 15, 1864. The couple had no children. The brothers were both captured at Plymouth on April 20, 1864, and taken to Andersonville Prison. Both survived until they were liberated in early spring 1865. William's health had deteriorated at that point. Most of the soldiers were sent to Camp Parole at Annapolis, Maryland. William was then given a hospital furlough and sent home. In one of his final acts, he wrote a will on May 31, 1865, specifying parts of the estate going to his wife and other parts to his brother Henry. The will says in part that he was "weak in body of disease contracted during my service in the army and while a prisoner." Also included in the will was this phrase: "now on hospital furlough and late a paroled prisoner from Andersonville." Both statements are telling in their damnation of conditions at the prison where thousands died. But before we point fingers at the Confederates, consider that their survival rate in Union prisons was nearly as low. Neither government was prepared for this war.

Many widows endured months and years of sending letters and testaments to the government to secure a pension. Elizabeth Dile's trek through the process was made even more arduous by her distance from William at the time of his death and by the circumstances surrounding that death. He was still technically on furlough when he passed away, and as late as April 1867, the pension office was still asking for documentation of where and how he died. Since Elizabeth was a citizen of the South, she had to swear allegiance to the government. William's pension file contains thirty-five pages of documentation, including a certification by his physician that his condition was caused by his service in the war.

William has a government-issued headstone in Ludolph's Cemetery in Little Germany near his boyhood home. He died on June 16, about two weeks after he dictated the will. The headstone is basic—just an abbreviated first name, his last name, and his company and regiment information. It sits beside his father's headstone. Dile is the name on William's stone; John Diehl is on his father's stone.

How much was a private's life worth to the government? The answer would seem to be not much when considering William Dile's experience. At the outset of hostilities, privates in the Union Army's artillery and infantry regiments were paid $13 per month. That amount was increased periodically, with the final jump coming in June 1864 to $16 dollars. The muster files for the 101st show that Samuel, William, and the other prisoners received three months' extra pay for being prisoners of war. Since so many did not survive the ordeal, they, or their beneficiaries, received $48 in 1865.

Government issued head stone for William Dile, Co. A, 101st PA Regiment, in Ludolph's Cemetery in Little Germany.

WILLIAM KITNER

John and Sarah Riggleman Kitner married in 1807 and had thirteen children spaced out over a thirty-five-year period from 1808 through 1837 as they farmed in Tyrone Township. They also produced patriots as five sons fought in the Civil War, some at an advanced age. John, born in 1820, served in the 47th; Abraham, born in 1830, served in the 177th and the 208th; David, born in 1834, served in the 149th; Henry, born in 1832, and William, born in 1821, were in the 101st.

William enrolled on January 4, 1862, and mustered into Company A the following day in Harrisburg. He was a Carroll Township farmer who was 5'7" tall, with a light complexion, light hair, and blue eyes. He gave an enrollment age of thirty-two, but he was clearly almost forty-one. He had wed Elizabeth Stone in August 1845 and had two living children when he went off to fight. The 1860 census reveals that a son, Peter, and a daughter, Mary, resided with William. Elizabeth had died in 1857. Another son, Samuel, had died in 1854, and a daughter, Sarah, had died in 1851. Possibly, these accumulated tragedies were incentive enough to leave for the war.

The 101st was engaged in some of the costliest battles of the early part of the war; Fair Oaks in Virginia was such a battle. William Kitner was killed in action there on the last day of May 1862.

THE MATCHETT BROTHERS

It seems that some families are destined to be stricken with early deaths. The Matchett family of Oliver Township was certainly one. John Andrew Matchett and wife Elizabeth (Ober) Matchett lived there with children Isaiah, Edward, George, and Emma according to the 1860 census. John was listed as a laborer. The children were all born in the 1840s. John and Elizabeth both died in 1854. Other information about the couple is extremely limited. Both are buried in the United Methodist cemetery in Halifax, where many other Matchett family members are buried.

In 1861, when Edward and Isaiah enrolled in Company K of the 101st, both were noted as farmers residing in Dauphin County. Edward gave an age of eighteen; Isaiah was shown to be twenty. Both were just one-half inch shy of six feet tall and described as having light hair, light complexions, and light eyes. Isaiah enrolled first on September 26 and Edward on December 14. Edward ran into problems exceedingly early on and ended up being hospitalized in Blackwell's Island, New York, where he died of "consumption" on September 6, 1862. He is buried at Cypress Hills National Cemetery. Isaiah served quite a bit longer and even reenlisted while the regiment was stationed at Plymouth, North Carolina, in April 1864.

Isaiah was among the captured members of the 101st who were sent to Andersonville. Once there, he did not last long, dying of pneumonia on June 16, 1864. It is interesting to note that his father, John, also died from pneumonia. And a parallel can be drawn to Edward's death as well, as "consumption" is what we know today as tuberculosis, which most commonly attacks the lungs. Isaiah is buried in Andersonville National Cemetery, where so many of his 101st comrades also rest.

CHRISTIAN ROTHE

Pvt. Christian Rothe (sometimes spelled Roth, Rath, or Rhodes) of Company A, 101st PA Infantry, was born in Germany. He stood 5'10" tall and had dark hair with blue eyes. Christian was among the dozens captured at Plymouth, North Carolina, and sent to prisoner of war camps. He was incarcerated at Andersonville, where he died of scorbutus (scurvy) on December 1, 1864, and rests in Andersonville National Cemetery. His index card shows a residence of Perry County. Christian, who was forty-two at enlistment, served from December 13, 1861, until his death.

I was uncertain of his inclusion in this book until I found his will, which proved to be both informative and interesting. He had his will prepared on October 24, 1864, just thirty-eight days before he died. Christian stated he was "late of Bloomfield, County of Perry, State of Pennsylvania" and that he was then "at the hospital attached to the military prison." In that will, Christian mentioned $240 that was "in the Carlisle Bank in Carlisle," as well as referencing monies due him from the U.S. government. He bequeathed money to six fellow soldiers from Company A: Sergeant Henry Johnston, Sergeant James M. Gillmore, Corporal Edmund Richards, and Corporal William Townsley were to receive $25 each. Private Calvin C. Diffenbacker would receive $50, and Private John A. Duffy would receive the rest of his property as well as being named the executor. Diffenbacker had been transferred to the hospital as a steward and likely was caring for Christian.

This will was witnessed by Company K's Sergeant Thomas J. Shorb from Adams County. Shorb testified on June 27, 1865, in Gettysburg as to the accuracy and authenticity of the will. The will was probated in Allegheny County on February 26, 1866, presumably because five of the will's beneficiaries lived in that area.

Christian and the other men of the 101st Regiment arrived in Andersonville at the end of April 1864, which was a time of extreme turmoil within the camp. A group calling themselves the "Raiders" was terrorizing their fellow Union inmates by stealing from them, beating them, and preying upon those with weakened conditions. With the blessing of Warden Henry Wirtz, a group known as the "Regulators," who were mainly sergeants, vowed to protect prisoners and bring the Raiders to justice. A showdown occurred on June 29th, with the Regulators defeating the Raiders and allowing the inmate population to try them. The six ringleaders were hanged and buried separately from the rest of the inmates who perished at Andersonville. No listing of the members of the Regulators has been found; therefore, we don't know if those mentioned in Christian's will were Regulators or merely men tending to a sick comrade.

ARMSTRONG SMILEY SIGLER

Carroll Township in the mid-1800s was and still is dotted with farms, large and small. Another farm family there was the Zeigler family. Their name is often seen as Sigler, even on their tombstones in St. Peter's United Church of Christ Cemetery near Bridgeport. There are the graves for father Samuel Sigler, mother Mary Ann Dunkleberger Sigler, and sons Samuel Sigler and Armstrong Smiley Sigler.

Government recordkeeping was extremely lax during the war, possibly due to family name confusions. Armstrong Smiley Sigler often went by his middle name, as is seen in the 1860 census for Carroll Township. In army records, his surname is consistently Zeigler. Armstrong, born on September 12, 1843, enlisted with Company A of the 101st Regiment on December 16, 1861, and was mustered in twelve days later. He was 5'8" tall, with hazel eyes and dark hair. His tenure in the service was one year before contracting disease. He was discharged on a surgeon's certificate on the last day of January 1863 and furloughed home.

But like so many others, his weakened condition was one from which recovery was not possible. Private Armstrong Smiley Zeigler died at home on March 16, 1863, and was laid to rest near Bridgeport, where brother Samuel joined him a year later.

BENJAMIN SMEIGH

Benjamin Smeigh traveled a long road with many stops along the way. He was born to George and Magdalena Messimer Smeigh in Baltimore County, Maryland, on November 13, 1816. Before settling in the Landisburg area of Tyrone Township, he resided in Walker Township, Juniata County, according to the 1850 census. The 1860 census shows him back in Tyrone Township with wife Mary (Foltz), son Michael, and daughters Susan, Jane, and Sarah. Benjamin was engaged in farming when he enrolled on December 14, 1861, at the age of forty-five. Private Benjamin Smeigh, sometimes spelled Smee, stood 5'6" tall, with black hair, gray eyes, and a dark complexion.

Michael had enlisted with Company H of the 47th PA three months prior to Benjamin's enrollment. He served until the regiment mustered out on Christmas Day 1865. Alas, that Christmas, like the two before it and many afterward, were celebrated without his father.

Benjamin was discharged due to disability on December 29, 1862, and sent home. He died just ten months later, on October 22. He has been included here for several reasons. First, he died during the war and because of it. Second, he is a further example of the cost of war. We often concentrate on the battlefield casualties alone when tallying the numbers, but the destruction goes far beyond. Thousands died from the lingering effects of disease and of wounds months or years afterward, with the shadow of death hovering over them all the while. Those months and years would have been fraught with pain, discouragement, and thoughts of "what if." What if I had not served? What if I die? What will my family do? But serve, they did. And die, they did.

Benjamin Smeigh lies in the Sandy Hollow Church of God cemetery under a government-issued headstone that simply reads, "Benj. Smeigh Co. A. 101st Pa. Inf."

SOLOMON SOUDER

Solomon Souder was born in 1842 to farmers William and Elizabeth (Smith) Souder of Carroll Township. The oldest of five sons, Solomon was twenty when he mustered on January 5, 1862, in Harrisburg. He was assigned to Company A of the 101st. A 5'8"-tall farmer, Solomon had a light complexion, dark hair, and hazel eyes.

He was another to be wounded at Fair Oaks, Virginia, on May 31, 1862. He was taken to Fortress Monroe for treatment of the wound and thence to New York City via the steamboat *Vanderbilt*. After treatment, he rejoined his regiment and was one of the many veterans who reenlisted at Plymouth in the spring of 1864. He was also one of the many who were captured on April 20 and taken to Andersonville Prison.

Like so many others, he quickly became sick and was finally hospitalized with dysentery. His condition worsened, and Private Solomon Souder succumbed to disease on August 18, 1864. The official cause was "marasmus," which is a fancy word meaning he was severely undernourished. He rests in Andersonville National Cemetery.

XXVI.

The 102nd Pennsylvania Regiment

JAMES Thompson Toland was born in the York Springs area in 1814, but by the 1840 census, he was married and raising a family on a farm in Perry County near Newport. His wife was the former Jane Hershey Elliott. The couple had the following children: George, John, Margaret, Amanda, Julia, Mary, and James Jr., who arrived on January 30, 1847. George served with the 17th PA Cavalry. John enlisted with the 133rd and suffered a wound at Chancellorsville. Despite being only seventeen, James Jr. enlisted with the 102nd Regiment on August 19, 1864.

The 102nd was a proud unit that fought throughout the war and was in the heaviest fighting from their organization in the late summer of 1861 through Lee's surrender. It was recruited in the Pittsburgh area and thus did not have any Perry Countians in the ranks until late in the action when attrition in virtually all regiments required reinforcements. Young James Toland was one of these men. He mustered in with Company F, and his military service was tragically brief.

In short order, James became ill; finally, being hospitalized with typhoid fever in the regimental hospital at Gettysburg. James had lost his mother a year earlier; his father later wed the widow of a soldier in October 1865. That soldier was William Hutton (featured on page 96), who ironically died the same day as Private James Thompson Toland Jr., November 15, 1864. Young James did not see his eighteenth birthday. He is interred at Duncannon Union Cemetery, surrounded by dozens of Civil War veterans.

XXVII.

The 107th Pennsylvania Regiment

A BLAIN native found his way to Harrisburg to enlist in Company H of the 107th Regiment. His name was Henry Berrier, son of John W. and Esther (Schaers) Berrier. Henry was born on January 5, 1829, and at the time of his enlistment, November 14, 1861, was a married father of four. His wife was the former Margaret Hockenberry. They had children Mary Ann, William, Elizabeth Jane, and Matilda Martha. Henry had moved to Fannett Township in Franklin County and worked there as a blacksmith to support the family until he was mustered into the 107th PA Volunteers on January 9, 1862, and then went south to fight the Army of Northern Virginia.

The Berrier family was well represented in the army as brother Samuel served in the 158th. Cousins John and David were also serving, John in the 9th PA Cavalry and David in the 20th PA Cavalry. The 107th fought in every major battle in the Eastern Theater of the war. They were a hardy bunch, commended many times. At Gettysburg, they were in the thick of the battle on July 1 west of the Seminary, where they were outnumbered and outgunned by the Confederates in the afternoon. They, along with the others in that sector, held out as long as they could before finally retreating through the town.

During the hasty retreat, many soldiers found themselves in a bottleneck as they tried to make their way through the narrow streets and alleyways. Henry was among those captured. He was marched to Virginia as a prisoner of war and held captive in Richmond. Henry fell sick and died from an unspecified disease on February 13, 1864. He is buried in Richmond National Cemetery, although there is a tombstone for him in Concord Cemetery as well.

XXVIII.

The 112th Pennsylvania Regiment

THE 112th Regiment was recruited as an artillery unit in eastern Pennsylvania. It became the 2nd PA Heavy Artillery Regiment and the largest artillery unit from the state. So large, in fact, that after recruits were added later in the war, it was split into two units for a time. Two of those 1864 recruits were brothers Johnathan and Isaiah Clouser of Miller Township, who both served in Battery L.

The brothers Clouser were born to Michael John Clouser Jr. and Elizabeth Catherine Powell Clouser in Saville Township; Johnathan in 1838, and Isaiah on November 13, 1840. Elizabeth was an aunt to the Powells we met on page 76 when discussing the 47th PA. Michael moved to Miller Township, where he farmed. The couple also had Samuel, David, Amos, Ezrah, Sarah, Lydia, Elizabeth, and Catherine. Samuel served in the 201st PA and David enlisted with the 36th Militia Regiment.

Samuel Bates notes in the index cards he assembled for this regiment that muster files are not available for all companies. For that reason, and since there was also an Isaiah W. Clouser from Centre Township who served in the war, information is incomplete and intermingled. Johnathan enlisted on January 4, 1864, and was mustered out with the company on January 29, 1866. Isaiah enlisted on January 24, 1864. On his index card at that time, he was shown to be a twenty-four-year-old laborer standing 5'6" tall, with a light complexion, brown hair, and hazel eyes. A death date of July 21, 1864, is shown.

Isaiah had previously served with Company I of the 133rd Pennsylvania as well as with Company D of the 36th Militia. Isaiah died from smallpox, but conflicting information exists as to the particulars. His index card indicates a death in a military hospital in Washington,

D.C., while the muster files cite a death at Petersburg, Virginia, on July 21, 1865. He was interred at Newport Cemetery where his tombstone, though difficult to decipher, seems to favor the Petersburg scenario.

XXIX.

The 12th Pennsylvania Cavalry

THE 113th PA Regiment was another cavalry unit, the 12th PA Cavalry. It was formed in 1861 and played an important role in the many battles in Virginia.

WILLIAM PENN CLEGG

Two brothers from New Bloomfield enlisted together in West Chester on February 16, 1864, and joined Company E. Christian Thudlum Clegg was twenty-four and, brother William Penn Clegg was thirty-one. Christian made it back to New Bloomfield, but William did not. Their parents were James and Mary Willard Clegg. James was fresh off the boat from England when he met and married Mary in Chester County. James may have died prematurely since Mary's 1860 census information shows her residing in New Bloomfield with her daughter, Ann, and sons William, James, Christian, and Joseph. Future census data doesn't include him either. Also in the household are her granddaughter, Rebecca, and William Clouser, who was listed as an apprentice shoemaker.

William Penn Clegg was also a shoemaker. He wed Mary Asper in the German Reformed Church on April 3, 1856. The couple had one daughter, the aforementioned Rebecca, on February 26, 1858. At that point, the young family seemed poised for happiness, but it was short-lived, as Mary died just seven months later on September 23. William then married Sarah Jane Baker in 1863. William enlisted as a private in the 113th PA Regiment, the 12th PA Cavalry. At enlistment, he stood 5'8" tall and was described as having dark hair and dark eyes.

William's cavalry career was relatively short, as he was captured at Winchester, Virginia, on July 27, 1864. He was sent to the prison camp at Danville, Virginia, where he suffered, as did a great many others, with chronic diarrhea. William died on December 5 of that same year and was interred at Danville National Cemetery.

As an interesting side note, the widowed Sarah Jane married a Centre County man, John W. Frownfelter, who had been in the 17th PA Cavalry. William Clouser, who apprenticed to William, would later wed William's sister, Ann. Clouser was also a cavalryman who enlisted with the Clegg brothers in the 12th Cavalry.

JOEL S. HUGGINS

A Newport-area man helped fill the 12th Calvary's ranks later in the war. In early spring 1864, most of the members who were still in the ranks reenlisted while the regiment wintered in the Martinsburg vicinity. Joel S. Huggins enlisted on March 23, 1864, and joined Company F for the action around Winchester, Harpers Ferry, and the Shenandoah Valley Campaign. Joel had previously been a member of the 6th Militia in 1862.

Joel was born to Joel and Susanna Huggins of Oliver Township. The census of 1860 shows the senior Joel Huggins was a boatman, and the younger was a student who had been born on October 16, 1843. He had brothers James, William, and Jacob. His sisters were Elizabeth, Susanna, and Lavinia. Joel was the youngest. William served with the 149th Regiment late in the war.

At enlistment, Joel was described as 5'5" tall, with a dark complexion, dark hair, and dark eyes. His occupation was listed as laborer. The life of a soldier was a hard one that exacted a heavy toll upon them; in particular, the cavalrymen. They were in the saddle for hours on end, day after day, in all weather conditions. Sickness was rampant, and Joel was not immune to it, even though he had youth on his side. He developed pneumonia and died while in the regimental hospital at Fortress Monroe, Virginia. Joel was returned to Newport, where he sleeps in Newport Cemetery.

XXX.

The 13th Pennsylvania Cavalry

THE first four companies of this regiment were initially recruited in Philadelphia in December 1861 and known as the Irish Dragoons. In the spring and summer of 1862, more companies were recruited, including Company F, which was formed in Cumberland County along with recruits from Camp Curtin in Harrisburg. A smattering of Perry Countians dotted the ranks.

The 13th served first in the Baltimore area, guarding rail lines, then was later employed in Virginia. This unit was decimated by battle losses, captures, and disease while first fighting in the Shenandoah Valley and at Winchester. Later, action near Richmond further weakened its ranks, as many men were captured and sent to prison camps. The 13th PA Regiment then headed south, where they fought in the Raleigh, North Carolina area until the war mercifully wound down in the spring of 1865. The remaining men were mustered out on July 14, 1865.

The war's second summer saw evolutions. One of the most significant was with the cavalry. Early in the war, Jeb Stuart's Cavalry manhandled the Union horse soldiers. Union generals didn't understand the value of cavalry, nor did they know how to use them. Men were astride horses they couldn't ride, let alone fight while riding. The commissary department bought anything with four legs and a tail. Horses were broken down because they were old nags whose time had come and because these cavalrymen had no clue how to care for the animals.

Commanders more in tune with strategy saw that cavalry should be used to screen the army's movements, flank the enemy, and create havoc among the opposing forces. Better mounts were secured and better men became horse soldiers, men who knew how to ride and care for these animals. Where better to find such men than in the rural counties of Pennsylvania?

JOHN B. ELLIOTT

A Miller Township farmer by the name of John B. Elliott answered the call for cavalrymen. Born in 1830 to Benjamin and Nancy Elliott, John knew all about horses and how to care for them. John was the oldest of four. His brother, Robert, enlisted in the 187th PA Regiment. The boys had sisters Sarah and Rebecca. Benjamin's brother David also was in the household. Benjamin died in 1859, leaving Nancy dependent upon her children. According to her petition for a mother's pension, John was her primary supporter prior to his enlistment. It would not be surprising if army pay was an incentive for John to leave home so he could regularly send back money.

John was missing in action during the Wilderness battle. He had been captured and sent to Andersonville Prison, where he died of "acute dysentery" on June 17, 1864. He was interred at Andersonville National Cemetery. The muster file shows John was a corporal, but interestingly, all of Nancy's pension file documents show he was a private. Hers was the typical battle of back-and-forth paperwork with the adjutant general's office. First, she had to have a commanding officer swear that John was in the 13th Cavalry and was indeed dead. Then, neighbors, friends, and even her son Robert had to testify as to John's benevolence to her. Finally, she was awarded an $8 per month pension on December 2, 1869, beginning the date of John's death five-and-one-half years earlier.

CHARLES FENICLE

Charles and John Fenicle hailed from Spring Township. Charles was born in 1842, John two years later. They were the sons of farmers Stephen and Ruth Murphy Fenicle. Others in the family were Margaret, Ellen, Sarah, Alfred, and Adam, who would join the 209th Regiment in 1864. They farmed in the area of Spring near Pisgah. When the brothers went off to war, it must have been quite a burden for their father and the rest of the family. Charles and John mustered in together on August 30, 1862, in Harrisburg. Neither man was married. John returned from the war and raised a family, but Charles did not. He was captured in the fighting near

Richmond on September 16, 1863, and imprisoned in the Virginia capital. Charles, like so many others, died of chronic diarrhea on December 13. Initially buried in Oakwood Cemetery, he was reinterred and now rests in Richmond National Cemetery. Stephen later applied for and was granted a pension.

MITCHELL WATTS

Mitchell Watts (military records use Watt) had a lot to live up to being the grandson of General Frederick Watts. Mitchell's father was Frederick Jr. His mother was Rachel Galbraith Watts, the daughter of another Revolutionary War hero, Major Andrew Galbraith. Mitchell was born to the Miller Township farm family in 1840. His siblings were Mary, Sarah Jane, John, Emiline, Andrew, Margaret, Susannah, Frederick, and Harriett. The youngest, Frederick III, joined the 208th Pennsylvania, while Andrew enlisted in the 3rd PA Heavy Artillery. Mitchell joined his cousin Frederick as both enrolled in Company H of the 47th on September 14, 1861. Unfortunately, cousin Frederick's term of service was brief (page 84).

Mitchell was discharged from the 47th on November 27, 1862, in order to join Company D. Army records show him as being a 5'7"-tall farmer with gray eyes, brown hair, and a fair complexion. Mitchell served out his three-year term and was honorably discharged on September 11, 1864. He wasn't finished with the war. On February 23, 1865, Mitchell became a member of Company F of the 13th PA Cavalry, however fate stepped in before he received his first pay. Mitchell was killed in action on April 11, 1865, near Raleigh, North Carolina. The muster file shows he was owed bounty money and pay in the amount of $473 by Uncle Sam. He lies now in the national cemetery in Raleigh.

XXXI.

The 132nd Pennsylvania Regiment

THE 132nd Regiment, a nine-month unit, was recruited in north central Pennsylvania. Perry County, however, had a presence in the regiment: Wilson Marshall Darlington of Centre Township. It is unclear why Wilson enrolled at Mauch Chunk on August 9, 1862, but perhaps he was working in that area. It is unusual given that the 133rd, which contained three full companies recruited in Perry County, was being organized at the same time. He mustered into Company G on August 15. The 132nd had its baptism by fire at Antietam, where it suffered 152 casualties but behaved like a veteran unit according to reports. It was again devastated when it fought at Fredericksburg, losing 150 of its remaining 340 men. It also engaged at Chancellorsville on May 3 and 4 before mustering out on May 24, 1863, after engaging in a trifecta of extremely costly battles.

Wilson, born on December 16, 1841, came from a large farm family that included six brothers and four sisters. Father Wilson had married Mary Barbara Lupfer on November 30, 1830, and was farming in Centre Township at least as early as 1840. Brother Meredith Darlington served in the 208th Pennsylvania.

Wilson survived Antietam but was not as lucky at Fredericksburg. He sustained a gunshot wound to the right leg on December 13, 1862. Wilson was sent to Harewood General Hospital in our nation's capital for treatment. He lingered until January 7, 1863, before dying of complications from the wound. Records show he was interred in Soldiers' and Airmen's Home National Cemetery, but a current examination of those buried there does not show his name. He does, however, have a tombstone in Poplar Hill Graveyard in Centre Township, which would indicate a reinterment there.

XXXII.

The 133rd Pennsylvania Regiment

THE 133rd Pennsylvania was organized as a nine-month unit in early to mid-August 1862. Three companies were recruited in Perry County, marking this regiment as having the second-highest number of county soldiers of any in the Union Army. Loysville, New Bloomfield, and Newport were the recruitment centers for the regiment; however, not every man in those three companies was a Perry County resident. Nevertheless, only the 208th, with four companies recruited there, was represented by more Perry Countians.

After a brief training period, this regiment was rushed to Antietam but arrived a day after the battle that recorded the largest single-day number of casualties in the entire war. The men got a taste of war, assisting in the gruesome task of burying the dead. They camped in the Sharpsburg area until November, moving later to Falmouth and then to Fredericksburg, where they were among the ill-fated regiments tasked with storming Marye's Heights. As did most Army of the Potomac regiments at Fredericksburg, the 133rd suffered dearly with 184 casualties. Later, after the infamous "mud march," the regiment was involved on the final day at Chancellorsville. Shortly after that debacle, the regiment was sent to Harrisburg, where it mustered out in late May 1863, after a brief but tumultuous term of service. Despite the cruelties endured, including the inadequate generalship of Burnside and Hooker, quite a few members later reenlisted to grace the ranks of the 208th.

SOLOMON BERKSTRESSER

Earlier, the Berkstresser/Baxter name was discussed in relation to William Harrison Berkstresser (page 11) of the 30th Regiment. Now we must acknowledge the sacrifice made by his father. Solomon was the son of David and Martha (Russell) Berkstresser, who farmed in Toboyne Township. Depending upon the source, Solomon's birth was sometime between 1813 and 1818. The earlier date appears to be the most logical based upon ages supplied during census taking and in a death notice. If 1813 is accurate, he would have been forty-nine at enlistment, an age when most people are content to leave war-making to the younger generation. But patriotism ran deep in the Berkstresser family—his brother Samuel mustered out of the 30th Regiment at the age of forty-five. Another son, David, served in the 130th PA Regiment.

Solomon married Margaret McGowan in Shippensburg in July 1834. The couple had the following children: Mary Jane, David, William, Sarah, Amanda, Margaret, Calvin, Anna, Wesley, and Theodore. In 1850 they were a farm family in Centre Township. By the 1860 census, they were in Spring Township, where Solomon was listed as a laborer.

Solomon's term of service was tragically brief. He enrolled on August 5, 1862, and mustered in six days later, joining Company G of the 133rd. He obviously was a hardy individual, but strange surroundings and exposure to new germs took a toll. Solomon died just two months later, on October 9, in the regimental hospital near Sharpsburg, Maryland. The U.S. Registers of Deaths of Volunteers lists the cause as typhoid. Solomon is listed as being buried in Soldiers' and Airmen's Home National Cemetery in Washington, D.C. He also has a memorial tombstone in Sandy Hollow Cemetery.

EDWARD C. BENDERRE

In *Hains History of Perry County*, Lieutenant Edward C. Bendere is shown as Edward C. Bender of New Bloomfield. However, all military records bear the name of Bendere. Not much is known about him, though it appears he may have been from Philadelphia. Bendere enlisted as a private in Company G of the 133rd at New Bloomfield on August 5, 1862. He provided information stating a residence in Perry County, however he does not appear in census data from 1860. He obviously exhibited an aptitude for leading men and was quickly promoted after the death of the regiment's adjutant at Fredericksburg. Bendere took that position, but it was a short-lived promotion. The 133rd saw limited activity at

Chancellorsville, but Lieutenant Bendere was killed in action on May 3, 1863. He is buried in Fredericksburg National Cemetery. His mother, Catharine, applied for his pension, indicating that Bendere was single. Little more is known about either of them.

DAVID BISTLINE

A May 26, 1859, article in the *Perry County Democrat* has this headline: "Typhoid Fever. – This disease prevails to an alarming extent in Juniata Township, in this county." It cites the following: "Within the past 18 days four members of one family have died – John Biceline aged about 67 years; his wife Margaret aged about 58; Samuel aged 22, and Isaac aged about 16. The old gentleman and his son Samuel were interred on the same day." Over the succeeding two years, sons Peter and Jonas, as well as John's brother and neighbor, Samuel, would join them in the grave. This family continued to be devastated by deaths, including at least six infants by 1867.

The Bistline family came to this country with the surname Baeuschlein. The Americanization of the name takes these forms: Biceline, Beistline, and Bistline. In fact, where many are buried, St. John's Church Cemetery in Markelsville, you can find members of this family with headstones reading Biceline and Bistline.

Farmers John and Margaret gave birth to another son in 1844, David. Perhaps to escape the raging epidemic, perhaps because of a sense of duty, David enrolled in Newport on August 6, 1862, becoming a member of a different family, Company I of the 133rd PA Volunteers. For his part, John had fought against the British in the War of 1812. Perhaps David was just carrying on a family tradition.

Typhoid fever also raged throughout the armies, but it was a Rebel Minié ball that felled David, who was killed in action at Fredericksburg on December 13, 1862. Private David Bistline rests in the national cemetery at Fredericksburg, far from disease, far from family tragedies, and far from home.

JOHN CARSON BRETZ

It must have been exciting to be an eighteen-year-old from Newport, marching off to war with new friends, old friends, and order-barking sergeants. It was like reliving history for John Bretz. His great-great-grandfather, Ludwig Bretz, had fought in the Revolutionary War. Now John Carson Bretz would get his chance to make a name for himself. He had been born to Jacob and Amanda (Henrie) Bretz on August 31, 1844. Jacob was a miller in Oliver Township. He and Amanda had just welcomed Irene into the family in May to join John, Mary, Margaret, Emma, Alice, Frank, Clark, and Jessey. The 1860 census shows John living with his grandfather John Bretz and employed as a farm laborer.

John enlisted at Newport on August 6, 1862, and mustered in a week later in Harrisburg just before turning eighteen. He was a member of Company I of the 133rd PA Volunteers. After training and adjusting to army life in the Washington area, the 133rd headed first to Maryland, then to Fredericksburg, Virginia, to what was exciting but entirely different from anything John or the other Perry County men sought.

Fredericksburg was hell on earth. Companies of men were sent toward an impregnable hill, where sheets of flame from Rebel muskets and cannons cut swaths through soldiers as easily as John had once wielded a scythe through wheat. John was one of many who died that cold December day, just twelve days before Christmas. He rests now in Fredericksburg National Cemetery among friends old and new.

ALEXANDER MCCORD BROWN

Another farm boy from the Newport area was Alexander McCord Brown. Brown enlisted in Newport the same day as John Bretz and mustered in a week later on August 13, 1862, in Harrisburg. Alex was born to Alexander and Eleanor (McCord) Brown on May 18, 1842. The Browns farmed in Tuscarora Township per the 1860 census. Alex had an older sister, Margaret, and an older brother, Samuel.

Alex became a member of Company I of the 133rd and headed to Washington, then to the Manassas area, and finally to Antietam. The 133rd missed the battle there but not the carnage, and certainly not the marching, which taxed many, including Alex.

The regiment stayed in the Sharpsburg vicinity for the next month. Many, like Alex, were ill. He was confined to the camp hospital in Frederick, Maryland, with typhoid fever. Private Alexander McCord Brown died from typhoid on November 6, 1862, and is buried in Millerstown

Memorial Cemetery, where interested county residents can view his headstone. The epitaph etched on his stone tells his story much better than I.

WILLIAM DUGAN

Emanuel and Margaret (Bear) Dugan moved to Perry from York County, where they had wed on November 25, 1840. They settled in the Dellville area of Wheatfield Township. The 1860 census reveals that Emanuel was employed as a master miller. Their children were Lydia, William, Barbara, John, and Elmira. Their surname sometimes appears as Dougan.

William was born in 1843 but is a bit of a mystery man. He enlisted in Loysville on August 8, 1862, mustered in five days later in Harrisburg, and was assigned to Company H of the 133rd. He is not listed in the U.S. Registers of Deaths of Volunteers, and there is some discrepancy about his death. One source lists his death as occurring in a hospital near Fredericksburg on January 24, 1863. However, the muster files for Company H reveal it to be Christmas Eve 1862 at the regimental hospital at Falmouth, which of course is near Fredericksburg. No record of his burial has been uncovered yet.

JOSEPH DUNCAN

We have just learned about several young men from Perry County who perished before turning twenty-one. Now we meet another elder statesman, Joseph Duncan of Newport. Joseph was born on September 16, 1820, and therefore did not have the youthful exuberance of younger men. No, at nearly forty-two years old at enlistment in August, Joseph was doing it because he believed he could make a difference. His wife, Caroline, listed her birthplace as Prussia for the 1860 census, and at twenty-nine, was nine years Joseph's junior. They had Josephine, Catherine, George, William, James, and a sixth child, Joseph, was born after the loss of his father. The elder Joseph listed an occupation of laborer.

Joseph joined Company I of the 133rd and marched off to war beside those much-younger men. He no doubt served as a mentor to them and helped steel their nerves as wave after wave of Union soldiers tried in vain to storm that hill at Fredericksburg. When it was Company I's turn, they went forward with the resolve of seasoned veterans, even though they had only been soldiers for four months. Four months was all many of them would get, including Private Joseph Duncan. He fell that cold December day and lay among many of those younger men.

Joseph is buried in Old Newport Cemetery. His tombstone is engraved with these words: "was killed at the battle of Fredericksburg Va. Dec. 13, 1862, aged 42 years 2 mos 27 days." Caroline's tragedies continued. Young Joseph lived only two years, dying in 1865.

CHARLES PRESSER FINLEY

Robert and Sophia (Presser) Finley moved to Perry County from Huntingdon in the 1840s. Son Charles was born there in 1842, but by the 1850 census, the family was farming in Toboyne Township. The other children in the family were William, Joseph, James, Mary, John, Harris, Sarah, and Martha. Data from the census ten years later shows them still in Toboyne. Charles was a farmhand, John and Harris were schoolteachers. The only others at home were Sarah and Martha. Unfortunately, we know more about Harris than Charles Presser Findlay, as it sometimes was spelled.

Harris and Charles both were members of the 133rd. Charles enrolled at Loysville on August 5, Harris on August 10. Charles mustered in on August 11, Harris not until the thirtieth. Charles became a member of Company G, and Harris was a member of Company K. Harris was promoted to corporal after just two days, which could explain the differences. His work as a schoolteacher gave him a leg up on others. Furthermore, there may have been more of a need for leadership in Company K than in Company G.

Harris survived the war, moved west, and settled in the Oklahoma Territory, where he had a distinguished career as a judge. Charles did none of those things; the war intervened. He developed typhoid and was hospitalized near Falmouth, Virginia. Charles died from this hideous disease on December 20, 1862, about six weeks after his mother, Sophia, had passed away. It seems that if Rebel bullets did not find these men, typhoid fever did.

FREDERICK P. FLICK

Private Frederick P. Flick spent time in Perry County as well as in Mexico prior to the Civil War. The twenty-six-year-old enrolled at Loysville on

August 8, 1862, and five days later became a member of Company H of the 133rd Pennsylvania. Most of what we know about Frederick has been gleaned from his mother's pension application file. He was a blacksmith who apparently traveled quite a bit from Brooklyn, New York, to Pennsylvania, and back. The twenty-six-year-old was a devoted son who regularly sent money home to his mother, Frances. Testimony given by family friends cites that a portion of his army pay, as well as the hundred-dollar bounty he received upon enlistment, went to support his widowed mother.

The disaster at Fredericksburg has been well documented as to the toll exacted upon the Union Army in general, as well as upon the local boys who fought with the 133rd. If a Rebel Minié ball didn't find them, diseases or exposure did. The conditions were brutal as men slept on the snowy ground without benefit of so much as a blanket. Captain Tressler testified that Frederick Flick was a "good and faithful soldier" and that he died from "fever resulting from exposure and hardship" the day after Christmas in 1862.

FREDERICK HAIN

It is painfully obvious by now that the 133rd was nearly decimated at Fredericksburg, but we are not done yet. The John Hain family moved to Perry from Northumberland County sometime in the 1840s. Both the 1850 and 1860 censuses show them living in Oliver Township, where they were farmers. Like many others, their surname is spelled differently at times. It appears as Hains in the 1850 data, Haine in the 1860 data, and many of Frederick Hain's military records show Haines. His tombstone in Center Union Cemetery in Bucks Valley shows Hain, so that is how we will address another man gone entirely too soon.

Frederick's mother was the former Catherine Snyder. His siblings were Isaac, David, John, Joseph, Henry, Jacob, and Sarah. Jacob and Isaac later served in Company G of the 208th PA Regiment. Frederick enrolled at Newport on August 8, 1862, and mustered into Company I five days later in Harrisburg. He was another casualty at Fredericksburg on December 13. He was moved to a hospital in Washington, D.C., where he succumbed to his injuries on December 23. Some records list his date of death as 1863, but the U.S. Registers of Deaths of Volunteers lists it as 1862.

JACOB HAIR

Different spellings of a surname are also true of Jacob Hair, whose name often appears as Hare or Haire. Jacob's parents, Peter and Sarah (Smeigh) Hair, were farmers in Carroll Township. They had the typically large farm family that included David, William, Carson, Susannah, Mary, Elizabeth, and Sarah in addition to Jacob, who was born in 1838. David served with the 201st PA later in the war.

Jacob enrolled at Loysville on August 8, 1862, mustered in at Harrisburg five days later, and became a wagoner in Company H of the 133rd. While this regiment was a nine-month regiment, many men did not even reach the halfway point. Fredericksburg got in the way, as did diseases. Jacob came down with an illness that grew worse until hospitalization was required. He was admitted to Harewood General Hospital in Washington, where he was diagnosed with typhoid. Sources vary as to his date of death, but he was interred at Soldiers' and Airmen's Home National Cemetery near the hospital. That record indicates it was November 25. The muster files show a date of November 27, and the U.S. Registers of Deaths of Volunteers shows a date of November 23. Like the spelling of his last name, these records provide no consistency.

ANDREW JACKSON HOUENSTINE

George and Elizabeth (Wilson) Houenstine farmed in Tuscarora Township. George was a patriot who served in the War of 1812 and not only gave his sons patriotic names but also gave them a patriotic spirit. In addition to Joseph and William, the couple had sons Andrew Jackson and George Washington.

Andrew, born on July 3, 1830, and William, older by three years, both enrolled at Newport and mustered into Company I of the 133rd. Both men were carpenters. Andrew was 5'11" tall, with blue eyes and light hair. He had wed Mary Duffield, and the couple had daughters Anna Laura and Carrie Elizabeth. William was later promoted to corporal, while Andrew served as a private. Andrew developed a sickness about four months after joining the regiment. The battle of Fredericksburg was fought in freezing weather, and shortly after the battle, Andrew came down with a cold. This developed into a pulmonary condition that precluded his returning to duty. The muster files show he was discharged on a surgeon's certificate on March 22, 1863, and sent home from Camp Humphreys, Virginia. Andrew's condition worsened quickly, and he passed away on April 21, 1863. He rests in Bull Hill Cemetery near Donnally Mills.

JOHNSTON KERR

William and wife, Margaret McClellan Kerr, who went by Nancy, farmed in Juniata Township and raised a large family that included three Civil War soldiers. Ephraim and Irvine served in Company F of the 104th Pennsylvania, while Johnston Fetter Kerr served as a sergeant in Company I of the 133rd. The boys had a tradition to uphold as their grandfather Matthew Kerr had fought in the Revolutionary War. Margaret passed away in 1843, leaving the boys and their siblings, Letitia, Nancy, John, David, Rebecca, Matthew, Robert, and William, to cope with her loss. Some were quite small. Johnston, born on March 8, 1834, was seven.

Johnston wed Sophia Rice on December 22, 1859. The couple had two boys, Johnathan and Johnson, when he enlisted at Newport. He joined a lengthy list of area men going to represent Perry County in the 133rd PA.

Like many of his comrades, Johnston's career was tragically short. A note in the muster files states, "Died Dec 5/62 of Typhoid Fever at camp near Potomac Creek, Va." Johnston was reunited with many of his fellow soldiers when he was buried in Fredericksburg National Cemetery. His young sons benefited, as so many others, from an education in the Soldiers Orphan School at Loysville, admitted on October 14, 1868.

JAMES MATHERS

Private James Mathers of Saville Township is another mystery man. His parents were William and Eliza. They farmed with an extended family that, in 1850, included children Catherine, Elizabeth, Samuel, James, Henry, Ann, and John. Also in the household were William's father James, and brother Peter.

At twenty-two, James enrolled on August 5, 1862, mustered in on the eleventh, and became a member of Company G of the 133rd. December 13, 1862, was one of the bloodiest days of the entire war for

Perry Countians. An examination of the muster rolls for Companies G, H, and I of the 133rd reveals a staggering forty-eight casualties. James Mathers also died in battle that day. His name does not appear in the records of Fredericksburg National Cemetery, not particularly unusual given the substantial numbers of unknowns buried there.

MEREDITH D. MCBRIDE

Strong family ties and patriotism ran in the McBride family of Centre Township. John McBride, born in 1720, emigrated from Ireland to Pennsylvania. His son John fought in the Revolutionary War. Matthew, Joseph, and a third John followed. Matthew had sons Matthew, Meredith, John, and Samuel. All were farmers.

The McBrides were a close-knit family as evidenced by the 1850 census that shows Matthew and Meredith farming and living in the same household as Matthew's wife, Mary, and their children Sarah, John, and Samuel. Though Mary's husband died in 1851, she, Meredith, and the children continued to reside and farm together.

Meredith felt the need to enlist and did so on August 8, 1862, at Loysville. He mustered in five days later and moved to the Washington area as a member of Company H of the 133rd PA Volunteers. In that same company was his cousin John McBride.

"Tomorrow at seven o'clock to parts unknown and uncertain that I will return again to my native home" are words contained in the last will and testament of Meredith D. McBride, written on August 18, 1862, at Camp Simmons as the regiment prepared to march to war. Many soldiers prepared for any eventuality before battles and campaigns. Perhaps Meredith had an uneasy feeling, or perhaps he was just a man who did not leave things to chance. In that will, he made provisions for Mary and her children so they could keep the farm and support themselves.

As for many, Fredericksburg got in the way of his return home. The muster files for Company H have these remarks: "missing since Battle of Fredericksburg 12/13/62." If you visit Fredericksburg National Cemetery, you will notice that some grave markers have rounded tops, and some are small square stones with flat tops. Of the thousands of markers at Marye's Heights, fewer than three thousand are the granite markers with rounded tops. Those are the stones that mark the graves of the soldiers who have been identified. Private Meredith D. McBride lies in a grave with a small square marker. His will was probated in the Perry County Courthouse on December 28, 1863.

FREDERICK OWEN MCCASKEY

Soldiering runs in some families, such as the Owen/McCaskey clan. Levi Owen fought in the Revolutionary War and had at least two grandsons fighting to uphold the Union he helped establish. One was Frederick Owen McCaskey of Carroll Township. Born to John and Mary (Polly) Owen McCaskey on March 30, 1839, Frederick helped his father farm their land. For a farm family at that time, the household was small, with just the parents and children Amos, Mary Jane, and Frederick.

Frederick and cousin Isaiah Owen went off to Loysville to enlist and joined Company H of the 133rd, mustering in on August 13, 1862. They headed south with the Army of the Potomac. Frederick found his way to Fredericksburg and suffered the same fate as so many of his comrades. Frederick's muster file reads "missing since battle of Fredericksburg Dec. 12, 1862." He is no doubt one of the hundreds of unknowns buried there.

His parents, his grandmother, and his remaining siblings moved west shortly after the war. The 1870 census shows the family resided in DeKalb County, Illinois. Mary died there in 1870.

JACOB MILLER

When Johannes Jacob and Christiana Jane Waltimyer Miller moved to Perry County, they settled for a time in Juniata Township. They began having children when Lydia was born in 1822. Over the next twenty-three years, Noah, Mary, David, Jacob, Henry, William, Andrew, and Jesse were added to the family. They relocated to Tyrone Township before some of the family moved farther west and settled in Iowa. In 1860, Jacob, William, Andrew, and Jesse resided with their parents, Henry lived next door with his wife and son. David was in Juniata County. William and Jacob were listed as laborers with no specified industry. It was common at that time for men to be day laborers who would hire out for various jobs, such as farming or wood cutting—anything where folks needed an extra set of hands.

Jacob, twenty-eight, and William, twenty-two, enrolled in Company G of the 133rd on August 5, 1862, and mustered in six days later. We know the regiment rushed to Sharpsburg and then to Falmouth before the big fight at Fredericksburg. William survived that battle, but Jacob did not. He was killed on December 13 by a round of grapeshot. He is buried in Poplar Hill Graveyard off Cold Storage Road. This tiny cemetery is the final resting place of eight soldiers who were veterans of the Civil War and the Revolutionary War. Two of whom were killed in battle.

HENRY MINICH

Henry Minich grew up on a farm in Tyrone Township. His parents were George and Margaret Rebecca (Koser) Minich. Samuel was the oldest child, followed by Sarah, Diana, Mary, Henry, Caroline, Benjamin, and John William. George's mother, Mary, also lived with them. George passed away in 1854, leaving Margaret Rebecca with the task of keeping up the farm and raising the younger children. John William was born in 1847, but he overstated his age and served with the 187th PA. Henry, born on August 2, 1839, had just turned twenty-three when he volunteered on August 8, 1862, in Loysville. He became Private Henry Minich, Company H, 133rd PA Volunteers, five days later in Harrisburg.

Even though the 133rd was recruited for only a nine-month term, a lengthy list of men did not finish out that term, and Henry is another name on that list. Near Potomac Creek, Virginia, later that fall, Henry was admitted to the regional hospital. He died from disease the first day of December. Henry lies in Lebanon Lutheran and Reformed Churchyard in Loysville. There he has been reunited with his parents and grandparents on both the Minich and Koser sides of the family.

GEORGE KEELY MYERS

The typical mid-nineteenth-century household was large and often consisted of extended family members. One such family was the George Myers household of Millerstown. George had wed Elizabeth Keely, and the couple already had children Catharine, Henry, George, Julia, and William by 1850. Elizabeth's father, George, and brother, Ulysses, also occupied the home. By 1860, Catharine and Ulysses had moved away;

daughters Elizabeth and Hannah had been added. George Keely was listed as a seventy-one-year-old carpenter. George Myers was a forty-two-year-old wagon maker.

Two of the sons enlisted in the army: Henry Keely Myers, age twenty, joined the 12th U.S. Infantry, while George Keely Myers, age eighteen, enlisted in the 133rd PA Regiment on August 6, 1862, at Newport. He mustered in a week later in Harrisburg and became a member of Company I. George was wounded at Fredericksburg on December 13 and sent to a hospital in Washington, D.C., according to muster files, where he died on December 18. That seems logical, but an entry in the U.S. Registers of Deaths of Volunteers shows a George K. Myers, Company I, 133rd Regiment, who died on April 5, 1863, of typhoid. His tombstone in Millerstown Memorial Cemetery is difficult to read, but I am inclined to go with the muster file information.

ISAIAH PARKER OWEN

Private Isaiah Parker Owen was the second grandson of Levi Owen, who saw his chance to establish his own identity in military service. He enlisted at Loysville on August 8, 1862, along with cousin Frederick McCaskey (page 159). He also mustered into Company H of the 133rd just five days later in Harrisburg and set off on his journey. After serving in the vicinity of Bull Run, the regiment marched toward the battle at Antietam. There, they arrived in time to help restore order to a horrific scene of carnage. They bivouacked near Sharpsburg, where it is probable that Isaiah became ill.

Isaiah was born to Wheatfield Township farmers Levi and Catharine Snyder Owen in 1841. Some records indicate a birth date of November 30 and some April 16. He was Catharine's youngest. She passed away in 1845. Levi remarried and had another son, George.

Regimental muster files show Isaiah was admitted to the regimental hospital near Sharpsburg, where he died on November 2, 1862. Civil War Veterans Burial Files indicate Isaiah was interred at Snyder's Church Cemetery, however their online records do not show that. It is tragic how poorly the government records detail the service and ultimate demise of these young men who served so briefly and so nobly. This is especially true of the first two years of the war.

JOHN A. REED

The 1850 census for Madison Township includes the Reed family. The patriarch, Robert, listed an unusual occupation as "scrivener." Though that has several meanings, he was probably a notary. By 1860, his occupation was farmer. He and wife Esther had the following children: Israel, Harriet, Sara, Emanda, David, John, Robert, Lucinda, and Samuel. Sara later married William Hull, who served in the 208th PA later in the war. Young Robert was also a member of that regiment. David joined the 16th PA Cavalry, and John enlisted on August 8, 1862, at Loysville and became a member of Company H of the 133rd.

John A. Reed was born on January 28, 1839. He was an apprentice millwright working with Samuel Behel. Like Isaiah Owen, John became ill at Sharpsburg and was admitted to the regimental hospital. He was well enough to accom ny the regiment to Fredericksburg but was hospitalized again there. John's stay in the hospital was lengthy and no doubt painful. He succumbed on March 5, 1863. The U.S. Registers of Deaths of Volunteers lists his cause of death as "apoplexy." John was brought home and interred at St. Paul's Lutheran Church near Andersonburg.

JOSEPHUS SMITH

While death is always a part of life, it was ever-present in some families, like the Jacob Smith family of Newport. Jacob and Mary A. Krewson Smith had five children together; only two of whom reached the age of twenty. Young Mary Ann died at age five, while sister Emma never reached age one. In fact, the elder Mary died at thirty-three in 1855. Jacob supported his family as an innkeeper in Newport. Josephus was the oldest, born on April 3, 1843. He was followed by Linford and Jacob E. Smith. Linford enlisted in the 20th PA Cavalry later in the war. Josephus enlisted in Newport on August 6, 1862, and became a member of Company H of the ill-fated 133rd PA Volunteers.

Along with his comrades, Josephus tried to storm an impregnable Rebel position at Fredericksburg and paid dearly. This action left such an indelible mark upon the survivors that after repulsing Pickett's Charge at Gettysburg on July 3 a year later, the shout went up along the Union lines, "Fredericksburg, Fredericksburg, Fredericksburg!" This was a sign of victory as well as a form of redemption. Josephus had received a wound at Fredericksburg and never saw the "redemption" that day. He was admitted to Emory U.S. Hospital in Washington, D.C., where he died from his wounds six days after the battle. He returned to Newport a final time and is buried in Old Newport Cemetery off Fifth Street.

ABRAM SPANOGLE

The typical migration pattern in the nineteenth century was east to west. The Jacob Spanogle family went the opposite way. Jacob was born in Huntingdon County, his wife, Hannah Shearer, in Franklin County. By 1860 they resided in Saville Township, where Jacob was a minister. Oldest son, Andrew, farmed while the younger boys, Abram, Samuel, and William, were farmhands. They had sisters Edna, Catharine, and Emma. By 1870, daughter Estella was born, and the family moved to Philadelphia, where Jacob served as a bishop.

Family and census records indicate that Abram was born in 1847. If true, that makes his stated enlistment age of twenty-two a bit far-fetched. He enrolled on August 11, 1862, and mustered into Company G of the 133rd. Abram's youth served him no better than his older comrades; he too fell to rise no more at Fredericksburg on December 13, 1862. He is not listed as being in Fredericksburg National Cemetery, but that is not unusual given all the unidentified bodies there.

DAVID TRESSLER WAGNER

St. Peter's Church Cemetery near Bridgeport is in an out-of-the-way location on top of a hill in the middle of farm fields. Farm boys growing up there had to be hardy and strong; the kind who made tough soldiers. It certainly seems as though Perry County farmers-turned-soldiers received more than their share of Rebel gunfire. Were these men always out front, leading the way? We will never know, but when examining the devastation wreaked upon our men, it seems as though we could make a case.

When it is all tallied, more than two dozen Perry Countians died while serving in a regiment that only existed for nine months. It is true that most suffered illness rather than gunshots, which is also understandable due to the relative isolation of men growing up in a rural area like ours. Once they were subjected to new germs and thrust amid thousands of unknown faces, the Grim Reaper had new weapons in his arsenal.

David Tressler Wagner (sometimes spelled Waggoner) grew up on a farm near Bridgeport. Born on March 1, 1842 (calculated from information on his tombstone), David was a middle child in a large family that included seven sisters and two brothers. Samuel Heckendorn and Elizabeth Tressler Wagner were the parents, who were, at the same time, proud and worried when David enlisted in Loysville on August 8, 1862, becoming a private in Company H.

David was mortally wounded at Fredericksburg on December 13 and would die on Christmas Day in the general hospital at Point Lookout, Maryland. David returned to that hill near Bridgeport and rests under an imposing spire that is a fitting monument to a brave young farm boy who turned soldier.

Monument for David T. Wagner in St. Peter's Cemetery near Bridgeport, Pennsylvania.

FINLAW WITHEROW

We find many examples of brothers enlisting together, like John and Finlaw Witherow of Centre Township. They were mustered into Company G of the 133rd PA on August 11, 1862, after enrolling in New Bloomfield on the sixth. Born on May 1, 1840, Finlaw's parents were

John and Margaret Sunderland Witherow. The 1860 census shows that the elder John Witherow was a clothier, an occupation he passed along to his eldest son, Samuel, who served with the 208th PA Regiment during the last year of the war. Margaret had passed on in 1841, and John was remarried to Maria Roth. Together they had John, Cyrus, Alice, and Charles.

When Finlaw enrolled, he was a twenty-one-year-old farmer in Centre Township. His military career was brief, like so many others. He contracted typhoid and was admitted to the regimental hospital at Falmouth, Virginia, where he died on January 4, 1863. His body was brought back to New Bloomfield, where he rests in New Bloomfield Cemetery.

HENRY L. YOHN

In the Jacob Yohn family of Tuscarora Township, children were spaced out over a twenty-two year period, as William was born in 1819 and eleven more children followed. Henry came along on September 13, 1839. Jacob and wife Margaret (Paden) Yohn farmed for a living.

Henry L. Yohn was a farmer upon enrollment on August 6, 1862, in Newport. A week later he was in Harrisburg and in the army as a member of Company I, 133rd PA Volunteers. The rest is a bit of a mystery. Muster files and his index card agree that Henry did not survive the war, but that is all on which they agree. Muster files for his company state that he "died date unknown." The Bates index cards state that he was another "killed at Battle of Fredericksburg 12-13-62." Whichever, if either is accurate, it is yet another example of the inadequacies of governmental recordkeeping. He is among the scores of unknowns at Fredericksburg.

XXXIII.

The Second Bucktails: 149th Pennsylvania Regiment

THE success and reputation acquired by the original Bucktails led to the desire for an entire brigade of such men. Major Roy Stone and Captain Langhorne Wister were dispatched to return to Pennsylvania in July 1862 and recruit those men. But the pair were recalled early from their missions due to the northward movement of Lee's army. Only two regiments were formed, the 149th and the 150th, with Stone and Wister respectively becoming their colonels. It was natural, then, for them to seek familiar and fertile recruiting areas, like Duncannon. Captain Francis Bacon Jones and twenty-one Perry Countians helped to swell the ranks of Company G of the 149th. They proudly displayed the symbol of the 42nd Regiment, the Bucktail.

The 149th received its baptism of fire on July 1, 1863, at Gettysburg, and what a baptism it was. This untested regiment, along with its sister regiment, the 150th, and the 143rd formed Stone's brigade. It was tasked with stopping the initial Rebel surge on the McPherson farm, west of town. They were stationed alongside the famous Iron Brigade, where their monument sits in silent testimony to the bravery and determination of that little band of warriors. At least eleven of those who enlisted in Duncannon saw action at Gettysburg. Out of that number, one man was killed in action, another mortally wounded (who would die en route to a hospital), one man was captured, and three sustained wounds in just a few hours' time; a staggering 55% casualty rate. The 149th achieved a reputation for toughness that day, and it carried that throughout its term. After Gettysburg, the next big test came at Spotsylvania Court House and the Wilderness. They were also heavily engaged at Weldon Railroad and Petersburg. The regiment paid with blood for the right to wear the Bucktail symbol.

JESSE BAIR

Private Jesse Bair from Buffalo Township missed the bloodbath at Gettysburg. He was drafted to help replenish the ranks and joined Company C of the 149th at Carlisle on October 6, 1863. Born to John and Mary (Moore) Bair in 1828, Jesse was a father of seven with one on the way. He was employed as a lockkeeper on the Pennsylvania Canal. His wife was the former Mariah Freet, whom he wed in 1847. Jesse's brother Jeremiah later joined the 208th Regiment about a year later.

Jesse saw action for the first time at Laurel Hill near Spotsylvania Court House, Virginia, seven months after mustering in. The battles in the beginning of May 1864 were fierce and deadly, as both sides fought for control of a piece of land known locally as the Wilderness. Jesse's first battle was his last. He was killed in action on May 8, 1864. Jesse is buried in Fredericksburg National Cemetery under the name Jesse Bear. His second youngest child, St. David Bair, was admitted to Tressler Orphans' Home in Loysville on September 3, 1866. None of the other children are listed in that roll.

JOHN BROOKHART

Another draftee was Private John Brookhart of Greenwood Township. He was born to John and Elanor Rider Brookhart on January 9, 1836. The 1850 census shows that John was a miller, as were his father and brothers William and Daniel. His life had some drama, as he married Charlotte Murray on July 10, 1859, and fathered Cora Ellen in March 1864. However, a gentleman named Benjamin Franklin Brookhart claimed to be his son, born to Rebecca Long on December 27, 1858. Benjamin filed for a minor's pension, but it was denied since John and Rebecca had not been married.

John mustered into Company C of the 149th on August 17, 1863. At that time, he was 5'6" tall, with blue eyes and brown hair and was still employed as a miller. The 149th was heavily engaged in the spring of 1864 in the Virginia theater. John was mortally wounded on May 23 at North Anna River. He was taken to the Fourth Division Hospital but died due to what the U.S. Registers of Deaths of Volunteers termed "cranial bone fractured." John was buried in Alexandria National Cemetery in Virginia.

JOHN A. BURTNETT

Getting the notification that you were drafted into the army in the second half of the war was likely received with mixed emotions. On the one hand, you were secure at home with a family, and wanted to stay that way. On the other hand, you wanted to serve and do your part. Being assigned to a Bucktail Regiment also carried mixed emotions. The Bucktails were known and respected throughout the North, but they were also in harm's way daily due to the reliance upon them from superiors who were either motivated by a powerful sense of duty or by a desire for glory—or a little of both.

When he registered for the draft in July 1863, John A. Burtnett was twenty years of age, unmarried, and listed as a laborer. Just six short weeks later, he stood in line at Carlisle, waiting to become a private in Company I of the second coming of the Bucktails. He was mustered in on August 16, and though he may have wished to be at home supporting his family, a sense of pride at being a Bucktail no doubt was evident.

Born in 1843, John was the oldest of eight children born to William and Elizabeth Burtnett of Tyrone Township near Landisburg. With William's health deteriorating, John sustained the family. His army pay was some help. John served without incident until the many battles in and around the Wilderness. He was listed as missing in action at Cold Harbor on June 8, 1864. In reality, he had been captured and was marching toward Andersonville. At that time, the POW camp was new. Construction had begun in February but was never completed. Designed to hold about ten thousand prisoners, by the time John got there, three times that many Union soldiers occupied the site. Conditions were deplorable. Disease was rampant. John contracted disease and perished on September 14.

Elizabeth filed for and was granted a mother's pension since John had no wife or children, and her husband was unable to work.

JOHN WESLEY CRILEY

John Wesley Criley had recently married Mary Lenig in 1861, and become a new father to Alice Elizabeth earlier in 1863, when he was notified that he had been drafted. He mustered into Company C on August 17, 1863, at Huntingdon, if his index card is accurate. Like his father and brother George, he was a wagon maker from Liverpool Township. John was born to father John and mother Mary Ann Williams Criley in 1837.

We have seen already that the 149th was devastated at Gettysburg, necessitating the influx of draftees. And it was hit hard at the Wilderness in the spring of 1864, suffering dozens of casualties, of which John was one. He was captured on May 5 and taken farther south to Wilmington, North Carolina. Wilmington's prisoners were liberated in February 1865, but some were quite sick, including John. He perished at the general hospital there on March 6. The U.S. Registers of Deaths of Volunteers does not list the cause of death, but it was likely dysentery, as the disease was rampant among these men. Strangely, no record of John's burial can be found. His widow remarried another Civil War veteran, Andrew Pines, a few years later.

BENJAMIN CUNNINGHAM

Benjamin Cunningham owns the distinction of settling what we now refer to as Dromgold, or Dromgold's Corner. He began farming the property in 1828 and married Amelia Henderson. The property remained in the Cunningham/Dromgold families until 2009, when it was donated to Perry County Historical Society. The connection to the Dromgold family was established when daughter Rebecca wed Michael Thomas Dromgold. Michael was a member of the 133rd PA as well as the 3rd PA Cavalry. Mother Amelia passed away in 1852, leaving Rebecca, Margaret, Elizabeth, Jane, and a son, Benjamin Henderson Cunningham, to be raised by their father.

The younger Benjamin registered for the draft in July 1863 and promptly mustered into Company F of the 149th in Carlisle a month later. He, like his father, was a farmer. Benjamin stood 5'8" tall, with brown hair and gray eyes. Like so many others, his tenure was relatively brief. Young Private Cunningham suffered from chronic diarrhea and died at the regimental hospital in Culpeper, Virginia, on January 17, 1864. Benjamin has been reunited with his parents and several sisters in the presbyterian cemetery on Windy Hill Road not far from the farm fields he once called home.

WILLIAM DICE

The Dice family moved north to Rye Township from their farmstead in York County sometime in the early 1850s. Johnathan Dice is listed in the York County census of 1850 as a farmer near Shrewsbury. Ten years later, the children all grown now, the family resided in Rye Township in Perry County. Mother Elizabeth passed away in 1850. Johnathan died and was buried in Rye Township's Grier Point Cemetery in 1854.

The draft registration files of 1863 show brothers William and John in Rye. Another brother, Levi, was already serving in the 1st PA Reserves with Company H. Levi was said to be the first volunteer from the Fishing Creek Valley near Marysville. John later served with the 208th PA, and William was drafted and joined Company D of the 149th in Carlisle on August 17, 1863. At his muster in, William was a 5'9"-tall farmer, with dark hair and blue eyes. He had married Leah Ramer in 1853 and was father to Sarah Jane, James Henry, Mary Ellen, and Leah Amanda.

At the North Anna River Battle on May 25, 1864, William suffered a gunshot wound. Hospitalized at Newton University Hospital in Baltimore, William lingered, not only suffering from the wound, but also an infection described by the doctor as pyemia. This blood infection is painful and deadly, as was the case with William. These infections were sometimes caused by the lead Minié balls in use at that time. He died from the infection on June 29, 1864, and was buried at Loudon Park National Cemetery.

ROBERT FOX

Robert and Margaret Fox farmed in Watts Township and raised six children. One, Robert, was born in 1837. The elder Robert Fox died in 1855. His will stipulated that young Robert was to remain on the farm with his mother. For whatever reason, that did not happen. Instead, the 1860 census shows that Robert married the former Caroline Kessler and had two small children, Catherine, three, and Robert, three months. Living in Penn Township, he was described as a day laborer.

By the time Robert enlisted with the 149th on August 14, 1862, a third child, George, had been born. But sadly, both little Catherine and little Robert had died. Perhaps it was this grief that caused Robert to enlist, to try to get away, or perhaps the family could use the fifty-dollar bounty being paid. At any rate, Robert Fox was mustered into Company G on August 26 and left for the war soon after.

Caroline Fox, who certainly had seen her share of tragedy by this time, was soon devastated again. Robert caught a musket ball in the neck at Gettysburg on July 1 and was carried from the field. He was transported to a hospital in Philadelphia but succumbed to his wounds on July 16, 1863, and was laid to rest in the national cemetery there.

Later census data shows Caroline continued living in Penn Township, where she worked as a housekeeper to support herself and young George. Obviously, Caroline had a tough life, which ended on January 21, 1902, at the relatively young age of sixty-two.

JOHN D. GENSLER

One could argue that our next man should not be included because he did make it back, only to die shortly thereafter. He belongs here since his death was caused by disease contracted in the service. Philip and Catherine Gensler lived in Tyrone Township in Sheaffer's Valley. Philip was listed as a laborer in both the 1850 and 1860 census data, though that census data is suspect. In 1850 the listed ages were as follows: Philip, thirty-five; Catharine, thirty-three; and John, seventeen. Ten years later, Philip was listed as forty-three; Catharine, forty-two; and John, twenty-three. Their other children were Philip, Catharine, Alexander, and George, who only lived a year.

John D. Gensler was twenty-six at draft registration. He was a laborer who stood 5'8" tall and had brown hair and gray eyes. John was drafted and joined Company I of the 149th on August 17, 1863, in Carlisle. Shortly after mustering in, he developed a severe case of dysentery. Admitted to Carver U.S. Hospital in Washington, he was discharged on a surgeon's certificate on January 25, 1864, and sent home. So many soldiers died from the effects of dysentery due to an inability to retain nutrients. John was one more example. He died at home on June 29, 1864. His tombstone in the Sheaffer's Valley Cemetery has the inscription, "Aged 31 y 9 m," which lends credence to his birthday being September 29, 1832.

WILLIAM H. HIPPLE

In the mid-nineteenth century, the Hipple family was quite large in Perry County's southern half. We find many in the townships of Carroll, Penn,

Wheatfield, and Rye. George and Elizabeth Bentzel Hipple were Rye Township farmers. They had children William, Elizabeth, John, Oliver, and Mary. John later joined the 173rd PA. William was one of the many men drafted to replenish the ranks of the 149th PA. He enrolled at Carlisle on August 17, 1863, and became a member of Company D.

His birth date is difficult to pin down. The 1860 census indicates he was born in 1828, but his enlistment information lists twenty-eight. William married Nancy A. Seiler and had two children by the time he went off to war. Emory was born on April 14, 1859, and Marion was born on October 26, 1862.

The fighting in the Wilderness exacted a huge toll on the Union Army in general; the 149th in particular. William was killed on May 6, 1864, according to the U.S. Registers of Deaths of Volunteers. He was "shot through the head while lying in line." Burial information has not been obtained.

Nancy filed for a widow's pension in June 1864, and her father, Henry, was appointed guardian of the children. The Soldiers Orphan School in Andersonburg received the two children for their educational needs: Emory on May 22, 1866, and Marion exactly one year later. There, the children were well cared for and received a fine education.

ROSS MCHUGH HOOD

One can only imagine how fourteen-year-old Ross Hood's heart swelled with pride as he watched big brother John march off to war with the rest of Duncannon's Morgan Rifles in May 1861. Then, when another brother, Nathaniel, enlisted on August 3, 1862, he had to fairly burst. At that time, no one younger than eighteen was admitted to the ranks of Lincoln's army, but about two weeks later, Ross McHugh Hood enlisted anyhow. Born on July 17, 1846, to Nathaniel Sr. and Catharine Hood, Ross had just turned sixteen. He listed his age on the enrollment papers as eighteen, and no questions were asked. He mustered into Company G of the 149th PA.

Like brother John, he pinned a bucktail to his forage hat and stood proud while learning the art of waging war. By the time the armies clashed at Gettysburg, both John and Nathaniel were out of the service. John was discharged on a surgeon's certificate on July 24, 1861, and

Nathaniel had mustered out with his company on May 20, 1863. Ross got his first taste of action on July 1—and his last. In the opening hours of this momentous battle, a boy not yet seventeen lay dead in a field on McPherson's Ridge.

There is a headstone over the graves of some members of the Hood family in Duncannon Union Cemetery. The names of parents Nathaniel and Catharine Hood on one side. The names of children Mary, Joel, and Ross on the other. The inscription under Ross's name reads "KILLED AT BATTLE OF GETTYSBURG. BURIED WITH UNKNOWN CO. G. 149. REGT. PA. VOL."

Cenotaph for private Ross Hood on his family's tombstone in Duncannon Union Cemetery. Note that he would have celebrated his seventeenth birthday had he lived just sixteen more days.

THE JACOBS BROTHERS

When discussing Frank Hench (page 24), it was noted that Frank lived for a time with and trained under William Jacobs, who was quite skilled as a blacksmith. William trained others, including three of his sons and a younger brother, Nicholas. Nicholas blacksmithed and farmed with wife Susannah Reisinger Jacobs and their ten children. One son, John, became a blacksmith as well. The farm couple also had Elanor, James, William, Elizabeth, Emaretta, Mary, Sara, Henry, and Martha. Three sons, James, William, and John, served in the war. James served with the 133rd Regiment while John and William served with Company K of the 149th. John and William mustered in together in Carlisle on August 16, 1863. James completed his term of service in May 1863, just as his brothers were preparing to depart for the front.

John, born on November 7, 1831, was married and had four daughters and two sons when he left for war. The year 1863 must have been a terrible year for John's wife, the former Elvina Spriggle. With her husband going off to fight, six children to care for, and the continuous news of Perry County men who did not make it back, life was harsh. Then, just three months after John's departure, her seven-year-old daughter Mary died. Thanksgiving, made an official holiday just that year, was dark.

Private John Jacobs stood 5'9" tall and had blue eyes, brown hair, and a fair complexion upon mustering in. He was with the 149th in the hell that was the Wilderness. Captured there on May 5, 1864, he was confined to the POW camp in Florence, South Carolina, where he died of dysentery on December 6, 1864, and was buried in Florence National Cemetery in South Carolina. Four of John's children were later enrolled at Soldiers Orphan School in Andersonburg.

By the time John was captured, brother William had been dead for three months. Born on March 19, 1838, William was a 5'8"-tall farmer with light hair and blue eyes when he was drafted and mustered in. William left behind a wife and three children. The children also were educated at Andersonburg. William did not take well to military life. He became sick that fall. His condition worsened and the decision was made to hospitalize him. En route to the hospital in Washington, D.C., he died of typho/malarial fever on February 1, 1864, less than six months into his term. William was returned to Ickesburg, where he was buried in Buffalo Cemetery at Saville.

DAVID KITNER

The Kitners of Carroll and Tyrone Townships could be called the typical Perry County farm family of the mid-1800s; large, hardworking, and well represented in the PA Volunteer Regiments. John and Sara Riggleman Kitner raised a baker's dozen children, five of whom were in the service. Earlier we introduced William (page 134) of the 101st. Henry, who did time at Andersonville, was also in that regiment. Abraham was in the 177th as well as the 208th, John in the 47th, and David in Company G of the 149th.

When David registered for the draft in July 1863, his information stated he was a twenty-eight-year-old married stonemason in Carroll Township. He mustered in at Carlisle on August 17, 1863, and began his tenure with the second Bucktails, although the drafted replacements were not considered Bucktails by the veterans.

The spring campaigns saw the Army of the Potomac heavily engaged after crossing the Rapidan River and moving toward Spotsylvania. The fighting around the Wilderness Tavern was especially cruel, with dense underbrush that easily caught fire, burning anything and anyone in its path. Musket fire was responsible for death in many ways. Many differing reports cloud the facts as to what happened to Private David Kitner. The muster files state he went missing in action on May 5, 1864. Other reports claim he was captured. Most probably, a statement made by Lieutenant Henry Fissel that David "was killed on the line" is most accurate.

David left behind his wife, Sarah. There was also a son, Benjamin, who tragically died in 1865. Sarah applied for a widow's pension on September 12, 1865. There was a burial card issued for David that shows him buried in Sandy Hollow Cemetery, but that does not appear to be the case. This is just one more example of a man who laid down his life for his country but whose country cannot be sure of his fate nor its circumstances.

ELIAS MESSIMER

Not every soldier volunteered immediately after President Lincoln's call. Many waited until drafted, but that does not mean they were any less patriotic or any less willing to fight for their country. There were always extenuating circumstances: life got in the way then, just as it does now. Perhaps being newly married and having two youngsters was why Elias Messimer chose to wait. Whatever his reasons, when he was called in the summer of 1863, he willingly went to Carlisle and enlisted on August 17, 1863. Elias became a member of Company G of the 149th PA and went to war.

Brother George Washington Messimer had just completed his stint with the 133rd when Elias left. They were the sons of David and Mary Magdalena Bair Messimer. Lemuel, Josiah, Catharine, and Nancy were the other children.

Elias Messimer was born in 1837 and was the oldest of the siblings. He had married Frances (Fannie) Kochenderfer in 1860. The couple had David and Molly Ann before he left for Virginia. In 1864, General Grant had come east. His relentless style was piling up casualties for both sides, but the reality is that the North could afford personnel losses better than the South. Generals Meade and Grant were hampered by their loss of men due to the heavy casualties in the battles of the Wilderness and Spotsylvania, and by the terms of enlistment expiring for many soldiers, who had signed on for three years in the spring of 1861. Nevertheless, by that point, the result was becoming clear despite being clouded by the blood that remained to be spilled. Grant and Meade had to keep applying pressure, so they did.

Private Elias Messimer was wounded and captured on May 27, 1864, during the fighting near the North Anna River. Messimer was taken to Richmond and incarcerated with what was described as a "severe wound of the right arm," which required amputation, the normal treatment for that type of injury in the 1860s. Today, chances are exceptionally good that the arm, and his life, could have been saved. In 1864, it was not. Elias languished for six weeks before succumbing to the wounds on July 8, 1864. He was buried in Richmond National Cemetery.

It is interesting to note that as a tribute to their fallen brother, all his surviving brothers, Lemuel, Josiah, and George, enlisted on March 1, 1865, and were mustered into Company D of the 47th PA. Of course, for George it was his second term in the army. Lemuel had married Mary Jane Baxter/Berkstresser, daughter of Solomon (page 149) and sister of William (page 11). In the 1860s and for years afterward, the Civil War wove its way through everyone's lives, touching virtually every family in both the North and the South. Young David Messimer was admitted to the Soldiers Orphan School on May 31, 1865, shortly after the war his father helped to fight had ended.

MARTIN VAN BUREN ORWAN

We were introduced to the Orwan family when we discussed Samuel (page 3), one of the earliest Perry Countians to perish in the war. The family was well represented in Company D of the 2nd Infantry Regiment with brothers George, Martin, and Samuel as well as Cousin Lewis. The surviving brothers all had a second term with Martin, serving in Company K of the 149th. He was drafted and enrolled in Carlisle on August 17. Family and census records date his birth to May 10, 1841, which jibes with his stated age of nineteen at enlistment in April 1861. However, when he mustered into Company K of the 149th, his stated age was thirty-four, an obvious error. Martin was a farm laborer in 1863.

The muster files for Company K show that Martin was captured at the Battle of the Wilderness on May 5, 1864, just five days before his birthday—a cruel present. Private Martin Van Buren Orwan joined the thousands of Union prisoners at the dreaded Andersonville Prison in Georgia. He also joined the thousands who died there. He was admitted to the hospital on September 10 and died ten days later from "chronic diarrhea" according to the U.S. Registers of Deaths of Volunteers. He rests in Andersonville National Cemetery. The Orwan family is representative of the long-term misery that gripped this nation. Samuel died on July 4, 1861, three months after the misery began. Martin died about seven months before it ended, with three years and three months in between.

SILAS E. POTTER

It is sounding like a broken record to illustrate the demise of another draftee into the 149th, but we have one more, Silas E. Potter of Penn Township. Silas grew up on a farm in Wheatfield Township, the son of Samuel and Ruth Ann Willis Potter. He had older siblings James, Sarah, and Catharine. Younger children in the household were Hiram, Caroline, William, Jesse, and Margaret. Silas was born in 1838, as shown when he registered for the draft in July 1863. At that time, he was a twenty-five-year-old married schoolteacher. Education was important to the Potters. Samuel served as secretary of the local board of education after the war. Silas had wed Mary A. Weldon and had three children, Harriet A., Hiram Monroe, and Florence Alice, who had just been born in March when he mustered in at Carlisle and joined Company G of the 149th. His brother William was serving in the 9th PA Cavalry and had a remarkable career that saw him rise through the ranks to become a captain. Another brother, Hiram, served in the 9th Cavalry as well. All three brothers suffered wounds.

Silas's career was of a much shorter duration. Another casualty at the Wilderness, Silas was listed in the company muster files as "missing in battle of Wilderness 5-5-64." Mary Ann had some difficulty attaining a widow's pension due to the uncertainty surrounding the end to Silas's term of enlistment. One of the lieutenants in Company G of the 149th, Henry Fissell of Duncannon, testified on her behalf that Silas was indeed killed that fateful day. Others were called to testify that she had wed Silas and had given birth to his children. We are left to ponder how the effects of her battle to secure a life-sustaining pension coupled with the devastating loss of Silas, would affect her life for years. As far as we know, his body was not recovered: a common occurrence in the Wilderness, where fires consumed so many.

XXXIV.

The 151st Pennsylvania Regiment

PENNSYLVANIA'S 151st Regiment was mustered in for a nine-month term in September and October 1862. Most of these men came from Berks County, but Company D was recruited in Juniata County. They were present at Chancellorsville but not heavily engaged. Their first real action came on July 1 in Gettysburg's Herbst Woods just west of the Lutheran Seminary. After the war, the regiment was universally referred to as the "Teachers Regiment" since so many of its men had been teaching prior to enlistment. Company D had at least sixty teachers in its ranks, most of whom taught at McAlisterville Academy. The regiment was decimated at Gettysburg, with the majority of losses occurring on the battle's first day, before moving to Cemetery Ridge to help repel Pickett's men.

The 151st went into action with 478 men. Only 141 men were unscathed. Their loss of 72% was the second-highest casualty rate of any Union regiment at Gettysburg. However, directly opposing them was North Carolina's 26th Regiment, which had the highest percentage (80%) of casualties on the Rebel side. The 151st was tasked with protecting First Corps as it retreated into town. It did its job so well that General Abner Doubleday remarked, "I believe they saved the First Corps." High praise indeed. If you have been to the Pennsylvania Monument at Gettysburg, you know that stars beside the names of soldiers on the regimental plaques indicate that the man was killed or mortally wounded during the battle. The plaque for Company D contains an awe-inspiring eleven stars.

At least two Millerstown area residents enlisted at McAlisterville: Malcolm Buchannon and John Haines. Buchannon survived Gettysburg,

Haines did not. John H. Haines was born to Frederick and Elizabeth Anna Charles Haines on April 28, 1839. The farm family appears in the census for Liverpool Township in 1850. Ten years later they were in Juniata County. Thirty years later they were in Platte County, Illinois, but minus son John.

John enlisted on October 24, 1862. He was a farmer and gave his address as Millerstown. John was one of many who fell in Herbst Woods, valiantly holding the Rebels at bay and enabling the rest of First Corps to retreat. Since the Confederates gained possession of Seminary Ridge, John and his fellow soldiers remained where they lay until after the battle. By the time they were buried, many were unrecognizable. They were reinterred at the national cemetery, where they remain; however, many are unidentified. The monument to these stalwart men is just south of the mound that marks the location of General Reynolds's death.

XXXV.

158th Pennsylvania Infantry

THE 158th was known as drafted militia. It was a nine-month unit of soldiers mostly from Cumberland, Franklin, and Fulton Counties. They rendezvoused in Chambersburg and were mustered into service there on November 1, 1862. They were sent to the Suffolk, Virginia, area and then to New Bern, North Carolina. There, they assisted in the efforts to relieve besieged Washington, North Carolina. After several attempts, they accomplished their mission. They were then assigned to General Meade's forces in pursuit of Lee's army. They completed their term and returned to Chambersburg for muster out.

JOSEPH A. MCCASKEY

Joseph A. McCaskey, of Shermans Dale, was a member of Company C of the 158th. He enrolled at Carlisle on October 16, 1862, after being drafted. At the time, Joseph had a wife, Jane Ramsey Smiley McCaskey, and four children: Ellen, John, Joseph, and baby Anna. His parents were Carroll Township farmers Frederick and Ellen (Wallace) McCaskey. The family was the typical farm family.

There is much confusion as to what happened to Private Joseph McCaskey. The muster files indicate he died aboard the steamship *Thomas Collyer*. One report shows him dying of typhoid fever. The U.S. Registers of Deaths of Volunteers states that Joseph died of "chronic diarrhea" in the Broad and Pine Streets General Hospital in Philadelphia. Both give a date of death as July 11, 1863.

Burial information is no clearer. One report shows him being buried in Philadelphia's Lafayette Cemetery, which closed in the 1940s and was abandoned despite thousands being interred there. Though all the bodies were to be exhumed and relocated properly, it did not happen. There is also a stone in Shermans Dale Presbyterian Cemetery on Windy Hill Road that bears his name, but it is impossible to know if he is entombed there. It is discouraging when a man is called to defend his country, taken from his family, and then loses his life in his country's service, only to be lost by poor recordkeeping and carelessness.

WILLIAM P. SMITH

Daniel Smith was born in Northumberland County in 1805. By 1830 he had relocated to Perry's Toboyne Township, where he and wife Elizabeth, the former Elizabeth Kline, were engaged in farming. They had a large family that included Susannah, Joseph, David, John, Alexander, Samuel, Jackson, and their oldest, William, who was born on March 4, 1830.

William married Mary Jane Dayton in 1857. Mary Jane was the daughter of another Toboyne Township resident, Hezekiah Dayton, a local shoemaker. The couple had Samuel Alexander and Margaret Jane before William was drafted into Company K of the 158th. By that time, the young family resided across the mountain in Mifflin Township, Cumberland County.

William was drafted in October 1862 and mustered in at Chambersburg on November 4. William's military career was brief, as he contracted typhoid fever while stationed in Washington, North Carolina. He died in the regimental hospital there on June 5, 1863, and was interred at New Bern National Cemetery in Craven County, North Carolina, another example of a man dying far from family and friends. He would never again see his wife or young children.

XXXVI.

The 16th and 17th Pennsylvania Cavalry Regiments

THE 161st PA was also the 16th PA Cavalry Regiment. It was comprised of troops from nearly all parts of the state. It served with the Army of the Potomac in all battles from Chancellorsville to Gettysburg, then to Brandy Station, then to the Shenandoah Valley Campaign. It was present when Rebel cavalry commander Jeb Stuart fell. It was also at Gettysburg guarding the right flank of Meade's forces. The trip back from the Shenandoah was fraught with ice and snow, and many men became sick. Perry County can be proud of the record of all its cavalrymen who spent days on end in the saddle.

JAMES HILL

Certainly a contributing factor in the wave of Irish immigration to America was the Potato Famine of the mid-1840s to the early 1850s. That "Great Hunger," as it became known, resulted in tens of thousands of deaths and led to an influx of Irish and other Europeans to places like Perry County, where hardworking men and women could live off the land and benefit from the sweat of their brows. One such family was the James and Jane (Laurimar) Hill family, who emigrated in 1854. They arrived with children James, Joseph, Charles, and eighteen-month-old Jennie. An older son, Thomas, stayed behind in Northern Ireland. The Hills first settled in Harrisburg before coming to Rye Township, where they farmed. After their arrival, Mariah-Maria and Robert were born.

The younger James Hill was born in or near Belfast in 1840. He had been in America for about seven years when war erupted here. By 1862 he was caught up in the tumult, anxious to do his part for his new country. On October 24 he mustered into Company H of the 16th PA Cavalry. No available records indicate he was married. James gave his occupation as farmer upon enlistment.

Private James Hill led a typical military life for nearly two years before coming down with a disease that is curable today, yet at the time felled thousands of otherwise hardy men. The U.S. Registers of Deaths of Volunteers describes James's death as due to "chronic diarrhea." He died on October 25, 1864, two years after muster, at City Point Cavalry Corps Hospital. He was buried in the cemetery in Hopewell, Virginia. James and his family had traveled some 3,500 miles (about the width of the United States) to escape famine only to be brought down by another food-related malady.

DAVID A. REED

We met John Reed (page 162) earlier when discussing the 133rd. Now unfortunately, we are introduced to brother David. Robert and wife Esther Reed had the following children: Israel, Harriet, Sara, Emanda, David, John, Robert, Lucinda, and Samuel. They farmed in Madison Township. As noted previously, David joined Company F of the 16th PA Cavalry. He enrolled in Juniata County on September 10, 1862, and mustered in on the second day of October. He was described as 5'8" tall, with black hair and brown eyes. David was two years older than brother John, and, like John, was single.

From available records, David had some bouts of sickness throughout his term of enlistment—not altogether unusual for cavalrymen, who were often pushed to the limits of endurance and beyond. But with David, these bouts foretold a major problem. He was hospitalized in Cavalry Corps U.S. Hospital at Brandy Station, Virginia, where, on April 29, 1864, Private David A. Reed died. The U.S. Registers of Deaths of Volunteers lists the cause as "typho-malarial fever." David was laid to rest in Culpeper National Cemetery in Virginia, the second Reed son to perish in the war.

JOHN SMITH

John Smith was from a large family in Wheatfield Township. John F. and Rachel Steigelman Smith were prosperous farmers who had five sons and two daughters. Additionally, they employed extra hands on the farm, one of whom was David Rose, who also joined the 16th Cavalry. Originally from Dauphin County, the Smiths farmed in Perry County before continuing their migration westward, first to Illinois, and then ultimately to Clay County, Kansas.

Johannes Schmidt fought alongside George Washington in the Revolutionary War. A son, Conrad, fought in the War of 1812. Another son, Elias, was John F. Smith's father. The family name was altered to Smith somewhere along the way, a frequent practice in that era of American history.

With a lineage like that, the younger John Smith might have felt compelled to enroll in the service of his country. On September 10, 1862, at the tender age of nineteen, he did just that. He mustered in eighteen days later at Camp Curtin and became a cavalryman in Company G of the 16th. John did not fare as well as his ancestors. Sadly, John never returned to Perry County.

Wounded in the battles at the Wilderness, Smith succumbed to his wounds on a yet unknown date. John's is another of the many examples of confusing military records. Muster files for the 16th contain this remark: "dropped from the rolls date unknown by general order #42 Hdqrs., Brig., Lynchburg, Va." That file further states that John was "wounded in action 6-9-64 at Battle of Wilderness, Va." This may have been John's date of death, as the Wilderness Battle was fought in the first week of May. We have read many instances of the mass confusion during this battle. It was fought in dense underbrush on Rebel home turf, which provided an advantage that negated the Union Army's numbers of troops engaged.

No record of John's burial, if any, has been found.

BENJAMIN WHITE

James and Margaret (McClintock) White farmed in Carroll Township and raised a family there in the 1830s through the 1870s. The girls in the family were Priscilla, Rachel, and Margaret. The sons of James and Margaret, born between 1836 and 1850, were Isaac, Joseph, Benjamin, John, James, and Franklin. The elder James died in 1869, and, soon after, many of the clan relocated to Indiana. However, their stay in the Midwest was short-lived.

Mother Margaret sadly outlived many of her sons. Joseph died at age thirty in 1870. John passed away at age twenty in 1866. Franklin, with whom Margaret resided for a brief time in Indiana, died in 1876 at age twenty-six.

Isaac served in the 165th PA Infantry. Joseph enlisted in the 15th PA Cavalry. Benjamin served in the 16th Cavalry. Only Isaac lived to see the twentieth century. Benjamin, born in 1842, enlisted on September 13, 1862, in Chambersburg. He mustered in nine days later to become a private in Company H. At enlistment, Benjamin was 5'7" tall, with red hair and gray eyes. His term of service, slated for three years, would only last three months. He contracted smallpox and died exactly ninety days after mustering in while a patient in the Kalorama U.S. Hospital in our nation's capital. Benjamin was laid to rest there in Soldiers' and Airmen's Home National Cemetery.

JAMES C. CAMPBELL

President Lincoln's call for more cavalry in July 1862 was answered by the 161st and 162nd Regiments, recruited from across Pennsylvania. Company I of the 17th PA Cavalry contained forty Perry Countians. Its organizer and first captain was Perry County District Attorney John McAllister. This regiment was put to the test at Chancellorsville, where it drew high praise from General Pleasanton for its coolness despite being new. It was assigned to Colonel Devin's brigade and fought with him throughout its term, earning more accolades at Gettysburg on McPherson's Ridge on July 1, 1863. In addition to service at Gettysburg, the 17th fought at nearly every battle in the Eastern Theater of the war, then played a vital role in General Sheridan's Shenandoah Valley Campaign—an arduous task that helped bring the South to its knees. The information on the veteran's index cards is not complete regarding the men of the 17th, and discharge information for some is incomplete as well.

Most enlistees did not muster in at the rank of corporal, but New Bloomfield's James C. Campbell had a lot going for him when he became a member of Company I. His father was Hugh Campbell, who at the time was Perry County Sheriff. Young James inherited some of his father's leadership and disciplinary abilities. He was also employed as a compositor (printer) in the office of the *Perry County Democrat* newspaper, indicating an education and organization skills. His mother was the former Elizabeth Finley Bausum. James, born in 1838, had siblings Amanda, William, Francis, Martha, Elizabeth, Charles, and David. Amanda later wed John McCroskey, who served in the 149th PA. Francis served in the 133rd.

When James enlisted on September 6, 1862, he was twenty-four, with brown hair and blue eyes. Tall for that era, he stood one inch shy of six feet. James is not listed on the 17th Cavalry's plaque at the Pennsylvania Monument, which may mean he was on furlough at the time. James was shot in the breast at White House Landing, Virginia, on June 21, 1864, and was buried in Yorktown National Cemetery in Virginia.

JEREMIAH HIPPLE

Some battlefield names are familiar to us—Fredericksburg, Gettysburg, Chancellorsville, Bull Run—but how about Occoquan Creek? This lesser-known but deadly confrontation took place on a part of Bull Run near Manassas, Virginia. In fact, Bull Run is a tributary of the Occoquan River. This engagement, officially classified as a skirmish, was part of the fighting that took place around Fairfax Station, Dumfries, and Chantilly as 1862 reached its bloody close. Engaged in the action was the 17th PA Cavalry and young Jeremiah Hipple.

Hipple was the son of John and Mary Ann Seiler Hipple of Carroll Township. He was shown to be twenty-three at enlistment on September 16, 1862. At that time, he was a carpenter living in New Bloomfield. The seventh of eleven children, Jeremiah was probably born in 1839, though some records show 1840. A younger brother, Wesley, served with the 97th PA Infantry in 1864 and '65.

After mustering into Company I on September 26, 1862, Jeremiah served for only three months. He was mortally wounded on December 28 and sent to a hospital in Fairfax, Virginia, where he languished until New Year's Day, passing from what was officially stated in the U.S. Registers of Deaths of Volunteers as "paralysis." His body was returned to New Bloomfield, where he rests in Bloomfield Cemetery.

WILLIAM KOCHER

Private William Kocher enlisted at Harrisburg on September 26, 1862. His veterans card file indicates he resided at Ickesburg; however, some information shows a New Bloomfield residence in 1860. Possibly since he didn't have much time to make his mark on history, we don't know much about this soldier. Most of what we know is gleaned from his pension file. That document shows he was the son of Peter and Sarah Kocher and enlisted in Harrisburg at the stated age of twenty. As was attested by men who swore an oath that they had personal knowledge of the Kocher family, William was the sole support for his mother. He earned money by working for neighbors, as they needed help planting and harvesting farm crops. His enlistment information shows him to be a farmer, though no record has been found indicating land ownership. Sarah needed his support since her husband, Peter, had died in 1853.

William may have enlisted due to the need for a regular paycheck. Testimony given in the pension application shows that he sent the majority of his pay home to Sarah. Since William was unmarried, Sarah applied for the pension. She applied in Perry County, though at the time, she was a resident of Northumberland County. The pension file shows page after page of documentation by friends as well as William's superior officer, Lieutenant Lewis Orwan of New Bloomfield, who testified that William was indeed a member of his company and that he "died in Corps Hospital Head Quarters Cavalry near Falmouth, Virginia of Typhoid Fever April 9, 1863." It is tragic that this young man died so soon and that Sarah then had no means of support. It is also quite sad that William has faded into history—not even his burial location has been identified.

SAMUEL MYERS

We first encounter Samuel Myers in the 1850 Oliver Township census. He is staying with, and/or working for, the Abraham Deardorff family on their farm. Abraham and wife Susannah also have their children living there, one of whom, Peter, enlisted with the 36th Militia during the Gettysburg crisis in 1863.

It is unclear what the relationship may have been between Samuel and the Deardorffs until reading his tombstone, but we will get to that later. When Samuel mustered in at Carlisle on October 18, 1862, he gave his age as twenty-five and his residence as Bloomfield. He also gave his name as Samuel Deardorff. He became a member of Company F of the 17th PA Cavalry and served in all its engagements, including Gettysburg.

Samuel was with the unit all through 1863 and most of 1864, but at Newtown, Virginia, Samuel Deardorff was "killed in skirmish" on October 11, 1864, according to the muster files for his company.

Samuel Deardorff has a tombstone in Winchester National Cemetery in Virginia. To make matters more confusing, Samuel Myers has a tombstone at the Deardorff/Gantt Cemetery near Newport. The engraving on that stone makes the mystery a tad clearer. It reads in part, "Samuel s/o Eve Deardorff Oct 11, 1864; Enlisted at Harrisburg Sept 23, 1862, in U S service Co. F 17 Regt Cav. Killed near Manchester Va."

ELIAS REED

Perry County supplied men for Company I of the 17th PA Cavalry from all occupations and of all ages. We have met some young men who volunteered, and now we will meet one who was quite a bit older than the typical cavalryman—Elias Reed of the Liverpool area. Elias was the son of David and Susannah Reed of Greenwood Township. Susannah died in the 1830s and David then moved to Centre County. Elias stayed behind, where he lived with the Josiah Grubb family in Liverpool Township.

At enlistment on September 16, 1862, Elias was thirty-six years old, married to the former Mary Ann Crane, and was a father to five. He was a laborer according to the 1860 census. The children were James, Elias, Emma, Mary, and John. The couple also had just buried their son Joseph, who had only lived about one month. Perhaps that heartache was what inspired Elias to enlist. Perhaps he just wanted to serve. Whatever the reason, Elias became a member of Company I on September 26 and headed south to fight for his country.

Elias later fell sick and brought more heartache to Mary Ann. He was confined to a hospital near Windmill Point, Virginia, and passed away in January 1863. The muster files indicate the date was January 24; the U.S. Registers of Deaths of Volunteers shows it to be January 29. The diagnosis was typhoid fever. He was buried at Windmill Point.

Mary Ann's heartache did not end on January 29. Emma died at the age of ten in 1865. Young Elias passed away at fifteen in 1870, the same year Mary died at twelve. John Crane Reed and Robert Luther Reed reached adulthood. They both were educated in the Tressler Orphans' Home, admitted on January 26, 1866, three years after their father's death. The pension files show a long ordeal for Mary Ann, with many back-and-forth correspondences until she finally received her widow's pension.

THOMAS SPEASE

Ludvig Spies was born in Elsoff, Westfalen, Prussia, in 1808. Catharina Gellbach was born there as well a year earlier. They married in 1833 and set sail for America the following year, arriving in Baltimore that summer. It is unclear whether their oldest son, Ludvig Jr., was born in Prussia or Pennsylvania. Ludvig and his young family appear in the 1840 census for Wheatfield Township. Ten years later, George, Sophia, Thomas, Catherine, William, and John have joined the household. That census lists all the children as being born in Pennsylvania; however, some of Junior's information shows a birth in Germany. The 1860 census shows Ludvig Sr., now known as Ludwick or Lewis Spease, engaged in farming on land just east of Dellville Union Church, now Dellville Methodist Church. Thomas resided in New Kingstown.

Twenty-one-year-old Thomas Spease enlisted in Carlisle on September 15, 1862, and mustered into Company F of the 17th PA Cavalry a week later. The winter of '62–'63 was bitterly cold, with plenty of snow, even in Virginia. Thomas became ill and was hospitalized in Washington at Emory U.S. Hospital. He had contracted typhoid, which put him in his grave at Military Asylum Cemetery, now known as Soldiers' and Airmen's Home National Cemetery, on July 12, 1863.

Lewis Spease Sr. and Catharina had lost a son. Two more died at early ages. John, born in 1850, died in 1879 when a tree he was cutting down fell on him. Lewis Jr. died in 1883, one year after his mother and nine years before his father, a sad ending to a story of hope for a bright future in a new land.

BENJAMIN SPRIGGLE

Repeatedly, we see men enlisting from Saville Township. They served in many of the state's infantry regiments as well as cavalry units. This was a fertile area for Union Army recruits, another of whom was Benjamin Spriggle. Benjamin was from a large family that included brothers George, David, and Samuel. His sisters were Maria, Rebecca, Sarah, and

Catherine. Their father was Jacob and mother was the former Leah Powell. Benjamin was listed as being nineteen on the 1860 census, but he stated two years later that he was nineteen at enlistment. He enrolled on September 10, 1862, and mustered in on the twenty-sixth as a member of Company I of the 17th Cavalry.

His name is not shown on the Pennsylvania Monument at Gettysburg. Perhaps he was on detached duty or furlough, but he was with the regiment immediately afterward while they dogged Lee's army on its retreat. Just a week after the final shots were fired at Gettysburg, cavalry and some infantry troops engaged in a bloody skirmish near Funkstown, Maryland. Nearly five hundred casualties resulted on July 10, 1863. Benjamin Spriggle suffered a severe wound to his left leg. He was hospitalized in Frederick, Maryland, where the leg was amputated. As so often happened during the war, the damage was too great. Private Benjamin Spriggle struggled to get well but could not. Though some records indicate a death on August 12, the U.S. Registers of Deaths of Volunteers lists it as occurring on August 16. Since that is the date of burial, it seems more likely. His body was taken to nearby Sharpsburg, where he rests in Antietam National Cemetery. Saville Township sent dozens of its sons to war. Many did not return.

JOHN STOUFFER

A pair of brothers from near Shermans Dale helped fill the ranks of Company I. George Washington Stouffer and younger brother John grew up on a farm in Carroll Township. Born to Jacob and Anna (Smeigh) Stouffer, the pair helped with farming until George moved over the mountain and began to work for the Abraham Spotts family. He was still engaged in farm labor when he enlisted on October 26, 1862. John was already mustered in as of September 26.

John gave his age at enlistment as twenty, so he would have been born in 1842 or '43. Some men, like George, were transferred to provisional cavalry units after the 17th was mustered out on June 16, 1865. This was done to complete their terms. George mustered out of Company I of the 2nd Provisional Cavalry on August 7, 1865. John was not so lucky. Though information is incomplete, John died of disease in Campbell General Hospital in Washington, D.C., on an unknown date.

XXXVII.

The 173rd Pennsylvania Drafted Militia

THE 173rd PA Regiment was known as drafted militia. It was organized in October and November 1862 as a nine-month unit. The Militia Act passed by Congress in July, gave President Lincoln authority to draft three hundred thousand men for up to nine months of service. It also allowed African Americans to enlist in the army to perform menial tasks that freed up front line soldiers to fight instead of labor. Men still volunteered due to the threat of more drafts that potentially could be for three years rather than nine months. So the 173rd had many enlistees, and one unit, Company E, was recruited in Perry County. Not every man in the company was a county resident but most were. The 173rd never entered battle. Instead, it performed provost guard duty in the Norfolk area and along the Orange and Alexandria Railroad. Still, that duty could be hazardous.

With the absence of any skirmishes or other actions against Rebel forces coupled with the relative shortness of its term of duty, the 173rd had few casualties. But two men lost their battle with disease: both Perry Countians.

GEORGE J. CLEMENS

It had to be both exciting and terrifying to march off to war as a sixteen-year-old. But having your father marching beside you every step of the way was likely reassuring and comforting. George J. Clemens gave his age as eighteen when he volunteered. His father, Peter, was forty-four. In reality, George had been born on May 7, 1846, making him just over sixteen. He was the oldest of eight children born to Peter and Harrietta

Burroughs Clemens. Peter was a laborer living in Greenwood Township according to the 1860 census.

For quite some time, the 173rd was stationed at Camp Viele in Norfolk, Virginia. This overall was not a bad duty except for the humidity and bugs—bugs that carried disease. Young George probably had never been away from home before, and his immune system could not fight disease. He contracted typhoid and died on April 3, 1863, just five months after mustering in. George's body was returned, and he lies in St. James Cemetery which is near Oriental just over the Juniata County line. As for Peter, he was mustered out with his regiment on August 17, 1863. About a year later, Peter enlisted in Company K of the 69th PA and completed his service on July 1, 1865.

JOHN DUNKLE

The 1850 census shows John Dunkle was a blacksmith in New Buffalo, while by 1860 he was a boatman. That industry was quite active with the Susquehanna River and the Pennsylvania Canal on the town's doorstep.

John was the son of George and Susannah Greiner Dunkle. One of John's brothers, Peter, served with the 18th PA Cavalry. John had wed Elizabeth Rineberger in January 1848. The couple had four children, Sarah, George, Ira, and John by the time John Sr. became a soldier at the age of thirty-five on October 21, 1862.

His term of service was especially short. John contracted smallpox and was hospitalized in the regimental hospital at Norfolk, Virginia, where he died on January 10, 1863, less than three months into his term. He was buried at Norfolk, then reinterred in Hampton National Cemetery six days later.

The comparisons between the 173rd PA and the 177th PA are striking. They were both recruited in October 1862. They were both known as drafted militia, enlisted for a nine-month term. They each contained a company recruited in Perry County, though not all members were from the county. Each Perry County company suffered no battle-related fatalities but had multiple deaths due to disease. Each company's deaths were all Perry County men.

XXXVIII.

The 177th Drafted Militia

THE 177th left for Washington on December 3, and then went south to the Virginia coast. Whereas the 173rd went to Norfolk, the 177th went first to Suffolk. There, the first order of business was clearing a several hundred-acre pine forest of its trees across the river from the camp. This arduous task accomplished, the regiment moved to Deep Creek, where it controlled the local trafficking of contraband. The regiment incurred no deaths in combat, however, one officer and twenty-three soldiers died of disease. Many hardy men fell ill while stationed at Suffolk.

JACOB CLESS

Adam and Sophia Hassinger Cless farmed in Centre Township. John was their oldest child, followed by William, Sarah, Catharine, Jacob, and Martin. Adam passed away in April 1862, leaving the boys to do the farming. Then, about eight months later, another farmhand was lost when Jacob was drafted into Company F of the 177th Regiment. Jacob, born in either 1842 or 1843, mustered in at Camp Curtin on November 2 and went to Virginia.

No doubt farm work had prepared him for the laborious task of cutting wood, but nothing could prepare him for the onslaught of typhoid. Jacob became one of the regiment's two dozen deaths. He passed away in the regimental hospital in Suffolk on January 22, 1863. He was buried in Suffolk, then later reinterred at Hampton National Cemetery in Virginia. Jacob's mother apparently had some difficulty obtaining a pension for her deceased son, as evidence exists of a declaration of facts obtained from a fellow soldier, attesting that he witnessed Jacob's burial.

WILLIAM LAY

Samuel Lay and wife, the former Anna Fought, were Blain area farmers who raised five sons and five daughters. Two of the sons went off to war: Samuel with the 7th PA Cavalry, and William with the 177th PA Infantry.

William was a farmer and cabinetmaker living in Jackson Township at the outbreak of hostilities. He had wed Carrie Kistler on December 23, 1858, and was already the father of Wilson, Ella, and Elmer when he registered for the draft. Carrie's brother John was a member of the 49th Regiment.

William received his draft notice on August 26, 1862. He enrolled on October 20 and was mustered on November 6. A look at the muster files for Company F of the 177th indicate that William was discharged with his company on August 5, 1863, and that he survived the war. Sadly, that information is inaccurate. At the time, the rest of the regiment mustered out at Harrisburg; William, however, was too sick to travel. Prior to coming to our capital city, the regiment had been stationed at Maryland Heights, and it is unclear whether he stayed in Maryland or was in Harrisburg.

Private William A. Lay died on May 19, 1864, after being ill for nearly a year. He was buried in Blain Union Cemetery.

JESSE SHANNON

Remarks made by officers of the 177th Regiment acknowledge the prevalent sickness within the ranks while stationed in the Suffolk vicinity. It would have been a relief to get orders to move inland, even if it meant the probability of combat. Unfortunately, Jesse Shannon could not take advantage of the better living conditions away from the coast. He was already one of the sickest.

Jesse was born to John and Catharine Metz Shannon, of Madison Township, in 1845 according to the 1860 census that shows him to be fifteen. He was the oldest of six children. John at the time was a millwright.

Jesse enrolled on October 16, 1862, at the stated age of eighteen. He mustered on November 2 and became a member of Company F of the

177th. Jesse was too sick to accompany the regiment when it relocated to Deep Creek, Virginia. He died in the regimental hospital on March 4, 1863. No record of his death appears in the U.S. Registers of Deaths of Volunteers.

HENRY SHEARER

It is interesting to see the diverse backgrounds and differing ages of the men in each regiment. Jesse Shannon was probably seventeen at enlistment; Henry Shearer was a dozen years older. Both were in Madison Township in the 1860 census. Henry was a married father of two who supported his family as a laborer in an unspecified industry; possibly taking work where and when he could get it. Many men at that time classified themselves as "day laborers."

In that census, Henry and his wife, the former Margaret Catharine (Kate) Perry, were joined in the household by children Samuel and Martha, as well as Henry's father, John. Henry's mother, Elizabeth, was not in the picture. Henry's brother Peter later served with the 202nd PA and Margaret's brother with the 208th.

Henry did not fare well along Virginia's coast any better than fellow soldiers Jesse Shannon and John Cless. He accompanied the regiment on its move to Deep Creek, Virginia, but he died in the regimental hospital of "pleuritis" according to his diagnosis. He was buried at Deep Creek, but we do not know more than that. Son Samuel was later educated at the Tressler Orphans' Home in Loysville.

XXXIX.

The 21st Pennsylvania Cavalry

THE 21st PA Cavalry Regiment was also the 182nd of the line for Pennsylvania. Recruited initially in August 1863, it was equipped at Harrisburg, then sent to Chambersburg for training. Its service prior to February 1864 consisted of escort and guard duty at various outposts. In February of '64, the men rendezvoused at Chambersburg, where they welcomed new recruits. Afterward, their duty became more combat-oriented, as they saw plenty of action at Cold Harbor, then Petersburg. One of the new recruits was a young man from Penn Township named George B. Parsons.

In 1860, George lived with his parents, James and Elizabeth Morris Parsons. Sisters Margaret and Anna Lavinia lived there also. Brothers James, John, William, and Leonard rounded out the family. George was a boatman who stood tall in the saddle at 6 feet, with light hair and gray eyes. John had been a corporal with the Bucktails before being discharged on a surgeon's certificate. William served in the United States infantry.

George got his chance to serve when he mustered into Company C of the 21st PA Cavalry on February 19, 1864, and headed to Chambersburg. That is as far as he got. George contracted a disease and died in camp at Chambersburg one month later. The muster files cite a death date of March 14, but his headstone gives a date four days later. His body was returned to Duncannon, where he has been reunited with his parents, as well as brothers John and William in Duncannon Union Cemetery.

XL.

The 184th Pennsylvania Regiment

THE 184th PA had a relatively brief term of service, organizing in early May 1864. However, its battle experiences were anything but brief. The regiment left Pennsylvania for the front on May 14 and almost immediately saw action. Five hundred men crossed the Pamunkey River and skirmished with Rebel forces all the way to Cold Harbor, where the regiment lost heavily but was highly commended for meritorious service. Then it went on to Petersburg, again losing heavily. After just twenty-five days at the front, only 150 men answered roll call. Three Perry Countians were among the 350 who were unavailable.

HENRY F. CLAY

Martin Clay farmed in Carroll Township between Crum's Corner and Dromgold with wife Sarah (Casner) Clay and children John, William, Samuel, Jacob, Henry, Mary, and Sarah. The Clay family was large, prosperous, and patriotic, with ties to other patriots, like the Hartzells, Ebrights, and Robinsons. Henry, born in 1845, was eager to do his part. Enrolling on May 12, 1864, at Harrisburg, Henry F. Clay had an eventful, though brief, tenure with Company A.

Henry was one of the many who were captured and taken to Andersonville Prison. Once there, he could not overcome the rampant diseases and meager rations at the overcrowded facility. Private Henry F. Clay died of "diarrhea acute" according to the U.S. Registers of Deaths of Volunteers on September 1, 1864. He rests there along with thousands of comrades. Incredibly, Henry was one of nineteen men from Company A who perished at Andersonville.

SAMUEL HARTZELL

The fortunes of war have neither rhyme nor reason. Why the Minié ball found one man and not the next can only be pondered. The Hartzell brothers of Wheatfield Township stand as an example. Born to Samuel and Elizabeth Clay Hartzell—Isaiah on December 10, 1841, and Samuel on March 30, 1843—the Hartzells were farmers. Isaiah enlisted with Company B of the 42nd Regiment, better known as the Bucktails. He saw action at the bloodiest battles in the eastern theater, among them were Antietam, Fredericksburg, Gettysburg, and the Wilderness, serving from June 1861 to June 1864. He survived the war and went back to Perry to marry and raise a family.

Samuel mustered into Company A of the 184th PA in March 1864, just three months before Isaiah mustered out. Samuel's service was brief, equally eventful, and deadlier. He was wounded in the left arm at the first battle of Petersburg in June 1864. The arm was amputated, but Samuel did not survive his ordeal. He died at Harewood Hospital in our nation's capital on July 1, 1864. He was among the first generation interred at Arlington National Cemetery; alas, thousands of others have followed.

EMANUEL JONES

The 1850 census for Carroll Township shows the Jones family lived just two doors away from the Clays. Benjamin and Elizabeth Souder Jones were also farmers and no doubt worked together, as was the custom with farmers in that era. It was common for one farmer to help another with planting or harvesting, then that farmer returned the favor. Families tended to be large, in part because all the labor was manual. Families helped one another, went to church with one another, became friends, and often intermarried. Another reason for large families, though not stated in so many words, was the high death rate among children. Once a son survived his early years and became big enough to help with farm work, he was an indispensable part of the farming operation. Having one or more boys go off to war put a tremendous weight upon those left behind.

The Jones family was small compared to most others. A daughter, Maria, and sons, Benjamin and Emanuel, were born in the 1840s. Emanuel was listed as four years of age in 1850, so he was probably born in 1846. He and Henry Clay most assuredly were friends, and each was probably eager to make his mark on the world by entering the war. Each had to wait until reaching the legal age to enlist, which they did together on May 12. From there, they went their separate ways.

Shortly after mustering in, Emanuel became sick. He was sent to the hospital at Davids Island, New York, where he was diagnosed with typhoid and died on September 17, 1864. Emanuel rests in Cypress Hills National Cemetery in Brooklyn. Henry Clay and Emanuel Jones are now separated by nearly one thousand miles.

XLI.

The 186th Pennsylvania Regiment

THE 186th PA Regiment was recruited in the spring of 1864, primarily in Philadelphia. The men were assigned to provost guard duty there. Their role was to guard prisoners and supply depots, a necessary job, if not a glamorous one. With no skirmishes or battles, one would consider this a safe assignment, but as we have seen, nowhere was safe.

EPHRAIM P. SANDS

Little is known about Ephraim P. Sands of Centre Township. Another Ephraim Sands, in a different regiment, also served in Philadelphia. The two men have had their military files confused, even to the point where Ephraim's government-issued grave marker has an inaccurate date of death.

We know Ephraim was born on October 2, 1830. The 1860 census shows him as a farm laborer in Centre Township, married to the former Susan Slade. Two children are there as well, John, born in 1858, and Clement, born in 1859. Two more children later followed: George in 1861, and Edith in 1862. Private Ephraim P. Sands mustered into Company F of the 186th Regiment in Philadelphia on February 29, 1864. At some point he became ill and did not complete a year's service. The U.S. Registers of Deaths of Volunteers states he died at the regimental hospital on February 3, 1865, of an "unstated cause."

Ephraim was returned to Perry County and buried in the old New Bloomfield Cemetery next to Carson Long Military Academy. The bronze burial plaque shows a date of death as 1881, which is the date for the other Ephraim Sands. His wife, Susan, applied for a widow's pension on March 3, 1865. The children were admitted to the Tressler Orphans'

Home in Loysville, the boys on July 1, 1865, and Edith on May 23, 1866. Sadly, Susan experienced more heartache as young John died just three months after entering school at Tressler.

XLII.

The 187th Pennsylvania Regiment

THE 187th PA Regiment was organized from members of the 1st Battalion and new recruits brought in during the spring of 1864. It first went to our nation's capital on May 19, and then went to the front in eastern Virginia. It was assigned to the Fifth Corps, commanded by G. K. Warren, and became part of Joshua Chamberlain's 1st Division; both men had been hailed as heroes of Gettysburg. At the fierce battle in front of Petersburg, the regiment lost 10% of its number on June 18 and was highly commended by General Chamberlain. After being deployed to Philadelphia near the end of the war, it was given the honor of leading President Lincoln's funeral procession from the railroad station to Independence Hall. It contained some Perry County men, three of whom never participated in that memorable and solemn occasion.

WILLIAM P. GENSLER

John and Elizabeth Easterline Gensler raised the typical large farm family in Perry's Tyrone Township. They had a fruit orchard, so lots of hands were needed. The boys were John F., Jonah, James, George, Scott, Clay, Samuel, and William. The girls were Martha, Elizabeth, Catharine, Isabella, Nancy, and Anna. John F. enlisted at Loysville and served with the 133rd. Later, he and William became members of Company D of the 187th.

William P. Gensler was born in 1835. He married Elvina Jane Kiner in 1851 and settled down to farm in Madison Township. Three boys were born to the couple: James Franklin, Clark William, and John Westley. One of Elvina's brothers, William Kiner, also joined Company D with the Gensler brothers. They enrolled on February 23, 1864, and moved south to the war.

Fighting was almost nonstop from late May until mid-June. Cold Harbor, near Mechanicsville, Virginia, and the battles for control of Petersburg's transportation hub cost many lives on both sides. The battle on June 18, so praiseworthy per General Chamberlain, proved costly to Elvina Kiner Gensler, who became a widow that day. Her little boys lost their father, Private William P. Gensler, near Petersburg. James Franklin and Clark William were admitted to the Soldiers Orphan School at Andersonburg on October 19, 1866. There is no word as to why the youngest, John, did not attend.

JOSIAH LENIG

Company K of the 187th PA Regiment had many Perry County soldiers in its ranks. Josiah Lenig was the son of William and Mary Ann Lenig, who farmed in Centre Township. Born on September 5, 1840, Josiah was the second of five children, and the oldest son.

It seems Josiah was often called Joshua in army records, as evidenced by the muster files for Company B of the Bucktails. A Joshua Lenig, our Josiah, enlisted with the Bucktails on March 6, 1862. He served only two months before being discharged on a surgeon's certificate on May 12. The reason was merely stated as "disability." When Josiah registered for the draft in July of the following year, he was an unmarried farmer. A notation behind his name notes "private in Co. B. 1st Pa. Rifles discharged on account of disability."

Josiah was not deterred. He became a member of Company K in the 187th Regiment on May 4, 1864. His index card describes him as being 5'9" tall, with dark hair, a dark complexion, and black eyes. Information about his service is scarce until his name appears in the U.S. Registers of Deaths of Volunteers. The entry denotes death came to Private Josiah Lenig on September 20, 1865, well after the war ended but nevertheless caused by the war. The cause was listed as "complications fractured femur in line of duty." Josiah rests in New Bloomfield Union Cemetery with his parents.

HENRY NONEMAKER

One well-worn path for German immigrants to Perry County was to arrive in Philadelphia, spend some time getting acclimated in York

County, and then move to Perry. The Samuel Nonemaker family was an example. Sometimes spelled as Nunemaker or Nunemacher, the name was one of many German names to be Americanized. The Nonemakers settled in Kennedy's Valley to farm. Their children included Lydia, Daniel, Jacob, John, Samuel, Henry, Jeremiah, and Abraham. Susannah Snyder Nonemaker, like her husband, was born in Germany. Samuel served in the 17th PA Cavalry. Henry, born in 1845, enrolled with Company D of the 187th on February 10, 1864, at Carlisle.

As an interesting side note, the oldest child, Lydia, married a Kennedy's Valley native named Jacob Keck. Jacob drove a supply wagon from the Carlisle Army Depot to the battlefield at Antietam. He related a story that, as he approached the front, the bodies were strewn so thickly that he had to clear a path to continue his journey to bring much-needed supplies to a battered army.

Henry's tour of duty with the 187th was brief. He became sick in the summer heat and was hospitalized at Division General Hospital in Alexandria, Virginia. He died of typhoid fever on July 14, 1864, and was buried in Alexandria National Cemetery. One more spelling of the surname appears in the U.S. Registers of Deaths of Volunteers—Nummaker.

DAVID SHERIFF

Despite its remote location, Toboyne Township residents were not beyond the reach of the draft. An early map of the township shows Johnathan Sheriff's property near the base of Buck Ridge. The Sheriffs raised a large family amid impoverished circumstances. An 1838 listing of pauper children shows four Sheriff children who met that criterion, one of whom was David, born in 1830.

Married to Elizabeth Stumpf since August 20, 1849, David had seven children when he left for the war. Mary was born in 1851, followed by Alexander, Levi, Jennie, Benjamin, James, and Sarah. David farmed in Toboyne Township. After joining Company D of the 187th on February 19, 1864, David's record gets a little fuzzy. His service information is intermingled with another David Sheriff, who served with the 158th Regiment.

Private David Sheriff was hospitalized with smallpox and given a furlough. The disease took his life on December 18, 1864, while he was at

Newville. Elizabeth secured a pension for herself and the minor children, who were all under the age of sixteen. Elizabeth later married Robert Finley, also of Toboyne Township, where she resided in 1880. Mary, Jane, Benjamin, and Sarah were all shown as stepchildren of Reverend Finley in that census.

If the name Finley sounds familiar, it is because, ironically, Charles Finley (page 154) was a son of Robert's to his first wife. Charles P. Finley died of disease while serving with Company G of the 133rd PA, proving once again how this war touched almost every family, often repeatedly.

NICHOLAS SWEGER

Nicholas Sweger enlisted twice, first with the 133rd and later with the 187th. His date of birth is in question. The 1850 census shows him to be three. Then, ten years later, as you would expect, his age was shown to be thirteen. However, some records show his birthday as February 8, 1846, while his grave marker shows his birth year to be 1847. Either way, he was young when he volunteered with Company G of the 133rd on August 5, 1862. He served with that regiment throughout its term and was discharged with his company on May 26, 1863. Even at discharge, he was at most seventeen, probably sixteen.

He was the third-oldest of the children born to John and Margaret Comp Sweger. John was a stonemason in 1850 and a farmer in 1860. Nicholas was a farm laborer in 1860. Nicholas was eager to get back in uniform, as he volunteered on April 11, 1864, and was mustered into Company K of the 187th on May 4, 1864. Just one week later, he was transferred to Company A.

An example of a flat bronze tablet for Nicholas Sweger in the old New Bloomfield Cemetery near Carson Long Military Academy. Nicholas survived his term with the 133rd Regiment. However, he reenlisted with the 187th PA Regiment and was mortally wounded near Petersburg, Virginia.

Nicholas was another who fell in front of Petersburg on either June 17 or 18 with a serious wound. He was sent home on furlough, but despite his youth, the wounds were too severe for him to recover. He died on July 30, 1864, after languishing for six weeks. Burial was in the old New Bloomfield Cemetery off High Street.

HENRY TOOMEY

It seems that the primary regions from which families moved into Perry County were either Berks County or York County. Daniel Toomey moved up from around the Dover area of York. He settled in Tyrone Township. Annie Moudy Toomey was the mother of his children, but both the 1850 and 1860 censuses for Tyrone show his wife to be Sarah. In fact, he and Sarah are buried side by side in a small hilltop grove of trees known as Waggoner's Cemetery just off Kennedy's Valley Road. It is unclear what happened to Annie. Daniel was jobless according to both censuses and passed away in 1863. The children were Harriet, Samuel, Mary, Rebecca, Sarah, Daniel, Henry, Amanda, and Susannah. In the 1850 census, nine-year-old Henry was living with sister Rebecca, her husband John Warner, and their son Theodore.

Like every other able-bodied male of the time, Henry registered for the draft on July 1, 1863. He was an unmarried laborer. Henry joined Company D of the 187th on February 25, 1864, at Chambersburg. He participated in the battles at Petersburg and emerged unscathed. The army then moved toward the Weldon Railroad with the intent to destroy it. Severe fighting ensued during which Henry was killed on August 19. The entry in the U.S. Registers of Deaths of Volunteers shows he was killed at "Yellow House," which was at Blick's Farm. Records show he was buried there, then exhumed and reinterred at Poplar Grove National Cemetery near Petersburg.

XLIII.

No Cannons But We Have Plenty of Muskets

THE 188th PA Regiment was organized in April 1864 from the excess soldiers who had volunteered with the Third Heavy Artillery. The 188th was sent to Virginia and quickly saw action in battles at Bermuda Hundred, Drewery's Bluff, and Cold Harbor. They suffered heavy casualties throughout the summer and fall campaigns, as well as being decimated by disease. Perry County sent men to this regiment, but not everyone made it back.

ANDREW BURKHART

Johann Andreas Burkhardt was born in Württemberg, Germany, on September 8, 1820. At the age of twelve, he came to America with his parents, George Martin Burkhardt and Catharina Barbara Schwab Burkhardt. As most German immigrants were wont to do, their surname became Americanized and morphed into Berkett, Burkhart, and Burkett. Johann most often went by Andrew Burkhart. He wed Catharine Sherriff on May 1, 1845. Five years later, they were in Spring Township with a daughter, Sarah. The 1860 census shows them farming in Toboyne Township, where the family grew to include Mary, Susannah, Margaret, George, and Martha. Levi joined the household in 1862. Andrew was still farming in Toboyne Township when he registered for the draft in July 1863.

His index card shows a residence of Montreal, Canada, when he was mustered on February 27, 1864. That does not seem plausible and could be explained as either a clerical error or a mistake made through poor communication. Andrew was one of the men transferred to the 188th on

April 1, joining Company D. He went to fight with a musket rather than a cannon. He was described as a forty-three-year-old farmer who was 5'6" tall, with brown hair, a fair complexion, and gray eyes.

Andrew remained uninjured throughout the regiment's many battles; however, on picket duty at Point of Rocks, Maryland, he became ill. He was transported to McDougal General Hospital at Fort Schuyler in New York. There, his condition deteriorated steadily until he died on November 5, 1864. The U.S. Registers of Deaths of Volunteers lists the cause as "dropsy from hepatic disease." That sounds like a severe case of pneumonia that caused swelling due to a buildup of fluid. Andrew was buried in Cypress Hills National Cemetery in the Bronx.

We have seen before that war's devastation went far beyond the battlefield. Catharine was suddenly a widow with seven children, all under the age of fourteen. Though she received a pension, she later ran into financial trouble that culminated in some of her land being auctioned off at a sheriff's sale. Furthermore, she endured the loss of daughter Margaret, who committed suicide by drowning herself when she was just twenty-two. Were Margaret's demons a result of losing her father?

FREDERICK ROADS

Many of the Perry County men in the 188th came from the eastern part of the county. Frederick Roads (spelled variously as Rhoads, Rhodes, and Rodes) was the son of Henry and Mary Ann Roads. Henry died young, leaving Mary Ann in a tough financial position, one from which she never escaped. Frederick is shown in the 1860 census as a farmhand with the Jacob Troutman family. Later testimony given during Mary Ann's lengthy effort to secure a mother's pension shows Frederick was a devoted son who supported his mother for several years by working at neighboring farms. In lieu of pay, Frederick took grain and other farm products for his mother's benefit.

Frederick enrolled on February 26, 1864, and mustered in at Carlisle, becoming a private in Company D of the 188th. Frederick was a nineteen-year-old farm laborer who stood 5'3" tall. He had a fair complexion that matched his brown hair and hazel eyes. Chances are good that the army pay, sufficient but not overly so, was sent home to Mary Ann, who was then married to John Scott of Liverpool Township. The marriage was not one of convenience, as John could not work; in fact, he had been "a pauper in the Perry County poorhouse."

The army pay was short-lived, as Frederick was one of the thousands of Union casualties at Cold Harbor, Virginia, on June 1. He was "killed in battle." After many months of effort, a pension was awarded to Mary Ann by virtue of Frederick having no wife or minor children. Further, she was entitled since her husband could not support himself or his wife, a sad but all-too-common situation for the time.

SAMUEL SMITH

Samuel Smith was born to Jacob and Sarah Saucerman Smith, who farmed in Juniata Township. This was the typical large farm family of the time, with sons James, Andrew, and Samuel. The girls were Catharine, Mary, Eliza, Margaret, Helen, and Juliann. Andrew joined the 208th in September 1864, about six months after Samuel mustered into Company D of the 188th.

Thirty-six-year-old Samuel listed his occupation as a laborer. He stood 5'5" tall, with black hair, a fair complexion, and hazel eyes. He married Mary Long at her father's home in Greenwood Township on January 18, 1853. When Samuel went off to war on February 26, he left behind Catharine, Sarah, Hiram, and William, four children between the ages of seven and two. Samuel was one of dozens in the regiment who became sick in the fall of 1864. He was admitted to White Hall General Hospital in Bristol, Pennsylvania, where he died of "chronic diarrhea" on November 9, 1864.

GEORGE W. ZARING

Another young man who signed on, hoping to pull the lanyard of a cannon and instead found himself firing a musket, was George W. Zaring of Liverpool Township near Montgomery's Ferry. George was the son of Samuel and Sarah Long Zaring, who farmed in the fertile ground near the Susquehanna. Their surname is seen variously as Zaring, Zearing, and Zareing. Born in 1845, George was a nineteen-year-old with light hair, a fair complexion, and hazel eyes. He stood 5'6" tall when he mustered in on February 26, 1864.

His military career was brief, as he was seriously wounded at the Battle of Cold Harbor. The muster file for Company D of the 188th merely states, "Died June 29/64 of wounds received June 1, 1864." George was hospitalized in Washington, D.C., when he died and was then interred at Arlington National Cemetery.

XLIV.

New Regiments for Old Reserves

ON May 31, 1864, with the end of their three-year commitments in sight for many of the PA Reserves, the decision was made to disband the Reserve Corps regiments. However, the end of the war was not yet in sight. Men who had enlisted later than May 1861, as well as newer recruits, still had to serve out their terms, still had to fight savage battles, still had to get sick, and still had to die.

Two of the Veteran Reserve Regiments created to absorb these men were the 190th and 191st PA Regiments. Many men who rose through the ranks of the Reserves were now officers in these new units. One was Captain James B. Thompson of Port Royal. He now led Company F of the 190th. Thompson, a Congressional Medal of Honor winner for heroics while serving as a sergeant with the Bucktails on July 3 at Gettysburg, had enlisted as a private and was discharged as a major at war's end. The 190th was organized during the Wilderness Campaign and saw fierce fighting at Cold Harbor, Petersburg, and the battle at Weldon Railroad. There, it was unsupported despite being in an advanced position. That left the men vulnerable to an attack by an old Gettysburg adversary, Henry Heth.

Heth's troops surrounded the 190th and separated them from the rest of the Union Army. This led to the entire regiment's capture. The men were incarcerated until Lee's surrender, serving time at Virginia prisons in Danville and Richmond, and at Salisbury, North Carolina.

WINFIELD SCOTT DUFFIELD

Another of the many Saville Township residents who enlisted with the 41st Regiment was Winfield Scott Duffield. Winfield, born in 1843, was the son of Robert and Elizabeth Ritner Duffield, farmers in Saville Township. The second-oldest son in the family, Winfield had brothers Joseph, John, Thomas, and Andrew. Mary and Tabitha rounded out the family. Joseph joined Winfield in enrolling in Company G of the 12th Reserves, and both mustered on August 10, 1861. Young John also enlisted, as a nineteen-year-old in 1864.

Winfield stood 5'11" tall at enlistment. He had dark hair, a dark complexion, and gray eyes. He married a girl from Saville Township, Margaretta Welsh. The wedding took place at Miss Welsh's home on January 29, 1863, while Winfield was at home; possibly after going AWOL. The couple had no children. Winfield left again for the front two months later and even reenlisted as a veteran volunteer in February the following year. He then joined the many reserves who became members of the new regiments.

Winfield Scott Duffield was under the command of Captain James Thompson when he became a prisoner of war, first at Richmond, then at Salisbury, where he contracted dysentery and died on November 10, 1864. He was laid to rest in Salisbury National Cemetery, becoming the fourth member of the little band of Saville Township soldiers who perished after enlisting in the 41st.

JAMES C. DUFFY

Pennsylvania has always had local militia companies, but in the late 1850s, many more communities formed militias. With the escalating tensions between the slave states and the Union, this activity was further hastened. Examples of these early patriots in Central Pennsylvania were Lewistown's Logan Guards, who were among the first volunteers to arrive in Washington. In Perry County, we had the Morgan Rifles of Duncannon, who became the core of Company B of the 13th Reserves (Bucktails), and the Biddle Rifles of Liverpool, whose men became the core group of Company B of the 7th Reserves.

Private James C. Duffy enrolled with the Biddle Rifles and then mustered in with them in to the 7th Reserves on July 27, 1861. At enlistment, he gave Montgomery's Ferry as his residence. He was a butcher by trade, who stood 5'8" tall, with a light complexion, light hair, and blue eyes. I often marvel at the precision in the descriptions of these recruits since later on so many were lost to history. James reenlisted on February 16, 1864, and served with the 7th until he was transferred on May 31 to Company I of the newly created 190th PA Regiment. Many Reserves who had not completed their terms of service were transferred into this regiment when the Reserves were disbanded.

At Weldon Railroad on August 19, this regiment was in an advanced position without support, and dozens were forced to surrender. James C. Duffy was among the captured. He was sent to the Confederate prison at Salisbury, North Carolina, where he died on November 5, 1864, of an unidentified cause. James rests in the national cemetery at Salisbury, where he is misidentified as James O. Duffey.

JOSEPH B. EWING

Another man born in Perry on August 26, 1834, then moved to Juniata County was Joseph B. Ewing. His father, Joseph Sr., was born in western Cumberland County before relocating to the New Germantown area. The elder Joseph, a miller by trade, had wed Susannah Barnhart. Their other children were Anna, Katherine, Benjamin, David, and William, who enlisted with the 20th PA Cavalry Regiment. By 1850, the Ewings were in the East Waterford area.

Joseph Jr. was quick to volunteer, doing so in Carlisle on July 14, 1861, as he joined Company H of the 30th Regiment, otherwise known as the 1st Reserves, not to be confused with the Bucktails, who were the 1st Rifles (13th Reserves). Corporal Joseph Ewing was at Antietam, Gettysburg, and in the battles at the Wilderness. He sustained a wound while fighting at Jericho Ford, Virginia, on May 25, 1864. At that same time, all of the Reserves were being disbanded due to the expiration of their enlistment terms of three years, and due to dwindling numbers in their ranks. Joseph became a member of Company K of the 190th Regiment. Alas, Joseph's fighting days were over. He died at Totopotomy Creek near Richmond of "tetanus due to gunshot" on July 16, 1864. He is buried with his parents in tiny Morrison Cemetery near his former Juniata County home. Though he was officially a member of the 190th, the inscription on his headstone reads: "Joseph B. Ewing of Co. H, IP Reserve Corp of wounds received in front of Richmond July 16, 1864 aged 29 yrs, 10m, 20 d He gave his life for his country."

BENJAMIN E. LIDDICK

The Liddick families of eastern Perry County were true patriots. Just a look at their names alludes to that. In the mid-nineteenth century, there were names like Benjamin Franklin Liddick, Benjamin Harrison Liddick, and George Washington Liddick. There were so many Davids and Benjamins and Johns that most used their middle initials to lessen the confusion. These young men were also quick to answer the call for volunteers. Two of them were brothers: Benjamin and Jeremiah.

The boys were born to John and Elizabeth Liddick, who farmed in the Montgomery's Ferry area. Benjamin was born around 1842, five years after Jeremiah. John died in 1858. Elizabeth carried on with life as best she could. The 1860 census shows Benjamin, Jeremiah, and Lewis living with her. Jeremiah was first to volunteer, joining Company B of the 36th on May 4, 1861. Benjamin joined him on February 20, 1862. Both reenlisted two years later while at Alexandria, Virginia.

Both men were reported missing in action at the Wilderness on May 5. Both also were transferred to the newly formed 190th PA Regiment about that same time—on paper at least, because neither appears on the roster of the 190th. Jeremiah returned to the war, Benjamin did not. Benjamin had been captured and sent to the prison camp at Salisbury, North Carolina. At enlistment, Benjamin was reported to have been nineteen, with dark hair and gray eyes. At 5'8" tall, he was young and strong.

By February 1865, just three years removed from enlistment, he was in a Wilmington hospital fighting for his life. He lost that battle on March 25, 1865. The U.S. Registers of Deaths of Volunteers shows the cause of death "not stated." Also unstated is the location of Benjamin's grave. None of the North Carolina national cemeteries show a Benjamin E. Liddick, possibly indicating a burial outside the hospital. Those bodies were disinterred and relocated, but many were reburied as unknowns.

GEORGE WASHINGTON SHATTO

John and Sarah (Shade) Shatto raised daughters Sarah and Mary Ann along with sons William, Samuel, George, John, and Alexander in Penn Township. Alexander, George, and John all enlisted in Duncannon with the Morgan Rifles. The oldest of those three Shatto brothers to enlist was Private George Washington Shatto. George was already married to Margaret Jane Cleland and living in Rye Township when he enlisted, and was working as a cooper to support the growing family that now included daughter Laura Ann and a son, Irvine. Another son, George Elmer, joined the family in 1864. The Duncannon Iron Works employed coopers like George to make barrels for the storage and shipment of nails and other goods.

The elder George had been born on February 26, 1836. At enlistment he was described as having dark hair and complexion, with brown eyes. He was of average height for that time at 5'5½". The three brothers mustered in later than most of the rest of the regiment: George on August 6, John and Alexander on August 10. George served his term without incident until the Reserve Corps was disbanded on May 31, 1864, and Alexander and George both transferred to Company B of the 190th to complete their terms of service.

George Washington Shatto was among those captured and taken to Salisbury Prison in North Carolina. We have heard the horror stories surrounding prisoner of war camps on both sides of the conflict. Even hardy men like the Bucktails succumbed, including George, who died in prison on March 2, 1865, about six weeks before Lee surrendered. He was interred at the national cemetery in Salisbury, joining fellow warriors like Private Duffield. George's wife, Margaret, relocated to Williamsport to live out her days.

XLV.

The 192nd Pennsylvania Regiment

THE 20th PA Militia served three separate times. In 1862 and again in 1863, it was called upon for several weeks when Lee's army threatened an invasion of the state. Then, in late summer of 1864, it was again called up, this time for a term of one hundred days and was known as the 192nd Regiment. After mustering out on November 11, the unit reorganized as a one-year regiment with many of the one-hundred-day volunteers filling the ranks. New recruits were added to the mix, and the regiment moved south to aid in ending the war in Virginia. While the 192nd did not see much battle action, the men were still susceptible to the illnesses that were a more obstinate foe than the Rebel Army.

While the usual migratory pattern was from east to west in the 1850s, some, like the Benjamin Franklin Boltosser family, bucked that trend. The 1850 census shows the family engaged in farming in Jackson Township. Benjamin married Mary Ann Briner of Loysville on January 16, 1838. Their oldest child was Catharine Jane, then came David Franklin, George, John, Peter, and Samuel.

David Franklin was a single farmer in Oliver Township when he registered for the draft in July 1863. By then, his parents had moved east. The Boltosser name is seen as Baltosser, Baltozer, and Baltzer at various times. To make matters even more confusing, David Franklin often reversed his name to Franklin David. He served ten days in the militia in 1862 before mustering into Company C of the 192nd on Valentine's Day 1865. The war in Virginia ended fifty-four days later. Private David Franklin Boltosser died fifty-six days later of an unnamed disease in National General Hospital in Baltimore, Maryland, on April 11, 1865. There is a grave marked for him under the name Daniel F. Baltosser in Loudon National Cemetery. There is also a grave marked for him in Newport Cemetery on Middle Ridge Road, where his parents were also laid to rest.

XLVI.

The 200th Pennsylvania Regiment

THE 200th PA Regiment was recruited primarily in the counties of Cumberland, Dauphin, and York to serve for one year. They left for the front on September 9, 1864, and were initially assigned to the Army of the James but soon were transferred to General Meade's Army of the Potomac. They wintered near Fort Steadman and spent that time drilling and training to be ready for the spring campaign that everyone hoped would finally put an end to the misery. Indeed, they were ready. In March they were involved in heavy fighting near Fort Steadman and then in front of Petersburg, where losses were heavy. At Fort Steadman, the Ninth Corps commanding officer, General Hartranft, offered special praise for their steadfast gallantry. After the surrenders of first Lee, then Johnston, the regiment mustered out in the summer of 1865.

David Smiley Sr. and wife Mary Frances (Adcock) were Carroll Township farmers. Their children were Margaret, Mary, David Jr., and George. David Jr. was born on May 5, 1825, and was also a farmer in Carroll Township per the 1860 census. He married Frances (Fannie) Atchley in 1851 and was the father of Mary, John, James, Carrie, and William. David was a big man for the time at 5'10" tall, with sandy hair.

David mustered on August 31, 1864, and became a member of Company I of the 200th. He developed an illness and was admitted to hospitals twice in his short term. Returning to duty in February 1865, David participated in the fighting at Fort Steadman and at Petersburg. Wounded on April 2 during a final assault of the Rebel works, David was sent to Mower Hospital in Philadelphia.

The wound was a gunshot to his right forearm that did not at first seem serious. However, complications arose, and he was treated in the hospital for three weeks. Private David Smiley Jr. succumbed to his wounds on April 22, 1865. He was buried in Odd Fellows Cemetery in Philadelphia. There is a note in the Registry of Interments in Odd Fellows Cemetery files that states, "Removed April 27, 1865, to his home." A monument in the Shermans Dale Presbyterian Cemetery stands for David. On that stone are these words: "Died in the 40th year of his life. Wounded in the Battle of Petersburg April 2nd and died of his wounds. Co. I 200 Regt."

A *Carlisle Sentinel* article reprinted on Newspapers.com from December 17, 1927, relates a story about David's granddaughter receiving two small books David had carried during the war in which he kept notes. These arrived sixty-three years after David had died! That article also tells of the letter his widow received. Hoping it was good news because she had been planning a trip to Philadelphia for a visit, she instead received a letter that informed her of his passing. Thousands of others like it were sent to homes across this land.

XLVII.

The 201st Pennsylvania Regiment

THE 201st Regiment was raised primarily in Dauphin County but did have men from Cumberland and Perry sprinkled in. It was mustered in at Camp Curtin in the latter half of August 1864. A great many of the soldiers who made up this unit had been in the service previously. The men were sent from Harrisburg to Chambersburg, where they trained and drilled briefly before being deployed to various locations around Pennsylvania and Virginia. Their duty was primarily to round up deserters and guard prisoners. They were not involved in any real fighting; nevertheless, the Grim Reaper's shadow hovered over all encampments.

RICHARD M. DUDLEY

Some sources report that Richard M. Dudley was born in Cambridgeshire, England, on May 8, 1826. However, other sources show his parents wed in Marcus Hook, Pennsylvania, on January 13, 1825. Furthermore, both the 1850 and 1860 censuses show his birthplace as Pennsylvania, which makes more sense. Regardless of his origin, he resided in Penn Township. He was employed at the Iron Works, as was his father before him. John died tragically young in 1842. Richard's siblings were Elizabeth, John, William, Hannah, Mary Ellen, and Anna.

When Richard enrolled with Company A of the 201st Regiment on August 15, 1864, he was a puddler who stood 5'6" tall, with brown hair, a dark complexion, and hazel eyes. He wed the former Mary Wagner in 1854 and was father to Hiram Jefferson, Martin Luther, and Mary Ellen. Young Richard arrived four days after his father enlisted. It is unknown whether Richard ever saw his newest son because his military career was one of the briefest on record. He developed chronic diarrhea that resulted in his death just six weeks after enlistment. Richard died at a hospital in York on September 28 and was returned to Duncannon, where he was laid to rest in Young's Methodist Cemetery on Carver's Hill.

THOMAS J. EVANS

John and Ann Thomas Evans emigrated to the United States from Wales, eventually settling in Penn Township, where they farmed and raised a family. According to the 1850 census, all six children were born in Pennsylvania, beginning with Francis in 1833. Hannah, Thomas, William, Jane, and David followed. Ten years later, the three oldest children were out on their own. Francis, who died tragically young in 1863, had married; Hannah and Thomas resided in Harrisburg, employed as attendants in what was then known as the "State Lunatic Asylum."

Thomas, who often went by T. J. or Thomas J., enlisted with Company E of the 201st on August 19, 1864, while in the capital city. After that, information on him is extremely limited. His military career was brief, as he was sent home on a furlough and died while in Duncannon on November 9 of that same year. He was buried in Evergreen Cemetery, where a government-issued headstone simply reads, "T.J. EVANS Co. E. 201st PA INF."

WILLIAM A. HIPPLE

Lawrence and Sarah Heagy Hipple were parents to William Alfred, who was born on January 27, 1844. They farmed in Carroll Township. William's siblings were Anna, Oliver, Sarah, Eliza, Mary, John, and Margaret. Eliza married a neighbor, James W. Henderson. They soon moved to DeKalb, Illinois, to raise a family but could not escape the Civil War, as James became a member of the 15th Illinois Infantry. He survived the war. William and John joined Company C of the 201st PA Infantry. John became a corporal and survived the war. William did not.

The brothers mustered in at Harrisburg on August 19, 1864. William was 5'5" tall, with brown hair and brown eyes. It did not take long for illness to bring him down. He was admitted to the 2nd Division General Hospital in Alexandria, Virginia, where he died of typhoid fever on October 27, just two months after mustering in. William was returned to

Shermans Dale and buried in the Presbyterian Cemetery on Windy Hill Road next to both parents.

WILLIAM J. KENNEDY

Of the more than 288 sad stories included here none is more heart-wrenching than that of the Kennedy sisters of Carroll Township. Eva Tabitha, Margaret Eliza, and Eliza Jane were the daughters of William J. and Martha Jane Sutch Kennedy. Eva was born in 1856, Margaret two years later, and Eliza in October 1860. We first encounter Martha Jane Sutch when she resided with the Nathan Jones family, who farmed in Carroll Township. Martha had been born in 1833, and it is unclear why she was with that family. The 1860 census finds her married to William J. Kennedy, living still in Carroll, residing with daughters Eva and Margaret.

By the time little Eliza was three, William had registered for the draft in Carroll Township as a carpenter. He enlisted on August 18, 1864, and became a member of Company A of the 201st Regiment. The timing seems odd since tragedy had visited the family just six weeks earlier when Martha Jane died tragically young on July 8, 1864. The three little girls were without their mother, and now their father was leaving for war.

Private William J. Kennedy headed off to war, no doubt with a heavy heart. Alas, his misery soon ended with his death on October 29 from typhoid fever "at general hospital in Alexandria Va." according to the record of U.S. Registers of Deaths of Volunteers.

What of the three little girls now with both parents gone? An act of Congress from July 14, 1862, provided them some relief in the form of granting pensions to minor children under the age of sixteen. William Samuel Nesbitt, a farmer in Madison Township, became the guardian for the girls. He secured a pension to help them, as well as providing them a home.

XLVIII.

The 202nd Pennsylvania Regiment

THE 202nd Regiment mustered in about the same time as the 201st, in August and September 1864. Once established as a regiment, it did not go to the front but to the less glamorous duty of guarding railroads. It guarded strategic locations like Manassas Gap, Thoroughfare Gap, and toward the end of the war, it camped at Fairfax Station, Virginia, guarding the Orange and Alexandria rail line. The men might not have preferred the duty to battle since constant harassment by Mosby's Raiders and the local Confederate sympathizers caused much destruction and cost some lives. The 202nd also lost a substantial number of men to various diseases, seven in Company H alone. It mustered out in summer 1865, well after hostilities had ended. Company H was recruited in Cumberland County and contained some Perry County soldiers.

ALEXANDER W. FAGAN

Alexander W. Fagan grew up in Perry County before crossing the mountain and settling in Cumberland County's South Middleton Township. His father, Enoch Fagan, lived in Spring Township near Landisburg, where he was a shoemaker. Enoch had been a veteran of the War of 1812. Neither censuses from 1850 nor 1860 indicate Enoch had a wife. Siblings William, John, and Catharine do appear. In 1850, Alexander was a farm laborer living with the John Cree family in Spring Township. By 1860, he had moved to South Middleton Township, where he farmed with wife Mary Ann Heiser Fagan and children Isaiah, William, and Susannah.

Alexander enlisted on August 5, 1862, with Company A of the 130th PA, but his military career was cut short by a disability. He reportedly suffered from rheumatism and was discharged for disability on December 5 by order of Captain Lane. Alex was thirty when he enlisted; therefore, a birth year of 1832 is probable.

Alexander gave it another try when he enlisted in Company H of the 202nd on August 19, 1864. This tour of duty was brief also. He died just two months later on October 22. The muster files indicate he succumbed to disease, but the U.S. Registers of Deaths of Volunteers tells a different story. It states "traumatic festavis from gunshot wound." He was buried in Alexandria National Cemetery. Mary Ann applied for a widow's pension. In that petition, she cited Alexander's brother, John Fagan, as guardian of their children.

PETER SHEARER

We find Peter Shearer in the 1850 census not in Perry County but over the mountain in Cumberland's North Middleton Township. He was residing with his parents, John and Elizabeth, and working as a shoemaker. We next find him marrying Mary Elizabeth Albright on August 28, 1853. At that time, Mary lived in Carroll Township; Peter gave his address as Rye Township. By the time Peter registered for the draft in July 1863, his address was Carroll Township, where he continued in the trade of shoemaker.

Peter and Mary began a family that eventually included Sarah, Emma, John, Mary Catharine, and twins George and Philip. Peter mustered into Company H of the 202nd at Camp Curtin on August 29, 1864. The next stop for the regiment was Chambersburg for training and drill, then to Virginia.

In the spring, Peter was admitted to the regimental hospital at Fairfax Station, where he died from diphtheria on May 3, 1865, nearly a month after General Lee surrendered his Army of Northern Virginia. Peter is one of the more than sixteen thousand Civil War soldiers buried at Arlington National Cemetery.

Mary applied for and received a widow's pension, naming her father, William Albright, as guardian of the children. The twins, born on July 11, 1860, were admitted to Tressler Orphans' Home in Loysville in May 1867.

DANIEL STUM

Nicholas and Margaret Lay Stum relocated from Berks County to Perry sometime in the 1830s. Nicholas appears in the 1840 census for Toboyne Township. Nicholas died in 1849 and, while records are a bit unclear, the couple had nine children based upon that census. Daniel was born on February 20, 1828, and married Elizabeth Salsbury in 1853.

Daniel and two of his brothers, Henry and John, joined Company H of the 202nd Regiment in 1864. The men enlisted in August at Newville and mustered in at Camp Curtin on the last day of August 1864. During what was an uneventful yet unhealthy winter, Daniel became sick. He was admitted to Patterson Park General Hospital in Baltimore, Maryland, where he passed away from chronic diarrhea on February 28, 1865. Some records indicate a burial in Baltimore, but a definitive record has not been found. There is a grave marker for him in St. Peter's Upper Frankford Church Cemetery in Cumberland County. Many family members are interred there as well.

Elizabeth applied for a pension, naming her brother Joseph as guardian. Two of her children, William and Morris, were admitted to Tressler Orphans' Home in Loysville in 1865.

XLIX.

The 208th Pennsylvania Regiment

ASIDE from some regiments and independent unites designated as "colored," there were a total of 215 regiments raised in Pennsylvania during the Civil War. The 208th was among the last ones raised and sent to the front. Several later regiments were assigned to guard duty and the protection of Washington, D.C., as well as other strategic locations that could be targets for guerrilla warfare. The 208th contained a mix of new recruits and seasoned veterans who had previously served. Quite a few came from the ranks of the old 133rd which had three companies recruited in Perry County. Many of these veterans were now officers, both commissioned and noncommissioned. Four companies, Company E, Company F, Company G, and Company I, were recruited in Perry County. The captain of Company E was Francis Marion McKeehan of Centre Township, Company F was under the command of Captain Gardner Columbus Palm of Kistler, Newport's Benjamin Franklin Miller captained Company G, and Company I was led by Captain James Hill Marshall of New Bloomfield.

The 208th was mustered into service in early September 1864, and after training and drill at Bermuda Hundred, it was assigned to the Army of the Potomac on November 27. It was hotly engaged at Fort Steadman on March 25, losing four men killed and thirty-eight wounded. The 208th helped bring down the strategic rail city of Petersburg on April 2, 1865, losing nine men killed in action and another thirty-nine wounded. After Petersburg, the regiment joined in the dogged pursuit of Lee's army until the surrender a week later. On June 1, the regiment mustered out after a short but eventful tour of duty. Dozens of grave markers dot Perry County's cemeteries, proudly acknowledging veteran status in the 208th PA Regiment.

Company E of the 208th had five men named Foose in the ranks. Frank, two named Isaiah, and brothers Jacob and Henry. Jacob, Henry, Frank and Isaiah Carl were from Spring Township, the other Isaiah was from New Bloomfield. Company F had James Foose from the Blain area. James was one of the thirty-nine men wounded at Petersburg on April 2, 1865.

FRANCIS ELLIS FOOSE

Francis (Frank) Ellis Foose was born on October 29, 1842, to John and Rachel. John was a Spring Township mason, a trade he passed on to son Samuel. Frank was a farmer in 1860. The Foose family also included Elizabeth, Paul, John, and Susannah. Samuel, the oldest, enlisted with the 47th PA.

Frank enlisted on September 2, 1864, and mustered in a week later. He was 5'7" tall and was described as having a sandy complexion to go along with sandy hair and blue eyes. At enrollment, he was a twenty-one-year-old farmer. His youth and the hard labor of farming should have prepared him well to face the challenges ahead, but typhoid fever could bring any man down. It got Frank at City Point Hospital in Hampton, Virginia, on January 11, 1865. Frank was brought home and buried in Mt. Zion Cemetery in Elliottsburg.

HENRY FOOSE

The Daniel and Susannah Sheaffer Foose family of Spring Township were farmers in Little Germany. Their children were John, William, Henry, Jacob, Elizabeth, Sarah, and Margaret. Jacob and Henry joined the 208th. Older brother William was a member of the 54th PA. Jacob and William survived the war, Henry did not.

Henry, born in 1838, and Jacob mustered in together on September 2, 1864, at Harrisburg. Henry was a married man with three children at the time. He had wed Mary Jane Bear and fathered William, Edward, and Jemima. His occupation on the 1860 census for Spring Township was fence post maker. He stood 5'8" tall, with a light complexion, dark hair, and hazel eyes.

We have noted that nine men from the 208th were killed in the assault on Petersburg on April 2, 1865, just seven days before Lee surrendered.

One of them was Henry. The U.S. Registers of Deaths of Volunteers states he died from a gunshot wound that penetrated his lung. He was alive long enough to go to the hospital but perished eight hours later.

New Bloomfield's F. M. McKeehan, captain of Company E, sent a letter to Henry's father, Daniel. This letter, dated May 9, 1865, provided particulars concerning Henry's death. Henry "was wounded early in the morning" as the regiment attacked the Confederate stronghold of Fort Mahone. Private Jerome Toomey related to McKeehan that he had seen Henry at the "hospital at Meade Station about 10 ½ A.M." Toomey added that Henry "was not aware of being wounded in the side. He said it hurt him in the side when he breathes."

Captain McKeehan went on to say, "It was a gun-shot wound. Ball entering & passing through his right arm above the elbow and entering his body below the ribs." Showing how close these men had become, the captain added, "he wondered how many was wounded in the company and dies not wanting anything save water. He was then laying not able to turn himself."

Captain McKeehan ended the letter with these words: "I saw the list or register of graves and find that his grave is number 23. Henry was a good and obedient soldier. Hoping that God may be a husband to his widow and a father to his orphan children."

His body was brought home to Elliottsburg by Daniel Reeder. Mary Jane named her brother J. H. Bear as guardian for the children. Sadly, Mary Jane died in 1867, leaving three youngsters without parents. All three children were admitted to the Soldiers Orphan School at Andersonburg.

Isaiah, Isaiah Carl, and Jacob Foose all survived the war to return to their Perry County homes.

JOSIAH GRUBB

We have seen many men in their teens; now meet an elder statesman of forty who became a member of Company I of the 208th. Josiah Grubb of Perry Valley was born to Christian and Susannah (Pfoutz) Grubb on January 16, 1824. Josiah was one of ten children in the farm family.

Josiah wed Elizabeth Charles in 1843. They were parents to Emily, Uriah, Catharine, Christian, Elizabeth, and Ida. Like his father, Josiah was a farmer in Liverpool Township. He stood 5'9" tall, with dark hair and blue eyes. Mustered in at Harrisburg on September 3, 1864, he was approaching his forty-first birthday. Like so many men away from home for the first time, Josiah soon became ill. He was admitted to the 3rd Division, Ninth Corps Hospital near Petersburg, where he died on January 9, 1865, one week short of his birthday. The U.S. Registers of Deaths of Volunteers lists the cause as "inflammation of pleura," doctor-speak for what is commonly known as pleurisy, an inflammation of the membrane that surrounds the lungs. Private Josiah Grubb was returned to Perry County and buried in White Church Cemetery in Perry Valley.

JOSEPH HECKART

Joseph Heckart's time in Perry County was relatively brief, and his time in the army was tragically brief. The Heckart family was from Northumberland County. Joseph's parents were Peter and Eva Christine Witmer Heckart. Eva died in 1845. Sometime in the 1850s, Peter moved to a farm in Saville Township. Joseph and his wife, Sarah, whom he wed in 1857, came along. The rest of the family seems to have remained in Northumberland, at least until some members journeyed to the Midwestern states. By the 1860 census, Joseph and Sarah Grimm Heckart had welcomed sons Jeremiah and Benjamin into the home. Daniel arrived later in 1860, Charles two years later, and Joseph in 1863. Daniel and Charles died before the decade ended.

Joseph, born on January 11, 1837, enrolled with Company E of the 208th on August 30, 1864, and went to war in Virginia. Details are unavailable, but an entry in the U.S. Registers of Deaths of Volunteers for September 29, 1864, tells the sad story that he "accidently was killed while on picket duty by a shot from a comrade's rifle." Joseph's body was returned to Northumberland County, where he was laid to rest in the Union cemetery.

Sons Benjamin and Daniel were admitted to the Soldiers Orphan School at Andersonburg on March 1, 1867. Daniel died in November, adding to Sarah's woes. The boys address when not in school was shown to be Pillow, indicating that Sarah had moved back to Northumberland County.

EDMUND B. P. KINSLOE

Another man soon to be forty and also a member of Company E of the 208th was Edmund Burke Patterson Kinsloe. Edmund was born on either December 4, 1824, or April 12, 1824, depending upon the source of the information. He was the son of Francis West and Sarah McClain Kinsloe of Juniata County. His siblings were William, Thomas, Mary, John, Lucinda, Margaretta, and Adolph. Edmund seems to have moved around quite a lot. In 1850, he was residing with the Abrams family in Greenwood Township, Perry County, working as a merchant. When he registered for the draft in July 1863, he lived in Tyrone Township and was a laborer.

Edmund had wed Susan Elizabeth Titzel in 1858. Susan was born in Loysville, but the marriage took place in Thompsontown, where Edmund's father was the postmaster. Three children were born to the pair: Thomas West, Samuel Edmund, and Anna Margaret. Anna's death certificate cites a birthplace of Green Park.

Edmund became Private Edmund B. P. Kinsloe on September 10, 1864, in Harrisburg. He served with Company E through the winter and spring. He took part in the successful battle at Fort Steadman before moving onto Petersburg, where he became one of the casualties on April 2, 1865, in what was the final assault on the city. Ultimately, this action resulted in a Union victory. Edmund was taken to Carver U.S. Hospital in Washington. He lingered with what had to be an excruciatingly painful wound. The wound became infected, causing inflammation and abscesses. The official cause of death on April 25, 1865, in the U.S. Registers of Deaths of Volunteers was "shell wound rec'd in action phlegmonoid erysipelas."

SYLVESTER MCELHENEY

Sylvester McElheney's time in Perry County was brief, as was his time in the Army of the Potomac. He was born in 1838 to John and Judith McElheney in the Concord area of Juniata County, just over the Perry County line. The 1860 census shows Sylvester and his new wife living in Fannett Township. Sylvester had wed Harriet Ann Fegan on January 26, 1860. They had daughters, Mary Judith and Ann Elizabeth, as well as a son, Joseph. Young Joseph, born in September 1863, would sadly die in July 1865.

When Sylvester registered for the draft in July 1863, he was a twenty-five-year-old plasterer living with Harriet and the children in Jackson Township near Blain. He enlisted on September 3, 1864, with Company F of the 208th while in Perry. His younger brother Phillip also served in that company. In March 1865 the Army of Northern Virginia tenaciously defended the crucial rail hub of Petersburg, Virginia. If the army was to survive, that critical supply line had to remain open. The Army of the Potomac launched assault after assault upon that Southern citadel, knowing that keeping the pressure on was the clear path to victory. Fighting was savage and costly. Sylvester was wounded on March 25 at Fort Steadman. He was transported to Broad Street Hospital in Philadelphia, where he lingered until April 20 before he succumbed to the wounds. He rests now in Our Lady of Refuge Cemetery near Doylesburg with his parents, his wife, and his little son, who only survived Sylvester by three months.

An entry in the Soldiers' and Airmen's Home National Cemetery Interment Registry shows Edmund was buried there in Washington. There is also a tombstone in Centre Presbyterian Church Cemetery near Fort Robinson in Madison Township. His children were all admitted to the Soldiers Orphan School in Andersonburg; Thomas and Samuel on October 31, 1866, and Anna on March 1, 1869.

WILLIAM H. PERRY

Spring Township provided many soldiers for the Union Army in general and the 208th Regiment in particular. Although this area was rural, it was tight knit and contained many German and Swiss immigrants who worked together, worshiped together, and, in some cases, died together. A neighbor and friend of Henry D. Foose was William H. Perry, the son of Samuel and Mary Sheaffer Perry. By the time William joined the 208th Regiment, the Civil War had already brought grief to the family. Sister Margaret had married Henry Shearer (page 196), who had died of disease while serving with the 177th in 1863.

When William registered for the draft in July 1863, he was a twenty-one-year-old shoemaker living in Spring Township. His father, Samuel, had passed away in 1852. Two younger siblings, Ellen and Thomas, were also deceased.

William mustered in at Harrisburg and became a member of Company E on September 7, 1864. He marched off to war with many friends and neighbors. William survived the ferocity of the battle at Fort Steadman and joined in the assault on Petersburg on April 2, 1865. He, like neighbor Henry Foose, was killed that day. Both men may have been brought back to Perry County. Also, a Spring Township resident, Sergeant William R. Dum of Company E kept a journal in which this entry appears: "This morning at two Daniel Reeder came to us. His object in view is to take the bodies of Henry D. Foose & Wm H. Perry home to their friends." Daniel Reeder was himself a veteran who had lost his left arm while fighting with the 47th at Pocotaligo.

McKeehan added this note concerning Perry: "I have not been able to get the number of Perry's grave if it is numbered at all." Since no record of interment has been located for Private William Perry, he may have been buried where he fell.

JOHN REAPSOME

A look at pages seven and eight of the 1850 census for Spring Township reveals young lads growing up on neighboring properties. These lads were no doubt friends. Daniel Bistline was nine. William R. Dum was eight. William Perry was nine. John Reapsome was ten. The eldest of the boys was Henry Foose at seventeen. These boys had their whole lives ahead of them. They could revel in feeling free, running barefoot through the wheat stubble, fishing in the nearby streams, and getting together to romp and play.

Fast forward a mere fourteen years to the fall of 1864. Daniel Bistline had enlisted with the 47th PA and had been dead three years. The other four boys were now men serving together in Company E of the newly formed 208th PA. By virtue of a previous term in the 133rd, William R. Dum was a sergeant, the other three privates. All left their youth, their innocence, and their families behind. Dum, Foose, and Perry stormed the breastworks at Petersburg together the following April. Only Dum escaped unscathed. Reapsome was in the hospital and unable to join his friends on the field of battle.

Sometimes spelled Reapsomer, John was born in 1839 to George and Margaretha Bistline Reapsome, an aunt to Daniel Bistline (page 60). John's mother had died in 1846, and his father remarried. John wed Lucinda Wensel on Christmas Day 1862. The couple welcomed a daughter, Frances, on September 22 the following year.

Before Frances turned one, John enlisted in Company E on September 7. He developed "phthisis pulmonitis" and was hospitalized in March 1865. He not only missed Petersburg but was also absent when the rest of his company mustered out on May 25, 1865. According to affidavits in the pension files, he was mustered out three days later than his friends. His certificate of disability reads, "shows the incapability of soldier to perform military service." His condition most often was referred to at the time as "consumption," or tuberculosis.

John died on July 2, 1865, three months after Petersburg, and was laid to rest in Ludolph's Cemetery in Little Germany near the wheat fields he once called home. Though Private John Reapsome died after the war, he is included here for two reasons. Primarily, he died as a direct result of his army service. He is also included here as further evidence of the effects of war that carried over into peacetime. Tens of thousands of former Civil War soldiers suffered lingering effects from disease, wounds, and emotional scars. John's wife, Lucinda, eventually remarried. Daughter Frances was educated at the Tressler Orphans' Home in Loysville. No doubt both ladies suffered from the war's lingering effects, too.

GEORGE REMPFER

Johann George Rempfer and wife Margaretha Wagner were both born in Württemberg, Germany. They arrived in Philadelphia in August 1832, then moved to Perry County, settling in Saville Township. Their children were Johann George, Johannes, Jacob, Susannah, Catharine, Sophia, and Frederick. The elder George was a cabinetmaker, a skill he brought with him to America.

The younger George, born in 1836, was listed as a laborer when he registered for the draft in July 1863. He was living in Centre Township with wife Nancy Mickey Rempfer and their son, William, who had been born in 1862.

George enlisted and mustered on August 30, 1864, at Harrisburg. Despite the language barriers that often arose for second-generation German-speaking people, George became a corporal in Company E. He also became one of the nine men from the regiment killed in action on April 2, 1865, in front of Petersburg. Any death is tragic, but when you think that Lee's surrender was only a week away, it seems even more so.

JOHN LOY RITTER

John Loy Ritter was born on February 25, 1833, to George and Catherine Loy Ritter, who farmed in Madison Township. The 1860 census shows John residing with his parents on the farm, but he was now joined by wife Sarah Elizabeth and six-month-old daughter, Anna Catherine. Sarah and John had two more children, Ida Jane and David Bower, before war intervened.

John Ritter's military service records appear to be confused with other similarly named soldiers. When he registered for the draft in July 1863, he was a twenty-nine-year-old, married farmer in Tyrone Township. A little over one year later, he enlisted on September 7 with Company I of the 208th. The muster files for that unit show John being mustered out with his company on June 1, 1865. However, that was not the case. His military service was extremely brief, as he died at home on October 17, 1864. Wife Sarah Elizabeth posted an estate notice for John in the *Perry County Democrat* on November 10, 1864; therefore, the muster-out information is in error. John was buried in the old cemetery in Loysville known as the Lebanon Lutheran and Reformed Churchyard, where a younger brother who died in 1840 was buried, and where his parents are interred as well.

FREDERICK SHULL

Frederick Shull of Saville Township was another soldier rather long in the tooth. He was born on February 17, 1823, to farmers Samuel and Margaret Rebecca Rice Shull. Samuel died in 1832 shortly after Frederick's sister Catharine was born. Other siblings were Conrad, John, Samuel, William, and Sarah.

Frederick married Sarah Ellen Rice, also of Saville Township, in 1859. The Rice family had a history of volunteering for the military, dating back to the Revolutionary War. A great-great-grandmother, Abigail Hartman

Rice, was a nurse at the Yellow Springs Hospital during that war. Five of Sarah's brothers served in the Civil War. Absalom, David, Jeremiah, and William all served with the 36th Militia, mustered in to meet the Gettysburg emergency. Absalom also joined the 104th and Jacob served in the 201st.

In 1850 and 1860 Frederick was listed as a farmer. In 1860, he and Sarah were joined by new son, Lewis Ellerman Shull. A daughter, Emma Jane, was born in 1862. Frederick had two tours of duty, first with the 177th and then with Company F of the 208th. He enlisted with the latter regiment on September 6, 1864, and was soon promoted to corporal. He served in that capacity over the winter and into the spring campaign that saw the regiment engaged in retaking Fort Steadman on March 25, 1865. Unfortunately, he was killed in action that day. His body was returned to Saville Township, where he was buried in Buffalo Cemetery at Saville.

Sarah applied for a widow's pension, naming Frederick's brother William as guardian for the children. Sadly, Emma only lived six years. Lewis was admitted to the Soldiers Orphan School in Andersonburg on April 1, 1872. He received a solid education and was especially proficient at singing, a skill he took with him throughout his life. His obituary in the *Perry County Democrat* on April 4, 1934, noted that his nickname was "Lew the Singer."

JACOB TURNBAUGH

Of course, all battlefield deaths are tragic. Is it more tragic when the dying man thinks of the wife and children he will never see again? Or is it more tragic when the dying man is robbed of the opportunity to have a wife and children? Obviously there are no right or wrong answers, just pain and suffering.

Another Saville Township man went off to war with the 208th Regiment. This one at the age of twenty, with no wife or children but a girlfriend, someone he was making plans with. Jacob and Mary Elizabeth Souder Turnbaugh raised a large family on the income from Jacob's work as a shoemaker. The children were spaced out, from Henry, born in 1829, to William born in 1852: George, Sarah, Hannah, Isabella, Mary, Susan, and Jacob in between. Jacob was born in 1844.

He was a laborer, 5'7" tall, with a dark complexion, dark hair, and brown eyes. Jacob became a member of Company E of the 208th on August 30, 1864, at Harrisburg. He was uninjured at Fort Steadman but not so lucky at Petersburg. Jacob suffered a severe gunshot wound to his left thigh on April 2, 1865. Sent to the division hospital in Alexandria, Virginia, Jacob had an "amputation of lower third of left thigh." However, as so often happened with amputations, complications arose. Jacob lost his battle eleven days later. He was interred at Alexandria National Cemetery, never again seeing Saville Township or that special someone he had left behind.

GEORGE W. WEISE

Our last fallen member of the 208th was another older recruit by the name of George W. Weise of Centre Township. George W. was born on April 25, 1822, to George Sr. and Mary Elizabeth Apple Weise. George W. came from a family of eight children and had eight children himself with Barbara Fickes Weise, whom he had wed in 1843. In an uncommon happening for that era, the couple divorced on January 4, 1864. Their children were Emaline, Henry, William, Sarah, David, Winfield Scott, and George. Henry served with Company H of the 47th.

When George W. registered for the draft on July 1, 1863, he was a blacksmith in Centre Township. He looked the part of a blacksmith, standing 5'11" tall, with black hair and dark eyes. He enlisted on the last day of August 1864 and mustered into Company G five days later. George W. was assigned to the ordnance department of the 3rd Division and put his smithing skills to work there. At some point he returned to the 208th and was with them at Fort Steadman. In a case of being at the wrong place at the wrong time, George was standing in front of Avery House when a Confederate shell struck and killed him.

George W. is buried near his parents in Sulphur Springs Cemetery at Little Buffalo State Park. The engraving on his stone reads, "in memory of George W. Weise of Co. G. 208th Reg. P.V. Killed by a shell from a Confederate Battery in front of Petersburg, Va. March 25, 1865, Aged 42 years, 11 mo. and 29 days."

L.

The 209th Pennsylvania Regiment

THE 209th PA Regiment was recruited at a similar time as the 208th and served roughly in the same manner. These men were severely tested at Fort Steadman and again at Petersburg. Despite a relatively brief tenure in the war, they saw plenty of action and incurred plenty of casualties as the Army of the Potomac slowly tightened the noose around the Army of Northern Virginia. No companies were recruited in Perry County, but Companies A and F were raised nearby in Carlisle, and Company D nearby in Franklin County.

JOHN HERMAN GEES

We know precious little about John Herman Gees. The 1860 census shows him living in Penn Township, toiling as a day laborer. He was residing with wife Anna Mary, whom he had wed on February 1, 1859, in Harrisburg. The census reveals that John, who sometimes went by his middle name, Herman, was born in Prussia. He was shown to be thirty-one. Wife Anna Mary was twenty and listed a birthplace of Württemberg, Germany. According to Anna's application for a widow's pension, they had no children.

Also in that petition is a statement of facts of their marriage that places both as residents of Harrisburg in 1859. It also states that the names given to the Justice of the Peace were Herman and Maria. It seems that at various times, Anna Mary went by Maria, Anna, or Mary Ann, which may be attributed to some difficulty in handling the nuances of our language. At any rate, John Herman Gees must have had no trouble communicating as he enrolled in Company F of the 209th as a corporal. He mustered in on September 10.

Barely three months later, Corporal Gees was captured and sent to Salisbury Prison in North Carolina. Many soldiers died there, including John. He was admitted to the prison hospital two days before Christmas but died, as so many others, of chronic diarrhea.

ENOCH SYKES

Sometimes the irony in the life of an individual soldier nearly overshadows the story. Such was the case of Enoch Sykes. The 1860 census shows Enoch to be the son of James and Eve Sykes, who farmed in Carroll Township. Also in the family were Henrietta, Cecilia, Elizabeth, James Jr., Henry, and Ellen. Ten years earlier, the family was shown to be in York County's Hopewell Township, where the elder James gave an occupation of manufacturer. James had been born in England, Eve in Pennsylvania. It is unknown when the family relocated to Perry County, but the parents lived out their lives there and were buried in Grier's Point Cemetery, located along Route 850 near the village of Keystone.

Enoch enlisted in Carlisle on September 6, 1864. He was assigned to Company F of the newly formed 209th PA Regiment at the tender age of sixteen, though he supplied an age of eighteen at enrollment. Even though the war in the eastern theater ended just seven months later, the 209th, as well as the 208th, which contained four companies of Perry's best, faced heavy fighting as the Army of Northern Virginia fought savagely to hold on to their slim hope. The Battle for Petersburg's Fort Steadman was fierce and deadly. Young Enoch Sykes was killed in action on March 25, 1865, just two weeks before Lee surrendered. The story of Enoch Sykes began in Hopewell Township. It ended with his interment at City Point National Cemetery in Hopewell, Virginia.

LI.

An Illinois Soldier with Perry Roots

IT is difficult to know where to draw the line as far as whom to include in this book. One thing that surprised me as I researched these men is how often families used Perry County as a stopover on their way farther west. They arrived in search of cheap land and relocated to the Midwest later for the same reason. I have decided to include our next man even though he was probably only in Perry County for three years, yet his story is compelling and tragic, as they all are.

Benjamin Wade was born in Perry County to John and Anna Wade in 1843 while they were farming in Rye Township. His parents were both born in Dauphin County before settling briefly in Perry. Five children were born in Perry before they continued their western migration to Wheatfield Township in Clinton County, Illinois, when Benjamin was three.

Benjamin enlisted in Company D of the 15th Illinois Cavalry on October 1, 1861. He was a carpenter who was just over 5'3" tall, with a dark complexion, black hair, and hazel eyes. Benjamin proved to be a good soldier, but his tenure was tragically brief. The circumstances surrounding his death are shrouded in mystery, as he was killed by his own pickets at Jackson, Tennessee, on June 17, 1862.

LII.

A Minnesota Lad Returns to Pennsylvania

IT is uncertain whether our next subject was born in Perry or in Harrisburg. However, his family's story is compelling, nonetheless. Perry County can lay claim to five governors with county roots. Given its small population, could that be the highest number per capita in the land? Millerstown's James Beaver and Dromgold's William Bigler governed Pennsylvania. John Bigler, William's brother, governed California at the same time his little brother held the reins in Pennsylvania. Alexander Stephens, whose parents were from Duncannon, was Georgia's governor. And Stephen A. Miller, also from Dromgold, became governor of Minnesota.

First Lieutenant Wesley Funk Miller was the first-born son of Stephen A. and Margaret Funk Miller, both Perry Countians, who resided near Dromgold before relocating to Harrisburg when Stephen was elected prothonotary of Dauphin County. Wesley, the oldest of four boys, was born on April 1, 1841.

Seeking a better climate reputed to be better for his health, Stephen moved to St. Cloud, Minnesota, in 1858 and went on to become governor of his adopted state. In 1861, Stephen and son Wesley enlisted as privates in the 1st Minnesota Regiment, a unit later decimated at Gettysburg on July 2, losing 85% of its men in a heroic and successful charge that delayed an overwhelming Confederate force long enough for reinforcements to arrive.

However, in 1862, Wesley received a commission as lieutenant in Company E of the 7th United States Infantry. It was in that capacity that Wesley returned to Pennsylvania, where he fell on July 2 in battle near the Wheatfield, just a few hundred yards from where the 1st Minnesota gained immortality. Originally buried on the field, he was later interred in the national cemetery. His body was moved a second time and rests now in the Harrisburg Cemetery.

LIII.

Another Grand Old Man

IT seems appropriate that our last entrant is one of the oldest. Anthony Wox was born on October 26, 1811, in Tyrone Township of what was then Cumberland County. He was born to Peter and Anna Christiana Wox (sometimes spelled Wax or Wachs). Anthony's wife, Jane Elizabeth Shaw Wox, was born in Herkimer, New York. Records show their marriage was in Bryan, Ohio, in 1837, ten years before the Mexican War. Having missed the war with Great Britain and the war with Mexico, when we fought a war among ourselves, Anthony opted in. He mustered on September 16, 1864, becoming Private Anthony Wox of Company K, 210th PA Regiment, at the age of fifty-three. Forty-five was the upper limit for service at that time, so that is the age he gave, even though he was older. Perhaps his motivation to serve lay in the fact that three of his sons were in the army. Reuben was a member of the 149th, Lucious was wounded with the 101st but then reenlisted with the 17th Cavalry, and Sydney was also in the 17th. Other children were Alameda, Augustus, Fanny, and Alice. The Wox family farmed in Carroll Township.

As with members of the 208th, getting into the war in the fall of 1864 was still a dangerous assignment. Like the 208th, shortly after organization of the regiment, the 210th headed south for the front lines and was heavily engaged in the push toward Petersburg. Lee's Confederate forces fought stubbornly to protect their supply lines in Petersburg and their capital in Richmond. They also sought to stall long enough to link up with the armies in the Carolinas. The Union troops fought just as stubbornly to bring the war to a close. Many deaths marked the final two weeks of the conflict in Virginia. Battles at Five Forks, Boydton Road, Quaker Road, and Gravelly Run were waged between March 29 and April 1, with losses in the 210th of 35 killed, 115 wounded, and 150 missing. Anthony Wox was killed in action at Gravelly Run on March 31. He was buried where he fell and remains there, unmarked but not unmourned.

LIV.

Conclusion

AS a parent, I thankfully can only imagine the anguish one would feel at the death of a child, even though it was a more common occurrence in the mid-nineteenth century. Many children died at birth or shortly thereafter, as did their mothers. The sheer number of Civil War-era deaths were mind-numbing. According to many studies, the average life expectancy for men in 1860 was about forty. That rate increased if the man survived to adulthood. So, when your young man reached eighteen, as a parent, you no doubt thought things would be all right. Then, the Civil War raised its ugly head and put thousands in their graves.

We met 288 men who left Perry County: left their parents, left their wives, left their children, their sheltered lives. Some did not make it back. Some did, though briefly. Some returned in pine boxes. Hundreds of dinner tables throughout the county, as well as hundreds of thousands throughout the country, had empty chairs around them. Families were changed forever. Wives not only lost their soulmates, but they also lost the sole breadwinners. Few women worked outside the home. Many widows were forced to send their children to live with friends, relatives, or orphanages. Entire families were in many cases left destitute. This war caused heartache upon heartache during its four years. But the heartache went on for years after the cessation of hostilities. Families were torn apart not only by the deaths and horrific injuries but also economically. In 1860s America, bread was put on the table through the sweat of a man's brow. When that man was out of the picture, the image was dark indeed.

Some modern-day researchers think as many as three-quarters of a million men perished during the four-year war: 50-60% from disease. Of the men presented here, 44% died from battlefield causes while the remainder succumbed to disease, accidents, and other non-combat-related causes. It is interesting to note that battle-related deaths early in the war were more prevalent as a percentage than later in the war. That can be attributed to the practice of exchanging prisoners early on, while in the latter stages of conflict, prisoner exchanges were less frequent. Therefore in '64 and '65, incarcerations were of a longer duration, conditions were deplorable, rations were meager, and the ability to care for unhealthy prisoners was practically nonexistent.

We met one family, the Powells of Tuscarora Township, who lost three sons (page 76). Many other families lost two, including these families: Orwan (page 3 and 176), Hetrick (page 7 and 16), Kosier (page 72), Ebright (page 30 and 89), Matchett (page 134), Reed (page 162 and 184), Rice (page 18), Ricedorff (page 124), Kitner (page 134 and 174), Galbraith (page 33 and 65), Robinson (page 78), and Jacobs (page 173). Living through that pain once would be terrible; no words can adequately describe the horror of living it multiple times. This pain was felt everywhere, including the South. Few families escaped being touched by tragedy.

Yet, through all the pain, some good emerged. Medicine, so primitive at the outset, improved exponentially by war's end. Doctors developed a triage system that prioritized treatment of the most serious cases first, as well as concentrating on those with the best chance of survival. Born from the necessity to preserve bodies in extreme conditions for the lengthy trip home, embalming became a standard protocol.

Reconstructing land and lives after the war led to an age of great modernization. Railroads were built and expanded. Both coasts of our country were united due to transportation advancements. It took many years to heal the scars upon the land as well as the scars upon the hearts of America's people. Some scars never healed, as the great American tragedy known as the Civil War has been fought again many times over.

Earlier, I alluded to several cases where widows and mothers had an ordeal in garnering government pensions. Although our government was placing obstacles in the way of a deserving segment of the population, it was also acting as a prudent watchdog to rein in governmental spending that had spiraled out of control during the war and led to the initiation of a federal income tax.

We met 288 of Perry County's finest men. Were there others from the county who did not make it back? I am certain there were. Many militia and independent units operated during the four years of conflict, some with excellent recordkeeping and some without. Many men moved from Perry and enlisted where they resided.

A listing of men cited in the preceding pages follows for easy reference. Also included are sketches of men who did not survive the war and who have a connection to our county but do not seem to be the sons of Perry County.

My hope is that this volume may be used as a reference tool. To sit and read this from cover to cover would be a laborious task. I hope that this book has created a spark that might lead a reader to seek information about a soldier cited here, maybe a distant relative. If that occurs, I will be happy.

LV.

Personnel List for Soldiers Appearing

PRIVATE DAVID NEELY, Tyrone Twp, Co. A, 77th Reg., died May 20, 1864, in battle at Kingston, Georgia.

PRIVATE SAMUEL ORWAN, Centre Twp, Co. D, 2nd Reg., died July 4, 1861, of disease at his home.

PRIVATE THADDEUS C. RIDER, Newport, Co. D, 2nd Reg., died July 7, 1861, of disease in Baltimore, Maryland.

PRIVATE LOUIS H. VARNS, Watts Twp, Co. A, 3rd Reg., died August 23, 1861, cause and location of death unknown.

FIRST LIEUTENANT ALLEN S. JACOBS, New Bloomfield, Co. A, 11th Reg., died October 18, 1863, of disease at his home.

SECOND LIEUTENANT ARNOLD LOBAUGH, Newport, Co. I, 11th Reg., died September 26, 1862, in battle at Antietam, Maryland.

PRIVATE JACOB D. HETRICK, Greenwood Twp, Co. E, 15th Reg., died August 3, 1861, of disease.

CORPORAL WILLIAM H. SHADE, Centre Twp, Co. B, 36th Militia, died August 2, 1863, of disease in Gettysburg, Pennsylvania.

PRIVATE JOHN SLAUGHTERBECK, Greenwood Twp, Co. B, 36th Militia, died August 7, 1863, of disease in Gettysburg, Pennsylvania.

PRIVATE SAMUEL S. BAKER, Tuscarora Twp, Co. H, 30th Reg., died May 27, 1864, in battle at Spotsylvania, Virginia.

PRIVATE WILLIAM H. BERKSTRESSER, Spring Twp, Co. I, 30th Reg., died May 25, 1864, in battle at Washington, D.C.

PRIVATE WILLIAM H. QUIGLEY, Centre Twp, Co. H, 30th Reg., died June 26, 1862, in battle at Mechanicsville, Virginia.

PRIVATE JOHN F. ADAMS, Carroll Twp, Co. A, 36th Reg., died March 10, 1865, of disease in Annapolis, Maryland.

PRIVATE MATTHEW ADAMS, Wheatfield Twp, Co. B, 36th Reg., died March 5, 1864, of disease in Alexandria, Virginia.

PRIVATE GEORGE W. BROWN, Watts Twp, Co., B, 36th Reg., died June 27, 1862, in battle at Gaines Mills, Virginia.

PRIVATE FRANKLIN B. ELLIS, Duncannon Twp, Co. H, 36th Reg., died June 16, 1864, in battle at Wilderness, Virginia.

PRIVATE STEPHEN F. GLAZE, Montgomery's Ferry, Co. B, 36th Reg., died September 29, 1864, of disease in Andersonville Prison in Georgia.

PRIVATE AMOS W. HETRICK, Liverpool, Co. B, 36th Reg., died June 27, 1862, in battle at Gaines Mills, Virginia.

PRIVATE JAMES MCGLAUGHLIN, Liverpool, Co. B, 36th Reg., died October 27, 1862, of disease in Annapolis, Maryland.

PRIVATE JAMES H. MCCROSKEY, Carroll Twp, Co. A, 36th Reg., died November 13, 1864, of disease in Florence, South Carolina.

PRIVATE SILAS PORTZLINE, Liverpool, Co. B, 36th Reg., died November 16, 1863, of disease at his home in Liverpool, Pennsylvania.

PRIVATE ELIAS RICE, Landisburg, Co. B, 36th Reg., died September 9, 1864 of disease in Andersonville, Georgia.

TEAMSTER JOSIAH RICE, Landisburg, attached to various regiments, died September 28, 1964, of disease in Andersonville, Georgia.

PRIVATE DAVID SHATTO, Newport, Co. B, 36th Reg., died October 3, 1862, of disease in Washington, D.C.

CAPTAIN JOHN Q. SNYDER, Liverpool, Co. B, 36th Reg., died August 25, 1865, at his home, cause of death unknown.

PRIVATE JOHN W. VAN FOSSEN, Duncannon, Co. H, 36th Reg., died December 13, 1862, in battle at Fredericksburg, Virginia.

PRIVATE WILLIAM H. VAN NEWKIRK, Oliver Twp, Co. B, 36th Reg., died June 27, 1862, in battle at Gaines Mills, Virginia.

PRIVATE JOHN WAGNER, Montgomery's Ferry, Co. B, 36th Reg., died October 5, 1864, of disease in Florence, South Carolina.

PRIVATE HENRY N. WETHERALD, Duncannon, Co. H, 36th Reg., died November 22, 1864, of disease in Andersonville, Georgia.

PRIVATE PETER E. WILLIAMSON, Liverpool, Co. B, 36th Reg., died September 25, 1862, in battle at South Mountain, Maryland.

PRIVATE FRANK H. HENCH, Saville Twp, Co. A, 41st Reg., died July 3, 1863, in battle at Gettysburg, Pennsylvania.

CORPORAL WILLIAM A. FRY, Saville Twp, Co. A, 41st Reg., died November 2, 1863, of disease in Washington, D.C.

PRIVATE DAVID H. GRAHAM, Saville Twp, Co. E, 41st Reg., died September 17, 1862, in battle at Sharpsburg, Maryland.

PRIVATE JOHN C. LIGGETT, Saville Twp, Co. K, 41st Reg., died January 6, 1862, of disease in Camp Pierpoint, Virginia.

FIRST LIEUTENANT WILLIAM A. ALLISON, Penn Twp, Co. B, 42nd Reg., died September 17, 1862, in battle at Sharpsburg, Maryland.

PRIVATE CHARLES AUSTIN, Duncannon, Co. B, 42nd Reg., died July 28, 1864, in battle at Spotsylvania, Virginia.

FIRST SERGEANT THOMAS J. BELTON, Duncannon, Co. B, 42nd Reg., died July 3, 1863, in battle at Gettysburg, Pennsylvania.

PRIVATE GEORGE EBRIGHT, Wheatfield Twp, Co. B, 42nd Reg., died February 28, 1862, of disease at his home Duncannon, Pennsylvania.

PRIVATE PATRICK FORAN, Duncannon, Co. B, 42nd Reg., died April 13, 1862, of poisoning in Manassas, Virginia.

PRIVATE FRANCIS A. FOSTER, Duncannon, Co. B, 42nd Reg., died in 1862 at his home, of battle wounds, in Duncannon, Pennsylvania.

CORPORAL SAMUEL GALBRAITH, Miller Twp, Co. B, 42nd Reg., died December 20, 1861, in battle at Dranesville, Virginia.

PRIVATE SAMUEL TITLER, Toboyne Twp, Co. F, 76th Ohio Reg,. died July 15, 1865, in an accident in the Ohio River.

PRIVATE THOMAS W. GILLESPIE, Duncannon, Co. B, 42nd Reg., died June 30, 1862, in battle at Charles City Crossroads, Virginia.

PRIVATE WILLIAM H. JOHNSON, Duncannon, Co. B, 42nd Reg., date of death unknown, confined to U.S. Insane Asylum in unknown location.

PRIVATE CONRAD JUMPER, Centre Twp, Co. B, 42nd Reg., died September 14, 1862, in battle at South Mountain, Maryland.

PRIVATE PETER LEHMAN, Penn Twp, Co. B, 42nd Reg., died September 20, 1862, in battle at South Mountain, Maryland.

PRIVATE AMBROSE B. MAGEE, Carroll Twp, Co. B, 42nd Reg., died March 1, 1863, in battle at Fredericksburg, Virginia.

SERGEANT JOHN O'BRIEN, Penn Twp, Co. B, 42nd Reg., died June 3, 1864, in battle at Spotsylvania, Virginia.

PRIVATE THEODORE PARSONS, Penn Twp, Co. B, 42nd Reg., died June 30, 1862, in battle at Charles City Crossroads, Virginia.

PRIVATE GEORGE RAUB, Wheatfield Twp, Co. B, 42nd Reg., died December 20, 1861, in battle at Dranesville, Virginia.

PRIVATE GEORGE SPAHR, Duncannon, Co. B, 42nd Reg., died February 7, 1863, of disease in Hampton, Virginia.

PRIVATE JACOB STUCKEY, Duncannon, Co. B, 42nd Reg., died November 16, 1863, at his home in Duncannon, Pennsylvania, from wounds suffered in battle at Fredericksburg, Virginia.

PRIVATE AMOS BARGE, Carroll Twp, Battery G, 1st PA Light Artillery, died June 27, 1862, in battle at Gaines Mills, Virginia.

PRIVATE STINSON P. EVERILL, Madison Twp, Battery G, 1st PA Light Infantry, died July 1, 1862, in battle at Gaines Mills, Virginia.

PRIVATE SAMUEL S. LONG, Tuscarora Twp, Battery B, 5th U.S. Artillery, died August 11, 1864, of disease in Petersburg, Virginia.

PRIVATE WILLIAM ROUSE, Ickesburg, Battery G, 1st PA Light Artillery, died June 27, 1862, in battle at Gaines Mills, Virginia.

PRIVATE GEORGE W. TOPLEY, New Bloomfield, Battery K, 2nd PA Artillery, died June 14, 1864, in battle at Dinwiddie, Virginia.

PRIVATE ELI W. ORRIS, Ickesburg, Battery G, 3rd PA Heavy Artillery, died October 7, 1864, of disease in Baltimore, Maryland.

PRIVATE SAMUEL PECK, Saville Twp, Co. L, 2nd PA Heavy Artillery, died December 17, 1863, of disease in Washington, D.C.

PRIVATE JOHN F. KLECKNER, Saville Twp, Battery G, 2nd PA Heavy Artillery, died August 11, 1864, in battle at Philadelphia, Pennsylvania.

PRIVATE CASPER ROBINSON, Penn Twp, Battery K, 3rd PA Heavy Artillery, died March 23, 1864, of disease in Fort Monroe, Virginia.

PRIVATE STEPHEN D. WILLIAMS, Newport, Battery G, 3rd PA Heavy Artillery, died November 5, 1864, of disease in Millen, Georgia.

PRIVATE JOHN GEORGE BAIR, Buffalo Twp, Co. F, 46th Reg., died August 24, 1864, of disease in Andersonville Prison in Georgia.

PRIVATE DAVID B. SINGER, Buffalo Twp, Co. I, 46th Reg., died August 7, 1864, of disease in Nashville, Tennessee.

PRIVATE SAMUEL THOMAN, New Bloomfield, Co. D, 46th Reg., died May 27, 1864, in battle at Winchester, Virginia.

SECOND LIEUTENANT SAMUEL S. WOLF, Duncannon, Co. D, 46th Reg., died July 20, 1864, in battle at Peach Tree Creek, Georgia.

PRIVATE WILLIAM J. WRIGHT, Watts Twp, Co. I, 46th Reg., died October 14, 1864, of disease in Andersonville, Georgia.

CORPORAL GEORGE WASHINGTON ALBERT, Spring Twp, Co. H, 47th Reg., died April 29, 1864, of disease and buried at sea.

PRIVATE JOSEPH ACKER, Greenwood Twp, Co. D, 47th Reg., died October 19, 1864, in battle at Cedar Creek, Virginia.

PRIVATE DANIEL BISTLINE, Spring Twp, Co. H, 47th Reg., died November 6, 1861, of disease in Camp Griffin, Virginia.

PRIVATE WILLIAM H. CLOUSE, Landisburg, Co. D, 47th Reg., died September 12, 1864, of disease in Sandy Hook, Maryland.

PRIVATE WILLIAM F. DUM, Spring Twp, Co. H, 47th Reg., died April 9, 1864, in battle at Pleasant Hill, Louisiana.

PRIVATE JOHN F. EGOLF, Spring Twp, Co. D, 47th Reg., died October 19, 1864, in battle at Cedar Creek, Virginia.

PRIVATE JOHN EVANS, Miller Twp, Co. H, 47th Reg., died June 11, 1864, of disease in New Orleans, Louisiana.

PRIVATE GEORGE FOLEY, Liverpool, Co. D, 47th Reg., died April 23, 1864, of disease in a hospital in Philadelphia, Pennsylvania.

PRIVATE DANIEL FOOSE, Spring Twp, Co. H, 47th Reg., died October 22, 1861, of disease in Camp Griffin, Virginia.

PRIVATE JAMES GALBRAITH, Miller Twp, Co. H, 47th Reg., died February 2, 1862, of disease in Washington, D.C.

PRIVATE JACOB R. GARDNER, Miller Twp, Co. H, 47th Reg., died January 8, 1862, of disease in Camp Griffin, Virginia.

PRIVATE R. MARTIN HARPER, Landisburg, Co. D, 47th Reg., died August 16, 1862, of disease at his home Landisburg, Pennsylvania.

CORPORAL JOHN W. HOLMES, Miller Twp, Co. H, 47th Reg., died October 8, 1864, of disease in Annapolis, Maryland.

SERGEANT FRANK M. HOLT, New Bloomfield, Co. D, 47th Reg., died October 28, 1861, of disease in Washington, D.C.

PRIVATE SAMUEL HUGGINS, Greenwood Twp, Co. H, 47th Reg., died December 15, 1862, in battle at Hilton Head, South Carolina.

PRIVATE COMLEY IDALL, Miller Twp, Co. H, 47th Reg., died October 29, 1862, in battle at Hilton Head, South Carolina.

PRIVATE GEORGE S. ISETT, Liverpool, Co. D, 47th Reg., died May 17, 1862, of disease in Key West, Florida.

PRIVATE HARRISON JONES, Shermansdale, Co. D, 47th Reg., died October 19, 1864, in battle at Cedar Creek, Virginia.

PRIVATE URIAH W. KEIZER, Saville Twp, Unassigned, 47th Reg., died July 29, 1864, of disease in New Orleans, Louisiana.

PRIVATE SAMUEL M. KERN, Madison Twp, Co. D, 47th Reg., died June 12, 1864, of disease in a POW camp in Tyler, Texas.

PRIVATE HENRY R. KOSIER, Centre Twp, Co. A, 48th Illinois Reg., died April 10, 1862, in battle at Pittsburg Landing, Tennessee

PRIVATE JESSE KOSIER, Centre Twp, Co. D, 47th Reg., died August 30, 1864, of disease in a hospital in Sandy Hook, Maryland.

PRIVATE JOHN LIDDICK, Watts Twp, Co. H, 47th Reg., died November 8, 1864, in battle at Baltimore, Maryland.

PRIVATE STERRETT LIGHTNER, Landisburg, Co. H, 47th Reg., died November 3, 1864, of disease in Philadelphia, Pennsylvania.

PRIVATE MICHAEL LUPFER, New Bloomfield, Co. H, 47th Reg., died September 16, 1864, of disease in New Bloomfield, Pennsylvania.

PRIVATE WILLIAM MAYS, New Bloomfield, Co. D, 47th Reg., died March 30, 1864, of disease in New Orleans, Louisiana.

PRIVATE ALEXANDER MUSSER, Newport, Co. D, 47th Reg., died October 22, 1862, in battle at Pocotaligo, South Carolina.

PRIVATE NICHOLAS I. ORRIS, Saville Twp, Co. H, 47th Reg., died April 9, 1864, in battle at Pleasant Hill, Louisiana.

PRIVATE ANDREW POWELL, Tuscarora Twp, Co. C, 149th Reg., died September 6, 1864, of disease in Andersonville Prison in Georgia.

PRIVATE DANIEL POWELL JR., Tuscarora Twp, Co. D, 47th Reg., died October 19, 1864, in battle at Cedar Creek, Virginia.

PRIVATE JOHN POWELL JR., Tuscarora Twp, Co. D, 47th Reg., died August 29, 1862, of disease in Key West, Florida.

PRIVATE SOLOMON POWELL, Tuscarora Twp, Co. D, 47th Reg., died June 7, 1864, of disease in a POW camp in Pleasant Hill, Louisiana.

PRIVATE JASON T. ROBINSON, New Bloomfield, Co. H, 47th Reg., died October 22, 1862, in battle at Pocotaligo, South Carolina.

PRIVATE WILLIAM H. ROBINSON, New Bloomfield, Co. D, 47th Reg., died April 4, 1862, of disease in Key West, Florida.

PRIVATE JOSEPH SHELLEY, Rye Twp, Co. H, 47th Reg., died October 19, 1864, in battle at Cedar Creek, Virginia.

PRIVATE HENRY SHEPLEY, Landisburg, Co. H, 47th Reg., died December 10, 1864, of disease in Salisbury, North Carolina.

PRIVATE JEROME Y. SMALL, Centre Twp, Co. D, 47th Reg., died October 19, 1864, in battle at Cedar Creek, Virginia.

PRIVATE GEORGE H. SMITH, Centre Twp, Co. H, 47th Reg., died July 9, 1864, of disease in Natchez, Mississippi.

PRIVATE JEREMIAH SMITH, Saville Twp, Co. H, 47th Reg., died August 8, 1862, of disease in Beaufort, South Carolina.

PRIVATE EMANUEL SNYDER, Buffalo Twp, Co. D, 47th Reg., died January 8, 1863, of disease at his home in Liverpool, Pennsylvania.

PRIVATE HENRY STAMBAUGH, Spring Twp, Co. H, 47th Reg., died October 22, 1862, in battle at Pocotaligo, South Carolina.

PRIVATE JEFFERSON WAGGONER, Elliottsburg, Co. H, 47th Reg., died October 22, 1862, in battle at Pocotaligo, South Carolina.

PRIVATE SAMUEL WAGNER, Saville Twp, Co. D, 47th Reg., died May 15, 1864, at sea from wounds incurred in battle at Pleasant Hill, Louisiana.

PRIVATE JOHNATHAN WANTZ, New Bloomfield, Co. D, 47th Reg., died June 17, 1864, of disease in Pleasant Hill, Louisiana.

PRIVATE FREDERICK WATTS, Miller Twp, Co. H, 47th Reg., died February, 13, 1862, of disease in Key West, Florida.

CORPORAL JAMES THOMAS WILLIAMSON, Landisburg, Co. D, 47th Reg., died August 30, 1862, of disease at his home in Landisburg, Pennsylvania.

PRIVATE ANDREW WORK, Duncannon, Co. D, 47th Reg., died February 27, 1862, of disease in a Washington D.C. hospital.

PRIVATE WASHINGTON WORK, Duncannon, Co. D, 47th Reg., died September 21, 1862, of disease at his home in Duncannon, Pennsylvania.

PRIVATE WILLIAM ATTIG, Millerstown, Co. A, 49th Reg., died November 24, 1863, in battle at Washington, D.C.

PRIVATE GEORGE W. BEATTY, Saville Twp, Co. A, 49th Reg., died May 12, 1864, in battle at Spotsylvania, Virginia.

PRIVATE SAMUEL C. EBRIGHT, Penn Twp, Co. E, 49th Reg., died November 25, 1864, of disease in Winchester, Virginia.

CORPORAL JAMES ENDSLOW, Blain, Co. I, 49th Reg., died January 13, 1862, of disease in an Alexandria, Virginia, hospital.

PRIVATE GEORGE P. HARTMAN, Carroll Twp, Co. E, 49th Reg., died December 30, 1864, of disease in City Point, Virginia.

CORPORAL GEORGE E. HELLER, Millerstown, Co. I, 49th Reg., died August 25, 1862, of disease in Philadelphia, Pennsylvania.

PRIVATE JACOB REESE, Greenwood Twp, Co. I, 49th Reg., died November 9, 1862, of disease at his home in Millerstown, Pennsylvania.

PRIVATE WARREN STAHL, Millerstown, Co. I, 40th Reg., died November 27, 1862, of disease in Hagerstown, Maryland.

FIRST LIEUTENANT JACOB G. BEAVER, Millerstown, Co. H, 51st Reg., died November 17, 1862, in battle at Antietam, Maryland.

SERGEANT JOHN W. HEISER, Greenwood Twp, Co. I, 53rd Reg., died August 29, 1864, in a Washington, D.C., hospital of wounds suffered in battle.

PRIVATE WILLIAM H. HUTTON, Miller Twp, Co. B, 53rd Reg., died November 15, 1864, of disease in Florence, South Carolina.

CORPORAL ALEXANDER KOSER, Toboyne Twp, Co. H, 60th Reg., died May 22, 1862, in battle at New York, New York.

PRIVATE CULBERTSON KOSER, Toboyne Twp, Co. H, 60th Reg., died October 16, 1864, in battle at Newville, Pennsylvania.

PRIVATE DANIEL C. O'DONNELL, Toboyne Twp, Co. M, 65th Reg., died June 5, 1865, of disease in a Virginia Prison.

MUSICIAN DANIEL NAGLE, Liverpool Twp, 77th Regimental Band, died February 13, 1862, of disease at his home in Liverpool, Pennsylvania.

PRIVATE SYLVESTER MORTON, Shermans Dale, Co. K, 3rd U.S. Cavalry, died July 27, 1864, of disease in Little Rock, Arkansas.

SERGEANT JOHN TUDOR, Madison Twp, Jones Independent Cavalry, died October 18, 1863, of disease at his home in Madison Township.

PRIVATE JOHN W. CROOKS, Shermans Dale, Co. M, 7th Cavalry, died June 20, 1864, in battle at Shelbyville, North Carolina.

PRIVATE JOHN DURHAM, Carroll Twp, Co. I, 7th Cavalry, died March 21, 1863, of injuries suffered in Tullahoma, Tennessee.

PRIVATE HENRY S. FRY, Shermans Dale, Co. I, 7th Cavalry, died December 31, 1862, in battle at Murfreesboro, Tennessee.

PRIVATE DANIEL S. SHATTO, Tyrone Twp, Co. M, 7th Cavalry, died April 21, 1865, of disease in Montgomery, Alabama.

SERGEANT CORNELIUS BUFFINGTON, Liverpool, Co. K, 83rd Reg., died August 9, 1865, of disease at his home in Liverpool, Pennsylvania.

PRIVATE SAMUEL BAKER, Blain, Company C, 9th Cavalry, died April 13, 1865, in battle at Raleigh, North Carolina.

CORPORAL JOHN R. BOYD, Jackson Twp, Co. C, 9th Cavalry, died June 11, 1863, in battle at Triune, Tennessee.

BUGLER JAMES W. BUCKWALTER, Juniata Twp, Co. C, 9th Cavalry, died February 2, 1862, of disease in Jeffersonville, Indiana.

BLACKSMITH GEORGE L. DENTLER, Spring Twp, Co. C, 9th Cavalry, died April 18, 1862, of disease in Nashville, Tennessee.

PRIVATE DAVID T. DUM, Elliottsburg, Co. C, 9th Cavalry, died April 13, 1865, in battle at Raleigh, North Carolina.

PRIVATE BENJAMIN EBRIGHT, Penn Twp, Co. A, 9th Cavalry, died July 23, 1864, of disease in Andersonville Prison in Georgia.

PRIVATE CORNELIUS FOOSE, Duncannon, Co. A, 9th Cavalry, died April 3, 1863, in the Stones River battle in Franklin, Tennessee.

PRIVATE ISAAC GLADDEN, Wheatfield Twp, Co. M, 9th Cavalry, died February 5, 1865, of disease in Florence, South Carolina.

SERGEANT DAVIDSON U. HENCH, Madison Twp, Co. E, 9th Cavalry, died December 2, 1863, at home of injuries incurred in battle.

PRIVATE JOHN JONES JR., Juniata Twp, Co. G, 9th Cavalry, died March 10, 1865, in battle at Solemn Grove, North Carolina.

PRIVATE JACOB KEIM, Wheatfield Twp, Co. A, 9th Cavalry, died March 29, 1862, of disease in Bowling Green, Kentucky.

PRIVATE WILLIAM KUHN, Madison Twp, Co. E, 9th Cavalry, died August 5, 1862, in battle at Tompkinsville, Kentucky.

PRIVATE JOHN W. LIDDICK, Watts Twp, Co. A, 9th Cavalry, died April 24, 1864, in an accident in Mifflin, Pennsylvania.

PRIVATE ISAAC MCCLINTOCK, Carroll Twp, Co. I, 9th Cavalry, died July 9, 1862, in battle at Tompkinsville, Kentucky.

PRIVATE ALEXANDER MCCOY, Wheatfield Twp, Co. A, 9th Cavalry, died, date unknown, while in a POW camp near Goldsboro, North Carolina.

PRIVATE DANIEL W. RICEDORFF, Tuscarora Twp, Co. C, 9th Cavalry, died November 9, 1862, of disease in Lebanon, Kentucky.

PRIVATE JOHN W. RICEDORFF, Juniata Twp, Co. H, 29th Iowa, died September 1, 1863, of disease in Devall's Bluff, Arkansas.

PRIVATE SAMUEL SNYDER, Blain, Co. C, 9th Cavalry, died March 5, 1863, in battle at Thompson's Station, Tennessee.

SERGEANT M. B. P. STEWART, Duncannon, Co. A, 9th Cavalry, died November 22, 1864, in battle at Griswoldville, Georgia.

BUGLER JOHN A. STOTLER, Duncannon, Co. A, 9th Cavalry, died April 9, 1862, of disease in Leitchfield, Kentucky.

PRIVATE EDMUND WEBSTER, Greenwood Twp, Co. M, 9th Cavalry, died March 10, 1865, of disease in Wilmington, North Carolina.

PRIVATE ROBERT WILSON, Duncannon, Co. A, 9th Cavalry, died April 12, 1862, of disease in Springfield, Tennessee.

PRIVATE LEVI O. YOUNG, Shermans Dale, Co. C, 93rd Reg., died March 25, 1865, in battle at Petersburg, Virginia.

CORPORAL EDWIN M ESHELMAN, Liverpool Twp, Co. E, 99th Reg., died October 31, 1864, of disease in Washington, D.C.

PRIVATE WILLIAM A. DILE, Spring Twp, Co. A, 101st Reg., died June 16, 1865, of disease at his brother's home in Spring Township, Pennsylvania.

PRIVATE WILLIAM KITNER, Elliottsburg, Co. A, 101st, Reg., died May 31, 1862, in battle at Fair Oaks, Virginia.

PRIVATE EDWARD P. MATCHETT, Newport, Co. K, 101st Reg., died September 6, 1862, of disease in Blackwell's Island, New York.

PRIVATE ISAIAH J. MATCHETT, Newport, Co. K, 101st Reg., died June 16, 1864, of disease in Andersonville Prison in Georgia.

PRIVATE CHRISTIAN ROTHE, New Bloomfield, Co. A, 101st Reg., died December 1, 1864, of disease in Andersonville Prison in Georgia.

PRIVATE BENJAMIN SMEIGH, Tyrone Twp, Co. A, 101st Reg., died October 22, 1863, of disease at his home in Landisburg, Pennsylvania.

PRIVATE SOLOMON SOUDER, Shermans Dale, Co. A, 101st Reg., died August 16, 1864, of disease in Andersonville Prison in Georgia.

PRIVATE ARMSTRONG S. ZEIGLER, Carroll Twp, Co. A, 101st Reg., died March 16, 1863, of disease at his home in Spring Twp, Pennsylvania.

PRIVATE JAMES T. TOLAND JR., Miller Twp, Co. F, 102nd Reg., died November 15, 1864, of disease in Gettysburg, Pennsylvania.

PRIVATE HENRY BERRIER, Blain, Co. H, 107th Reg., died February 13, 1864, of disease in Richmond, Virginia.

PRIVATE ISAIAH CLOUSER, Miller Twp, Battery L, 2nd Heavy Artillery, died July 21, 1865, of disease in Petersburg, Virginia.

PRIVATE WILLIAM P. CLEGG, New Bloomfield, Co. E, 12th Cavalry, died December 5, 1864, of disease in Danville, Virginia.

PRIVATE JOEL S. HUGGINS, Newport, Co. F, 12th Cavalry, died April 7, 1865, of disease in Fortress Monroe, Virginia.

CORPORAL JOHN B ELLIOTT, Miller Twp, Co. F, 13th Cavalry, died June 17, 1864, of disease in Andersonville Prison in Georgia.

CORPORAL CHARLES FENICLE, Spring Twp, Co. F, 13th Cavalry, died December 13, 1863, of disease in Richmond, Virginia.

PRIVATE MITCHELL WATTS, Miller Twp, Co. F, 13th Cavalry, died February 23, 1865, in battle at Raleigh, North Carolina.

PRIVATE WILSON M. DARLINGTON, Centre Twp, Co. G, 132nd Reg., died January 7, 1863, in battle at Washington, D.C.

PRIVATE SOLOMON BERKSTRESSER, Spring Twp, Co. G, 133rd, Reg., died October 9, 1862, of disease in Sharpsburg, Maryland.

LIEUTENANT EDWARD C. BENDERE, New Bloomfield, 133rd Regiment Adjutant, died May 3, 1863, in battle at Chancellorsville, Virginia.

PRIVATE DAVID BISTLINE, Juniata Twp, Co. I, 133rd Reg., died December 13, 1862, in battle t Fredericksburg, Virginia.

PRIVATE JOHN C. BRETZ, Newport, Co. I, 133rd Reg., died December 13, 1862, in battle at Fredericksburg, Virginia.

PRIVATE ALEXANDER M. BROWN, Newport, Co. I, 133rd Reg., died November 6, 1862, of disease in Frederick, Maryland.

PRIVATE WILLIAM H. DUGAN, Dellville, Co. H, 133rd Reg., died December 24, 1862, of disease in Falmouth, Virginia.

PRIVATE JOSEPH DUNCAN, Newport, Co. I, 133rd Reg., died December 13, 1862, in battle at Fredericksburg, Virginia.

PRIVATE CHARLES P. FINLEY, Blain, Co. G, 133rd Reg., died December 20, 1862, of disease in Falmouth, Virginia.

PRIVATE FREDERICK FLICK, Loysville, Co. H, 133rd Reg., died December 26, 1862, of disease in Falmouth, Virignia.

PRIVATE FREDERICK HAIN, Newport, Co. I, 133rd Reg., died December 23, 1862, in battle at Washington, D.C.

PRIVATE JACOB HAIR, Carroll Twp, Co. H, 133rd Reg., died November 23, 1862, of disease in Washington, D.C.

PRIVATE ANDREW J. HOUENSTINE, Tuscarora Twp, Co. I, 133rd Reg., died April 21, 1863, of disease in Newport, Pennsylvania.

SERGEANT JOHNSTON FETTER KERR, Juniata Twp, Co. I, 133rd Reg., died December 5, 1862, of disease in Falmouth, Virginia.

PRIVATE JAMES MATHERS, Saville Twp, Co. G, 133rd Reg., died December 13, 1862, in battle at Fredericksburg, Virginia.

PRIVATE MEREDITH D. MCBRIDE, Centre Twp, Co. H, 133rd Reg., died December 16, 1862, in battle at Fredericksburg, Virginia.

PRIVATE FREDERICK O. MCCASKEY, Shermans Dale, Co. H, 133rd Reg., died December 13, 1862, in battle at Fredericksburg, Virginia.

PRIVATE JACOB MILLER, Juniata Twp, Co. G, 133rd Reg., died December 13, 1862, in battle at Fredericksburg, Virginia.

PRIVATE HENRY MINICH, Loysville, Co. H, 133rd Reg., died December 1, 1862, of disease in Potomac Creek, Virginia.

PRIVATE GEORGE K. MYERS, Millerstown, Co. I, 133rd Reg., died December 18, 1862, in battle at Washington, D.C.

PRIVATE ISAIAH P. OWEN, Wheatfield Twp, Co. H, 133rd Reg., died November 2, 1862, of disease in Sharpsburg, Maryland.

PRIVATE JOHN A. REED, Madison Twp, Co. H, 133rd Reg., died March 5, 1863, of disease in Fredericksburg, Virginia.

PRIVATE JOSEPHUS W. SMITH, Newport, Co. I, 133rd Reg., died December 19, 1862, in battle at Washington, D.C.

PRIVATE ABRAM SPANOGLE, Saville Twp, Co. G, 133rd Reg., died December 13, 1862, in battle at Fredericksburg, Virginia.

PRIVATE DAVID T. WAGNER, Bridgeport, Co. H, 133rd, Reg., died December 25, 1862, in battle at Point Lookout, Maryland.

CORPORAL FINLAW WITHEROW, New Bloomfield, Co. G, 133rd Reg., died January 4, 1863, of disease in Falmouth, Virginia.

PRIVATE HENRY L. YOHN, Tuscarora Twp, Co. I, 133rd Reg., died December 13, 1862, in battle at Fredericksburg, Virginia.

PRIVATE JESSE BAIR, Buffalo Twp, Co. C, 149th Reg., died May 8, 1864, in battle at Spotsylvania Court House, Virginia.

PRIVATE JOHN BROOKHART, Greenwood Twp, Co. C, 149th Reg., died May 24, 1864, in battle at North Ana River, Virginia.

PRIVATE JOHN A. BURTNETT, Landisburg, Co. I, 149th Reg., died September 14, 1864, of disease at Andersonville Prison in Georgia.

PRIVATE JOHN W. CRILEY, Liverpool Twp, Co. C, 149th Reg., died March 6, 1865, of disease in Wilmington, North Carolina.

PRIVATE BENJAMIN H. CUNNINGHAM, Carroll Twp, Co. F, 149th Reg., died January 17, 1864, of disease in Culpeper, Virginia.

PRIVATE WILLIAM DICE, Rye Twp, Co. D, 149th Reg., died June 29, 1864, in battle at Baltimore, Maryland.

PRIVATE ROBERT FOX, Duncannon, Co. G, 149th Reg., died June 16, 1863, in of wounds in Philadelphia, Pennsylvania, after battle at Gettysburg, Pennsylvania.

PRIVATE JOHN D. GENSLER, Landisburg, Co. I, 149th Reg., died June 29, 1864, of disease at his home in Landisburg, Pennsylvania.

PRIVATE WILLIAM H. HIPPLE, Rye Twp, Co. D, 149th Reg., died May 6, 1864, in battle at Wilderness, Virginia.

PRIVATE ROSS M. HOOD, Duncannon, Co. G, 149th Reg., died July 1, 1863, in battle at Gettysburg, Pennsylvania.

PRIVATE JOHN JACOBS, Ickesburg, Company K, 149th Reg., died December 6, 1864, of disease in a POW camp in Florence, South Carolina.

PRIVATE WILLIAM A. JACOBS, Ickesburg, Co. K, 149th Reg., died February 1, 1864, of disease in Washington, D.C.

PRIVATE DAVID KITNER, Carroll Twp, Co. G, 149th Reg., died May 5, 1864, in battle at Wilderness, Virginia.

PRIVATE ELIAS MESSIMER, Carroll Twp, Co. G, 149th Reg., died July 8, 1864, after being shot at Richmond, Virginia.

PRIVATE MARTIN V. B. ORWAN, New Bloomfield, Co. K, 149th Reg., died September 20, 1864, of disease in Andersonville Prison in Georgia.

PRIVATE SILAS POTTER, Penn Twp, Co. G, 149th Reg., died May 5, 1864, in battle at Wilderness, Virginia.

PRIVATE JOHN H. HAINES, Millerstown, Co. D, 151st Reg., died July 1, 1863, in battle at Gettysburg, Pennsylvania.

PRIVATE JOSEPH A. MCCASKEY, Shermans Dale, Co. C, 158th Reg., died July 11, 1863, of disease in Philadelphia, Pennsylvania.

PRIVATE WILLIAM P. SMITH, Toboyne Twp, Co. K, 158th Reg., died June 5, 1863, of disease in Washington, North Carolina.

PRIVATE JAMES HILL, Rye Twp, Co. H, 16th Cavalry, died October 25, 1864, of disease in City Point, Virginia.

PRIVATE DAVID A. REED, Madison Twp, Co. F, 16th Cavalry, died April 29, 1864, of disease in Brandy Station, Virginia.

PRIVATE JOHN SMITH, Wheatfield Twp, Co. G, 16th Cavalry, died August 9, 1864, in battle at Wilderness, Virginia.

PRIVATE BENJAMIN WHITE, Carroll Twp, Co. H, 16th Cavalry, died December 22, 1862, of disease in Washington, D.C.

CORPORAL JAMES C. CAMPBELL, New Bloomfield, Co. I, 17th Cavalry, died June 21, 1864, in battle at Whitehouse Landing, Virginia.

PRIVATE JEREMIAH HIPPLE, New Bloomfield, Co. I, 17th Cavalry, died January 1, 1863, in battle at Fairfax, Virginia.

PRIVATE WILLIAM KOCHER, Ickesburg, Co. I, 17th Cavalry, died April 9, 1863, of disease in Falmouth, Virginia.

PRIVATE SAMUEL DEARDORFF MYERS, Oliver Twp, Co. F, 17th Cavalry, died October 11, 1864, in battle at Newtown, Virginia.

PRIVATE ELIAS REED, Liverpool, Co. I, 17th Cavalry, died January 29, 1863, of disease in Acquia Creek, Virginia.

PRIVATE THOMAS SPEASE, Wheatfield Twp, Co. F, 17th Cavalry, died July 12, 1863, of disease in Washington, D.C.

PRIVATE BENJAMIN SPRIGGLE, Saville Twp, Co. I, 17th Cavalry, died August 16, 1863, in battle at Frederick, Maryland.

PRIVATE JOHN STOUFFER, Shermans Dale, Co. I, 17th Cavalry, died, date unknown, of disease in Washington, D.C.

PRIVATE GEORGE CLEMENS, Greenwood Twp, Co. E, 173rd Reg., died April 3, 1863, of disease in Norfolk, Virginia.

PRIVATE JOHN DUNKLE, New Buffalo, Co. E, 173rd Reg., died January 10, 1863, of disease in Norfolk, Virginia.

PRIVATE JACOB CLESS, Centre Twp, Co. F, 177th Reg., died January 22, 1863, of disease in Suffolk, Virginia.

PRIVATE WILLIAM A. LAY, Jackson Twp, Co. F, 177th Reg., died May 19, 1864, of disease in Maryland Heights, Maryland.

PRIVATE JESSE SHANNON, Madison Twp, Co. F, 177th Reg., died March 4, 1863, of disease in Suffolk, Virginia.

PRIVATE HENRY SHEARER, Madison Twp, Co. F, 177th Reg., died April 19, 1863, of disease in Suffolk, Virginia.

PRIVATE GEORGE B. PARSONS, Penn Twp, Co. C, 21st Cavalry, died March 18, 1864, of disease in Chambersburg, Pennsylvania.

PRIVATE HENRY F. CLAY, Carroll Twp, Co. A, 184th Reg., died September 1, 1864, of disease in Andersonville Prison in Georgia.

PRIVATE SAMUEL HARTZELL, Wheatfield Twp, Co. A, 184th Reg., died July 1, 1864, at Harewood Hospital, Washington, D.C., of wounds suffered in battle.

PRIVATE EMANUEL JONES, Carroll Twp, Co. A, 184th Reg., died September 17, 1864, of disease in Davids Island, New York.

CORPORAL EPHRAIM P. SANDS, Centre Twp, Co. F, 186th Reg., died February 3, 1865, of disease in Philadelphia, Pennsylvania.

PRIVATE WILLIAM P. GENSLER, Loysville, Co. D, 187th Reg., died June 18, 1864, in battle at Petersburg, Virginia.

PRIVATE JOSIAH LENIG, Centre Twp, Co. K, 187th Reg., died September 20, 1865, of injuries sustained in Philadelphia, Pennsylvania.

PRIVATE HENRY NONEMAKER, Kennedy's Valley, Co. D, 187th Reg., died July 14, 1864, of disease in Alexandria, Virginia.

PRIVATE DAVID F. SHERIFF, Toboyne Twp, Co. D, 187th Reg., died December 18, 1864, of disease in Newville, Pennsylvania.

PRIVATE NICHOLAS SWEGER, Centre Twp, Co. A, 187th Reg., died July 30, 1864, in battle at Centre Township, Pennsylvania.

PRIVATE HENRY TOOMEY, Tyrone Twp, Co. D, 187th Reg., died August, 19, 1864, in battle at Dinwiddie, Virginia.

PRIVATE ANDREW BURKHART, Toboyne Twp, Co. D, 188th Reg., died November 5, 1864, of disease in Fort Schyler, New York.

PRIVATE FREDERICK RHOADS, Greenwood Twp, Co. D, 188th Reg., died June 1, 1864, in battle at Cold Harbor, Virginia.

PRIVATE SAMUEL SMITH, Greenwood Twp, Co. D, 188th Reg., died November 9, 1864, of disease in Philadelphia, Pennsylvania.

PRIVATE GEORGE W. ZARING, Liverpool, Co. D, 188th Reg., died June 29, 1864, in battle at Washington, D.C.

PRIVATE WINFIELD S. DUFFIELD, Saville Twp, Co. F, 190th Reg., died November 10, 1864, of disease in Salisbury Prison in North Carolina.

PRIVATE JAMES C. DUFFY, Montgomery's Ferry, Co. I, 190th Reg., died November 5, 1864, of disease in Salisbury Prison in North Carolina.

CORPORAL JOSEPH B. EWING, Toboyne Twp, Co. K, 190th Reg., died July 16, 1864, in battle at Totopotomy Creek, Virginia.

PRIVATE BENJAMIN E. LIDDICK, Buffalo Twp, Co. I, 190th Reg., died March 25, 1865, of disease in Wilmington, North Carolina.

PRIVATE GEORGE W. SHATTO, Penn Twp, Co. B, 190th Reg., died March 2, 1865, of disease in Salisbury Prison in North Carolina.

PRIVATE DAVID F. BOLTOSSER, Oliver Twp, Co. C, 192nd Reg., died April 11, 1865, of disease in Baltimore, Maryland.

PRIVATE DAVID SMILEY JR., Shermans Dale, Co. I, 200th Reg., died April 22, 1865, of wounds sustained in battle at Philadelphia, Pennsylvania.

PRIVATE RICHARD DUDLEY, Duncannon, Co. A, 201st Reg., died September 28, 1864, of disease in York, Pennsylvania.

PRIVATE THOMAS J. EVANS, Duncannon, Co. E, 201st Reg., died November 9, 1864, of disease at his friend's home in Duncannon, Pennsylvania.

PRIVATE WILLIAM A. HIPPLE, Shermans Dale, Co. C, 201st Reg., died October 27, 1864, of disease in Alexandria, Virginia.

PRIVATE WILLIAM J. KENNEDY, Carroll Twp, Co. A, 201st Reg., died October 29, 1864, in battle at Alexandria, Virginia.

PRIVATE ALEXANDER W. FAGAN, Spring Twp, Co. H, 202nd Reg., died October 22, 1864, in battle at Alexandria, Virginia.

PRIVATE PETER SHEARER, Carroll Twp, Co. H, 202nd Reg., died May 3, 1865, of disease in Fairfax Station, Virginia.

PRIVATE DANIEL STUM, Jackson Twp, Co. H, 202nd Reg., died February 28, 1865, of disease in Baltimore, Maryland.

PRIVATE FRANK E. FOOSE, Spring Twp, Co. E, 208th Reg., died January 11, 1865, in battle at Hampton, Virginia.

PRIVATE HENRY D. FOOSE, Spring Twp, Co. E, 208th Reg., died April 2, 1865, in battle at Petersburg, Virginia.

PRIVATE JOSIAH GRUBB, Liverpool, Co. I, 208th Reg., died January 9, 1865, of disease in Petersburg, Virginia.

PRIVATE JOSEPH HECKART, Saville Twp, Co. E, 208th Reg., died September 29, 1864, in an accident in Bermuda Hundreds, Virginia.

PRIVATE EDMUND B. P. KINSLOE, Tyrone Twp, Co. E, 208th Reg., died April 26, 1865, in battle in Petersburg, Virginia.

PRIVATE SYLVESTER W. MCELHENEY, Jackson Twp, Co. F, 208th Reg., died April 20, 1865, in battle at Philadelphia, Pennsylvania.

PRIVATE WILLIAM H PERRY, Spring Twp, Co. E, 208th Reg., died April 2, 1865, in battle at Petersburg, Virginia.

PRIVATE JOHN REAPSOME, Spring Twp, Co. E, 208th Reg., died July 2, 1865, of disease at his home in Spring Township, Pennsylvania.

CORPORAL GEORGE REMPFER, Centre Twp, Co. E, 208th Reg., died April 2, 1865, in battle at Petersburg, Virginia.

PRIVATE JOHN L. RITTER, Tyrone Twp, Co. I, 208th Reg., died October 17, 1864, of disease at his home in Tyrone Township, Pennsylvania.

CORPORAL FREDERICK SHULL, Saville Twp, Co. F, 208th Reg., died March 25, 1865, in battle at Fort Steadman, Virginia.

PRIVATE JACOB TURNBAUGH, Saville Twp, Co. E, 208th Reg., died April 13, 1865, in battle at Petersburg, Virginia.

PRIVATE GEORGE W. WEISE, Centre Twp, Co. E, 208th Reg., died March 25, 1865, in battle at Fort Steadman, Virginia.

CORPORAL JOHN H. GEES, Penn Twp, Co. F, 209th Reg., died December 23, 1864, of disease in Salisbury Prison in North Carolina.

PRIVATE ENOCH SYKES, Carroll Twp, Co. F, 209th Reg., died March 25, 1865, in battle at Fort Steadman, Virginia.

PRIVATE BENJAMIN WADE, Clinton County, Illinois, Co. E, 15th Illinois Cavalry, died June 17, 1862, in an accident in Jackson, Tennessee.

WESLEY F. MILLER, St. Cloud, Minnesota, Co. E, 7th U.S. Infantry, died July 2, 1863, in battle at Gettysburg, Pennsylvania.

PRIVATE ANTHONY WOX, Carroll Twp, Co. K, 210th Reg., died March 31, 1865, in battle at Gravelly Run, Virginia.

Here is a listing of men who perished during the war and have a connection to Perry County, but remain to be proven that they are sons of the county.

JAMES A. BROWN

One of the oddest cases is that of Corporal James A. Brown of East Windsor, Connecticut. Brown enlisted with Company M of the 2nd Connecticut Heavy Artillery on February 13, 1864. He was promoted to corporal on March 19 after only about one month of duty, an indication that he must have been a good soldier. Muster files show he deserted just two and one half weeks later on April 5. At that time, the 2nd Connecticut was engaged in the defense of Washington.

The next thing we know is that he was in Duncannon when he died on August 23, 1864. We can only speculate that he was making his way home when illness claimed his life. Though no one in the town was a relative, Brown was buried in Duncannon Union Cemetery as an act of kindness by the townspeople. They erected a monument to James Brown that contains this information: "died August 23, 1864 of congestive chills at Alex Morrison's aged 18 years erected by the citizens of Duncannon."

WILLIAM B. DORRELL

Lieutenant Colonel William B. Dorrell, 3rd Delaware Infantry, was killed in action in front of Petersburg on June 18, 1864, at the age of twenty-five. William is buried in New Bloomfield Cemetery. His tombstone bears this inscription: "Beloved husband of V. Addie McGowan." This reference may be to Virginia Adilida, the daughter of James McGowan of Centre Township. James relocated to Ellicott City, Maryland, in the 1850s and operated a hotel there. William Dorrell was a salesman in Philadelphia prior to the war, so the two could have found each other there.

SAMUEL GARMAN JR.

The Samuel Garman family is an interesting group of people. Samuel Garman Sr. was married three times and outlived all of his wives. He had at least eleven children, including Samuel Jr., who, like his father, had three wives and outlived all of them. Census data shows that the family resided in Reed Township, though Samuel Sr. and seven of his children are buried in Duncannon Union Cemetery. Samuel Jr., Benjamin, and Edward fought in the Civil War. Edward was a member of Company C of 4th U.S. Regular Army.

Edward wed Anna Fox in 1860. The couple had one child, Elizabeth. Edward died in Andersonville Prison on September 16, 1864, or September 13 in Libby Prison, depending upon which government record you examine.

ROBERT LAUGHLIN JR.

Robert Laughlin Jr. was born in 1845 to Robert Sr. and Maria McVitty Laughlin. The farm family resided in Hopewell Township near Amberson Valley, which borders Perry County. He appears there in both the 1850 and 1860 censuses with siblings Mary, Noah, William, Emiline, Ann, and John. John later served with Company F of the 13th PA Cavalry.

At his enlistment on September 1, 1864, Robert provided information that he was a farmer residing in Perry County, though no proof of that has been located. He was nineteen, stood 5'8" tall and had light hair, a fair complexion, and blue eyes. Robert mustered into Company I of the 9th PA Cavalry and went to war in Georgia. In what was the first battle of Sherman's March to the Sea, Robert was killed in action at Griswoldville on November 22, just fifty-one days after enlisting.

SAMUEL SPEAR

A man from Company B of the Bucktails was killed in action July second at Gettysburg. Though it appears that Private Spear was a resident of Reed Township, just across the line in Dauphin County, his story is unclear, plus it is difficult to omit a Bucktail from this list. There is a Samuel Spears listed as a sixteen-year-old farmhand in the Reed Township census of 1860, living with the Philip Newbaker family. When Samuel enlisted in Duncannon on May 27, 1861, he gave "farmer" as his occupation and an age of eighteen, so they may be one and the same. Samuel's index card also shows the 5'4½"-tall, blue-eyed man to be a Dauphin County resident. However, those cards contain a multitude of errors. The final resting place for this Bucktail has not been defined. The certainty is that Private Samuel Spear was one of thousands who gave his all for his country and died far too soon.

William Rauch was the unofficial historian of the Bucktails. He records that in the charge by the Bucktails near the famous Wheatfield, a young soldier from Company B was hit by an artillery projectile that further killed a man from Company I, as well as wounding "seven or eight others." This young man had his right arm severed by the shot and bled profusely. In his delirium, the soldier ran in circles shouting, "I won't die." He bled to death in a matter of minutes. Since only one soldier from Company B was killed that day, it is probable that Samuel Spears was that young man. He fell near the "stone wall" according to regimental records. This wall was located at the eastern limits of this bloody field that was witness to some of the fiercest fighting of the entire war.

About the Author

Born and raised on a farm in western Perry County, **Terry F. Bender** has resided in the county all his life. He is a graduate of West Perry High School and attended Dickinson College in Carlisle, Pennsylvania. He spent nearly forty years in the oil industry; first as a truck driver, then later in mid-level management.

He and wife Donna celebrated their fiftieth wedding anniversary in November 2024. They have three sons, five granddaughters, and three grandsons.

Terry's hobbies include collecting and reading books on the Civil War, crossword puzzles, woodworking, cutting firewood, and doting on the grandchildren.

www.ingramcontent.com/pod-product-compliance
Lightning Source LLC
Chambersburg PA
CBHW010929180426
43194CB00045B/2841